Mastering Cash Flow and Valuation Modelling

PEARSON

At Pearson, we take learning personally. Our courses and resources are available as books, online and via multi-lingual packages, helping people learn whatever, wherever and however they choose.

We work with leading authors to develop the strongest learning experiences, bringing cutting-edge thinking and best learning practice to a global market. We craft our print and digital resources to do more to help learners not only understand their content, but to see it in action and apply what they learn, whether studying or at work.

Pearson is the world's leading learning company. Our portfolio includes Penguin, Dorling Kindersley, the Financial Times and our educational business, Pearson International. We are also a leading provider of electronic learning programmes and of test development, processing and scoring services to educational institutions, corporations and professional bodies around the world.

Every day our work helps learning flourish, and wherever learning flourishes, so do people.

To learn more please visit us at: **www.pearson.com/uk**

Mastering Cash Flow and Valuation Modelling

ALASTAIR DAY

PEARSON

Harlow, England • London • New York • Boston • San Francisco • Toronto • Sydney • Auckland • Singapore • Hong Kong
Tokyo • Seoul • Taipei • New Delhi • Cape Town • São Paulo • Mexico City • Madrid • Amsterdam • Munich • Paris • Milan

PEARSON EDUCATION LIMITED

Edinburgh Gate
Harlow CM20 2JE
Tel: +44 (0)1279 623623
Fax: +44 (0)1279 431059
Website: www.pearsoned.com/uk

First published in Great Britain in 2012

© Systematic Finance plc 2012

Pearson Education is not responsible for the content of third-party internet sites.

ISBN 978-0-273-73281-5

British Library Cataloguing-in-Publication Data
A catalogue record for this book is available from the British Library

Library of Congress Cataloging-in-Publication Data
Day, Alastair L.
  Mastering cash flow and valuation modelling / Alastair Day. -- 1st ed.
     p. cm
  ISBN 978-0-273-73281-5 (pbk.)
1. Cash flow. 2. Corporations--Finance--Mathematical models. I. Title.

HF5681.C28 D389
658.15'244--dc23

                                                          2011033610

10 9 8 7 6 5 4 3 2 1
16 15 14 13 12

Typeset in Garamond 11.5/13.5pt by 30
Printed by Ashford Colour Press Ltd, Gosport.

Contents

Acknowledgements

I would like to thank Angela, Matthew and Frances, for their support and assistance with the completion of this book. In addition, Christopher Cudmore, Martina O'Sullivan and Helen Savill of Pearson Education have provided valuable support and backing for this project.

About the author

Alastair Day has worked in the finance industry for more than 25 years in treasury and marketing functions and was formerly a director of a vendor leasing company specialising in the IT and technology industries. After rapid growth, the directors sold the enterprise to a public company and he established Systematic Finance as a consultancy specialising in:

- financial modelling – design, build, audit and review to provide a full range of modelling services;
- training in financial modelling, corporate finance, leasing and credit analysis on an in-house and public basis throughout Europe, Middle East, Africa, Asia and America;
- finance and operating lease structuring as a financial lessor and consultant advising on pricing and evaluation.

Alastair is the author of three modelling books published by FT Prentice Hall: *Mastering Financial Modelling*, *Mastering Risk Modelling* and *Mastering Financial Mathematics in Microsoft® Excel*. He has also written a number of other books and publications on financial analysis, credit and leasing.

Alastair has a degree in Economics and German from London University and an MBA from the Open University Business School.

Conventions

- The main part of the text is set in AGaramond, whereas entries are set in Courier. For example:

  Enter the Scenario Name as `Base Case`

- Items on the menu bars also shown in Courier. For example:

  Select `Data, What-if Analysis, Goal Seek`

- The names of functions are in Courier capitals. This is the payment function, which requires inputs for the interest rate, number of periods, present value and future value.

  `=PMT(INT,NPER,PV,FV,TYPE)`

- Cell formulas are also shown in Courier. For example:

  `=IF($C$75=1,IF($B25>C$22,$B25-C$22-C$23,-C$23),`
  `IF($B25<C$22,C$22-$B25-C$23,-C$23))`

- Equations are formed with the equation editor and shown in normal notation. For example, net present value:

$$NPV = \frac{(CashFlow)^N}{(1+r)^N}$$

- Genders. The use of 'he' or 'him' refers to masculine or feminine and this is used for simplicity to avoid repetition.

Overview

WHO NEEDS THIS BOOK?

Mastering Cash Flow and Valuation Modelling is a practical book for developing flexible financial models rather than an Excel textbook or a corporate finance manual. It seeks to bridge the gap between the two and describes a practical approach to developing an efficient financial model from a blank sheet. You can work through each of the chapters and build the model yourself in stages. The disk provides skeleton models with basic data on the disk for you to work on, modify and develop. Financial modelling is a practical subject and you need to work through each of the stages and overcome problems to understand the process of building a model. On completion you will be able to build better models with improved accuracy and analysis using a greater range of Excel functionality.

My other modelling books published by FT Prentice Hall, *Mastering Financial Modelling*, *Mastering Risk Modelling* and *Mastering Financial Mathematics in Microsoft® Excel*, provide further examples and combine finance with standardised, consistent model design using ideas of best practice coupled with methods of auditing and testing. These books use a tried and trusted design standard that many people have adopted and the author has received many emails praising the methodology. This book adheres to spreadsheet best practice and adopts the same basic style, method and layout as the other books.

The key objectives for this book are to:

- show how to build a model from a blank sheet rather than showing a series of individual examples;
- explain key methods needed for financial analysis and valuation;
- describe how to build in flexibility and what-if analysis;
- reduce coding and other errors through consistent adoption of the design method;
- provide a library of basic techniques for further development and use in other models.

This book aims to assist two key groups:

- practitioners who want a manual of financial analysis and valuation from which they can gain immediate use and payback;
- business students who need a textbook which is more geared to Excel solutions than some college manuals and corporate finance textbooks.

The areas of responsibility where the book should be of interest are:

- CFOs and finance directors;
- financial controllers;
- financial analysts and executives;
- accountants;
- corporate finance specialists;
- treasury managers;
- risk managers;
- academics, business and MBA students.

Therefore, people interested in this book range from an M&A specialist who wants a reference book to academics and business students who need a reference book for course work. The book has an international bias and provides examples that are relevant to the UK and overseas.

HOW TO USE THIS BOOK

- Install the Excel application templates using the simple SETUP command. The files will install automatically together with a program group and icons. There is a key to the file names at the back of the book.
- Work through each of the chapters and the examples building the model from the templates. There is a skeleton file with all the labels for you to use as a starting point.
- Use the manual, spreadsheets and templates as a reference guide for further work.
- Practice, develop and improve your efficiency and competence with Excel.

Alastair L. Day
Email: aday@system.co.uk or Internet: www.financial-models.com

Executive summary

This is a summary of the book by chapter presented in a tabular form to show
the progression from a blank sheet to a completed comprehensive model.

Chapter	Topic	Subjects covered
1	Introduction and overview	Scope of the book and the objective to write a generic cash flow model incorporating a range of Excel features and techniques
		Model design methodology and the need for modelling standards
		Example models to display the method
2	Functions	Finance functions for time value of money, discounted cash flow and loan analysis
		Mathematics functions such as SUMPRODUCT
		Time for producing robust timelines in a model
		Logic such as IF, OR and AND
		Text functions for joining and manipulating strings
		Analysis ToolPak and the extra functions and statistics methods
3	Model template	Framework and setting objectives
		Setting up sheets as modules
		Sheet templates for future use
		Efficiency techniques to enter code quickly without errors
		Planning for sensitivities and building in flexibility
4	Historic statements	Historic income statement components
		Entering the historic balance sheet and applying the modelling standard

Chapter	Topic	Subjects covered
5	Sales forecast	Generating income from volume and price
		Using sales forecast
		Fixed and variable costs
		Other elements of costs
6	Assets	Assets sheet
		Depreciation methods such as straight line, declining balance and sum of digits
		Calculations and required Excel functions
		Tax depreciation methods
7	Debt	Debt sheet and types of debt
		Setting out the debt calculations
		Interest rates and cumulative costs
8	Balance sheet	Forecast current assets
		Forecast current liabilities
		Equity
		Making the accounting statements balance
9	Cash flow	International IFRS statements
		Modelling techniques
		Ensuring integration of financial statements
10	Ratios	Financial ratios
		Debt ratios
		Returns ratios
		Reconciliation and checking
		Ensuring consistency
11	Cost of capital	Weighted Average Cost of Capital (WACC) theory
		Risk free and risk premiums
		Deriving betas
		Modelling methods
		Calculated cost of capital
12	Valuation	Terminal value methods
		Using different methods
		Single enterprise and equity valuation

Chapter	Topic	Subjects covered
13	Other approaches	Peer groups comparisons
		Market and multiples models
14	Alternative methods	Adjusted present value (APV) method
		Economic profit output as a comparison with free cash flow
15	Sensitivity	Building in sensitivities
		Flexing and stress testing the model
		Essential Excel techniques
		Dashboard methods for displaying multiple answers
		Charting techniques for reporting purposes
16	Optimisation	Excel methods
		Optimising outputs
		Checking for the 'best' mix of return, coverage and leverage
17	Reporting	Reporting and summarising data for reporting purposes
		Presenting results to different audiences
18	Auditing and review	Error detection
		Excel auditing techniques
		Other methods for ensuring consistency
		Documenting the findings
19	Documentation	User documentation
		Model maintenance
		Protecting the model for distribution
		Final model audit and review

Warranty and disclaimer

The financial models used in the book have not been formally audited and no representation, warranty or undertaking (express or implied) is made and no responsibility is taken or accepted by the author, Systematic Finance and its directors as to the adequacy, accuracy, completeness or reasonableness of the financial models and the company excludes liability thereof.

In particular, no responsibility is taken or accepted by the company and all liability is excluded by the company for the accuracy of the computations comprised therein and the assumptions upon which such computations are based. In addition, the reader receives and uses the financial models entirely at his own risk and no responsibility is taken or accepted by the company, and accordingly all liability is excluded by the company for any losses which may result from the use of the financial models, whether as a direct or indirect consequence of a computer virus or otherwise.

Microsoft, Microsoft Excel and Windows are registered trademarks of Microsoft Corporation.

Introduction and overview

File: MCFM_Template.xls

SCOPE OF THE BOOK

This book starts with the assertion that financial modelling should not be complicated. Many users have never been taught or shown how to develop models and consequently produce models of varying quality. Excel textbooks outline the features but do not show how to combine techniques to build more comprehensive models which add value. The requirement and purpose of this book is to build a cash flow valuation model and demonstrate the stages from initial annual accounts to final reporting. You could describe a spreadsheet as workings for your own use whereas a model as described here is for distribution or client use. The latter needs basic standards and an organised approach for flexibility and to reduce potential errors. It is not enough to allow a model to 'emerge' since this will magnify rather than reduce the incidence of error and most likely produce a suboptimum result. Many corporate models fail since they have not been planned and developed effectively or have been augmented by different individuals over time, which compounds weaknesses in the original method.

Common Excel errors include:

- single sheet for all inputs, formulas and outputs making navigation around the model difficult;
- lack of colour coding, particularly of inputs;
- inconsistency of design, colour and format;
- no control over user input with no validation or cell protection;
- lack of explanation of currency or units;
- complex formulas making the code hard to follow;
- mixed formulas, e.g. C6/12 or SUM(AA:BB) + 55, making it impossible to flex a model or apply sensitivity;
- inconsistent formulas or hard coded cells within calculation blocks breaking a direct line of calculation;
- no printing set-up or standards for headers and footers;
- no documentation or explanation meaning that users find it difficult to understand the model structure or what changes have been made to the coding;
- no version numbers and revision dates so that users do not know which is the latest usable file version.

The next section sets out some pointers on model design since the objective is to develop models quickly according to a tried and tested methodology which reduces as far as possible the propensity of error. Models can then be shared between members in a team and are easier to further develop, update and maintain. There is no one clear method of designing models and it is up to you to develop a method which delivers consistent results. Nevertheless, this is a tried and tested, easy-to-follow method which produces robust models with a minimum of development time and the potential for further maintenance.

MODEL DESIGN METHODOLOGY

Modelling should not be a complex task; however, there is no right or wrong way to build models. Some modelling houses create complex models with hundreds of range names or hidden sheets that make it difficult for clients to maintain or develop the models themselves. Conversely, end-users start by entering code and developing models in an ad-hoc fashion. Both approaches are not ideal and this author favours an organised approach which emphasises simplicity and consistency as the key objectives. All models are structured using the same methods whether they are project finance, lease evaluation, financial analysis or leveraged buy-out models. The following paragraphs do not constitute an exhaustive guide to modelling but rather lay down some of the ground rules which are followed in this book. The amount of effort and development time may depend on the value of funds moving through the model, the size of the audience and the importance of the result.

Defined objectives

There should be defined outputs from the model rather than starting with the inputs. It is often better to start with the required answers rather than trying to define the assumptions. What are the five to ten answers required? A leveraged buyout model may need to compute:

- overall firm value;
- equity value to the shareholders;
- purchase price as a multiple of EBITDA (earnings before interest, tax, depreciation and amortisation) or some other value;
- internal rate of return available to the firm and shareholders;
- debt service coverage for each tranche of debt in seniority order;
- maximum gearing during the forecast period;
- output value as a multiple of EBITDA or some other metric.

Sometimes on reviewing a model the answers are not immediately visible or are hidden within blocks of calculations. All the calculations in the model should lead directly to the calculation of these answers. These answers can then be presented as a range of outcomes in a single-page executive summary. This approach means that a summary is available to individuals who do not need all the detail of the interim calculations. Each user should receive the level of detail he needs rather than having to scan the whole model.

Modular

One theory of modelling suggests that all calculations should be located on one sheet. Since Excel audit arrows do not directly display arrows to other sheets, it can make a model complex and difficult to understand. Similarly, updating or revision need careful execution to avoid errors where rows are deleted by mistake. Finally, navigation can be difficult as all the code can use thousands of lines of code over multiple sheets with no apparent structure.

Models should be broken down into blocks of code that can be checked and audited in situ. For example, a schedule of asset depreciation and written down value logically should be situated on one sheet and loan payments and balances on another. Users can see the different tab names and it is easier to tab along the sheets using Control + PageUp and PageDown rather than scrolling down a single sheet which may extend to thousands of lines. Maintaining the file is also easier since you can insert new sheets without disrupting the existing code. For example, a valuation model can be extended with economic profit or adjusted present value by the inclusion of a new schedule and linking to the free cash flows and other variables on other sheets.

Layout – physical separation

Figure 1.1 shows the standard layout used by the author. It follows from the premise that each sheet in a model should look broadly the same and conform to standards of layout and measurement. It is logical to place a title at the top left together with a current version number on the right. The input variables should be placed together in a single area or input sheets rather than spread throughout the model. If somebody else uses the model, you have to be confident that they will update all necessary variables and produce the correct outputs. Similarly, all the calculations should be in modules or blocks as described above with no hard coded formulas. The answers should be clearly visible with a summary as close as possible to the inputs. The printed area should be clear and any workings not required in the reporting should be in marked areas outside the printed area. Workings can be hidden using grouping of hiding the cells. Figure 1.1 is a schematic for a single-page model and could of course be scaled up into a more complex application with multiple input, calculation and output sheets.

Column A and row 1 are not used for stylistic reasons to maintain a margin. If the row and column headers are removed there will still be a margin around the model rather than it being squeezed against the side and top.

Figure 1.1
Layout

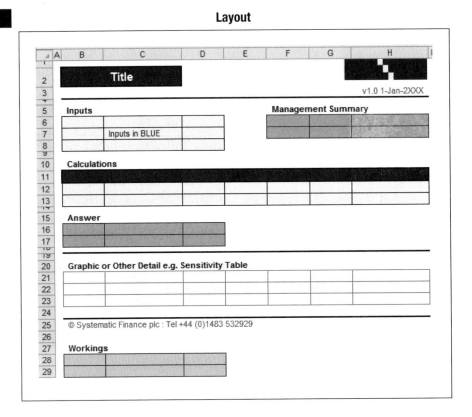

Information flow

If the planning starts from the outputs and you split the model into physical areas, information should flow through the model in a logical manner. Figure 1.2 illustrates the optimum flow of information through the sections in a model. There are several 'rules' that can be applied:

- south and east;
- left to right, top to bottom;
- like a book – logical succession of topics;
- information taken from a left-hand not a right-hand sheet.

It is more logical to order sheets starting with the income statement, balance sheet, cash flow and ratios rather than start with ratios. A user would expect to start at the first sheet and see the calculations build up to a final output area. Another rule could be that you always access information from the top or a sheet to the left as information sourced from all sides is confusing for an end-user.

Information flow

Figure 1.2

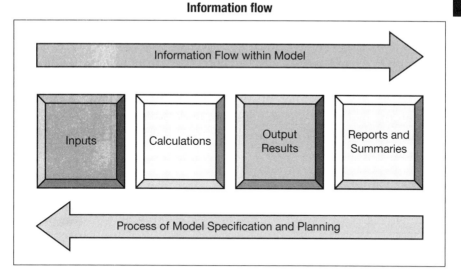

Informative labels

Superior models provide feedback to users and dynamically update information. Labels are more informative if they update as the user changes inputs. For example 'NPV at 5.2%' is easier to understand than 'NPV'.

For example, the formula would be:

```
="NPV at "&TEXT(XXX, "0.0%")
```

Also it saves the user immediately trying to find out the rate actually used to calculate the NPV. Where possible, models should 'cascade' information through the sheets providing direct links through the calculations.

Same columns

Users often start coding from blank sheets and unnecessarily duplicate effort. Each sheet should start from a basic template and will therefore use the same dimensions and layout. It is logical to start period one in the same column on every sheet so that all the code lines up. If you are in column F and the code uses a reference to column E on another sheet, it will immediately look odd and be worthy of investigation. If you 'zigzag' the formulas you will increase the risk of error. If you access different columns on different sheets, you will have to check each reference and errors will thus be harder to spot.

Colours

Colour is one way of differentiating between inputs and other types of cells. If a spreadsheet has no marking on input cells, a user has to show formulas or click aimlessly around the sheets in an attempt to understand the structure of the sheet and where to enter data. Inputs, outputs, workings and other cell types should be marked in a specific colour and format to ensure that others can understand where to enter data. The model in Figure 1.3 uses blue (shown in light grey in the figure) to mark the control or input area and (darker) grey for outputs. If the colour scheme is published in some form on the model then it is simple for any other user to understand the model. Ideally you should publish your basic format guide as part of the model explanation.

Figure 1.3

Specimen model

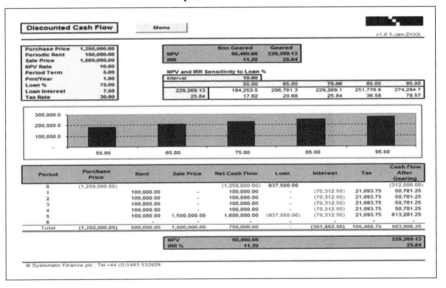

Styles

In the author's experience most users do not use styles in Excel but they do use basic styles for headings, paragraphs and numbering in Microsoft Word. Styles are a useful way to 'remember' what an input or header should look like and save time by applying the format quickly. It saves you formatting the cell type over and over again or using the format painter to carry the formatting forward. Figure 1.4 details the main styles used by the author in the model. Styles can consist of all the elements of border, colour, font and number or just one item such as number format in the style.

Styles

Figure 1.4

Name	Style	
(A) Area Styles		
SFL Sheet Title	AAA	
SFL Heading 1	**Heading 1**	
Heading 2	**Heading 2**	
Hesding 3	**Heading 3**	
Heading Row	Specimen Heading	Specimen Heading
Named Cell	*Tax Rate*	
Input	123,456.00 AAA	
Input Name/Label	Input Name	
Technical Input	1234 AAA	
Off sheet	1,234.00	1,234.00
On sheet	1,234.00	1,234.00
Info	Kg	sq mtr
External Link	5,443.00	
Empty Cell		
Totals Row	1,234.00	
Alert	v1.0 1-Jan-2020	Alert!
Check	0	1
Flag		
Column Total	-	-
Answer Box	**Specimen Answer**	**Answer**
Workings Box	Workings	Area
Do Not Cross Border Right	Do Not Cross	

Styles can be found at Home, Styles. The input style shown in Figure 1.5 does not include the number format so that it can be applied to a wide range of cells without affecting the existing number format. You can modify the style at any time and it should update throughout the model. This is similar to using CSS sheets in Javascript and web pages. When you copy a cell containing a style to another workbook the style is also copied, saving the time of re-entering the style. Used correctly styles provide a simple method of achieving the basic objective of consistency of numbers, fonts, colours, shading and borders across all workbooks.

Input style

Figure 1.5

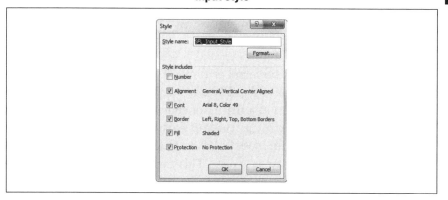

Number formats

Users are often illogical in their use of positive and negative numbers. In modelling, it is simpler if all costs or cash outflows are negative and all inflows are positive. It can cause errors and make reconciliation more difficult if you use positive costs, e.g. Sales – Cost – Depreciation. Where you see a positive extraordinary item in an income statement, you are not sure if it is a cost or benefit without examining the code. If cost and depreciation are negative you only have to add down the column using the shortcut 'Alt + ='. Excel does not include a built-in number format for negative numbers in red and so a suitable custom number format or style is:

```
Format ; Positive ; Negative ; Zero ; Text
#,##0.00 ;[RED](#,##0.00);-;"Please enter a number!"
```

Again, a limited number of formats are used in the model as styles. Rather than searching for the custom number format, it is easier to apply the existing number style (Figure 1.6). These do not contain any other formatting so they can be 'layered' on the top without overwriting the font, border or other existing formatting elements.

Figure 1.6

Number styles

SFL_Accounting_0	1,000,000	(1,000,000)
SFL_Accounting_1	1,000,000.0	(1,000,000.0)
SFL_Accounting_2	1,000,000.00	(1,000,000.00)
SFL_Eur_Acct_0	1 000 000	(1 000 000)
SFL_Eur_Acct_1	1 000 000.0	(1 000 000.0)
SFL_Eur_Acct_2	1 000 000.00	(1 000 000.00)
SFL_Round_000	1,000.00 T	(1,000.00 T)
SFL_Round_Mill	1.00 M	(1.00 M)
SFL_Percent_0	10%	(10%)
SFL_Percent_1	10.1%	(10.1%)
SFL_Percent_2	10.10%	(10.10%)
SFL_Yes_No	Yes	No
SFL_Short_Date	15-Jan-15	
SFL_Medium_Date	15-January-2015	
SFL_Long_Date	Thursday, 15-January-2015	

Printing

It is annoying if you want to print several pages from a workbook and find out that the author has not bothered to find out if they will fit on the sheet and print correctly. All sheets should be set up for printing with standard margins, headers and footers as a matter of course (Figure 1.7). This author uses file, sheet, date and time at the top with the sheet name and page number at the bottom. The model also includes a company name at the bottom together with the last save date. This can be achieved with a simple macro in workbook actions set to run whenever the user prints a page:

```
Private Sub Workbook_BeforePrint(Cancel As
Boolean)

    Dim wkSht As Worksheet

    ActiveSheet.PageSetup.LeftFooter = "(c)
Systematic Finance : Last Saved : " & Format
(ThisWorkbook.BuiltinDocumentProperties("Last
Save Time"), "yyyy-mmm-dd hh:mm:ss")

        End Sub
```

Printing

Figure 1.7

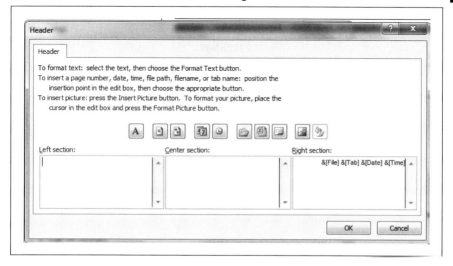

Units

Units and currencies should be clearly visible and where possible more than one currency should not be resident on the same sheet. Where models are multi-currency, it is usually better to input in the local currency and switch to the international currency for all calculations. The general currency and units should be visible in the same place on each schedule and the other units should be clearly marked in a specific column, for example:

Units: USD Millions

Where the numbers are formatted into millions using formatting such as #,##0.00', the units should be marked in the cell: #,##0.00', "Mill" to avoid any confusion. Otherwise, if the user sees '10' he may think that the number is ten rather than ten million.

Validation

Many errors emanate from faulty or incomplete data entry where user entry is not checked in any way. Data Validation allows a simple rule to be placed against individual cells requiring defined inputs. This means that if the model needs a percentage between 10 and 20 per cent, only this data is allowed and Excel generates an error message if the user tries to enter incorrect data.

The dialog box in Figure 1.8 displays the choices and when you click on one, other operators open up to allow logic and values to be applied. The objective is to have all inputs cells validated in some form and to ensure that data is entered to all input cells without blanks or incomplete data.

Validation

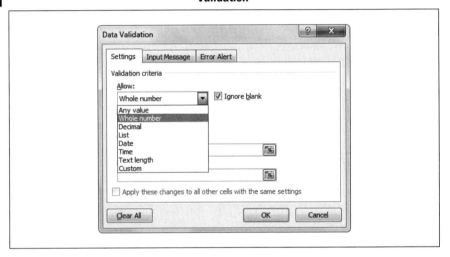

Self-checks

Models should include self-checks to ensure that any errors are immediately flagged. For example:

- assets and liabilities on balance sheets must be equal;
- cash generation should agree with the change in cash on the balance sheet;
- loan amortisation should write off the whole amounts.

A simple text string on each sheet can confirm that the model balances (Figure 1.9). If you place the model checks in the same place on every sheet, a user should be alerted immediately if the model is not synchronised.

Checks

Figure 1.9

Error checks	
Balance sheet	0
Forecast balance sheet	0
Balance sheet reconciliation	0
Cash flow	0
Cash reconciliation	0
Economic profit	0
Check	**0**

Error Check: Balances OK
N/A

Names

Named ranges can be an informative method of explaining formulas pro-vided the method is not overused. Referring to a cell as `CostofCapital` rather than `WACC!C5` may make the formulas more understandable; how-ever, defining hundreds of names without any hint as to their geographic location in the file can make the model too complex and hard for users to understand. Where developers use the `Create Names` method, it is simple to form hundreds of names at the same time. The author favours the use of some names and certainly the use of standard names in every file, e.g. Product, Author.

Functions – complexity

The next chapter provides simple examples of the majority of functions used in the model. The emphasis is on clarity and simplicity rather than nesting strings of functions together. The code below will work but is complex and difficult to audit. Such code has to be thoroughly checked for accuracy and every logical outcome. It would be better to break it down into multiple cells since a key advantage of Excel over compiled languages is that you can see the interim calculations and track through the calculations. It is not a 'black box' where you merely await the answer after a routine has run.

```
=IF(Method1="B",IF(SightType1=1,IF(Data!$D$9<>0,
Data!$D$9,C40),IF(SightType1=2,IF(Data!$D$9<>0,V
LOOKUP($C$16,Data!$B$16:$O$74,3),C40),IF(SightTy
pe1=4,IF(Data!$D$11<>0,Data!$D$11,C40),IF(SightTy
pe1=5,IF(Data!$D$12<>0,Data!$D$12,C40),IF(SightTy
pe1=6,IF(Data!$D$13<>0,Data!$D$13,0),IF(SightType
1=7,IF(Data!$D$14<>0,Data!$D$14,0),C40))))))),C40)
```

Formulas – mixed formulas

One key mistake that users new to Excel make is the use of mixed formulas such as C6/4 or SUM(C6:C12)+50. In both cases the formula contains a variable which should be located in the control or inputs area. The second formula could be a 'plug' number to make a balance sheet balance, but would constitute a severe weakness in the model. You have to be confident that you have a direct link from inputs through calculations to outputs, since any mixed formulas will render useless any flexing, sensitivity or scenarios. A hard-coded number will break the chain of formulas, as changing an input may not fully resolve its impact on the calculations.

Avoid circular references and links

Circular references or iteration occur when the answer is part of the calculation (Figure 1.10). For example, interest is payable on an average balance where the interest is rolled up at the end of the period. As the period end balance increases so does the interest payable on the average balances outstanding. Files should be checked to make sure that circular references are not ticked, as unintended circular references should be avoided. They make the file unstable, slower to recalculate and potentially inaccurate.

Figure 1.10   **Iteration**

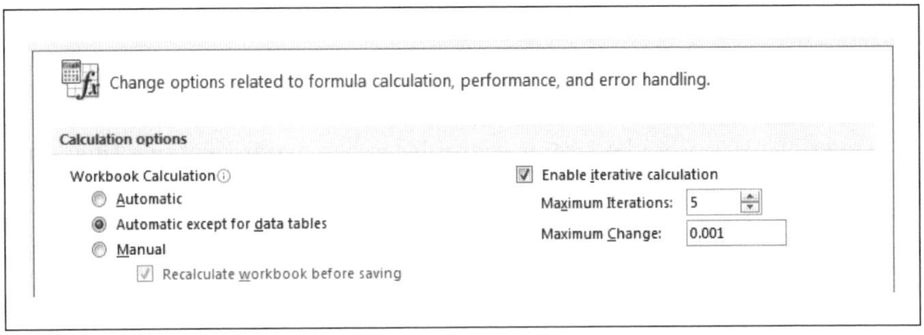

Similarly, links to other files do not necessarily show and `Data, Connections` should be checked, especially if named cells or ranges have been copied from another file. In Figure 1.11 `Edit Links` is 'greyed out', meaning that there are no links to other files. Excel will not warn you in the status bar that you have links and it is up to you to check for them.

Links

Figure 1.11

Graphics

Models should communicate results clearly and models with pages of tightly packed numbers do not show relationships or variances clearly. Charts can easily be produced with the shortcuts F11 or Alt F1 and are especially useful for checking cash flows or ratios. Charts can also reveal errors since the chart does 'look right'. The table in Figure 1.12 lists the main types of charts together with their possible uses.

Chart types

Figure 1.12

Type of graph	Use	Example
Line graph	Present continuous data, especially movements over a large number of time periods	Sensitivity chart
	Compare the behaviour of a large number of variables, especially when they are close together and would be difficult to distinguish between in a bar chart	GDP per capita for selected countries
Bar chart	Present discrete data	Product scales by region
	Compare the behaviour of a small number of different variables	Sales of three types of product by region
	Present movements over a short period of time, when a line graph may appear rather awkward	Product sales
Pie chart	Show the breakdown of a single variable into its component parts, particularly to emphasise that together the parts add to 100%	Sales split between divisions
	Never use two pie-charts side by side for comparison	
Stacked bar chart	Show how the breakdown of a variable into its component parts fluctuates, provided that the number of parts is limited	Cost breakdown
	Indicate the ranking in an example, by sorting the bars	Profitability by division
Area graph	Show the breakdown of a continuous variable into its constituent parts	Settlement exposure
X-Y (or scatter) graph	Understand the relationship between two variables	Correlation and regression

Front sheet

Models should have a front sheet detailing who developed the model, along with its owner, manager, purpose, last revision date and any other relevant information. The sheet shown in Figure 1.13 is common to many files and makes it easier for any user to gain assistance or to make sure they are using the correct version. The version number is of course repeated in the top right of every sheet to make it clear to any user.

Figure 1.13   **Front sheet**

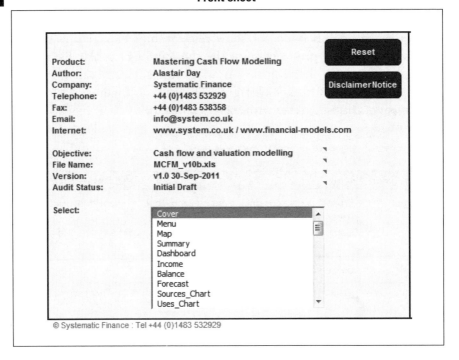

Navigation/hyperlinks

It becomes frustrating to navigate around a workbook once there are more than about ten sheets. Users need assistance and do not always understand the structure of a model especially if the calculations are not ordered logically. Users should be able to click on a button to return to a menu and then click on a chosen page in a table of contents. This means they can access any item in the file with a maximum of two clicks. Maps of models as shown in Figure 1.14 are useful since they can tell the user the order in which to enter data, and how to view calculations or the reports available.

Navigation can be achieved with macros or hyperlinks to named cells on the relevant sheets. Shapes and pictures can also accept hyperlinks as well as macros in the same way as web pages.

Hyperlinks

Figure 1.14

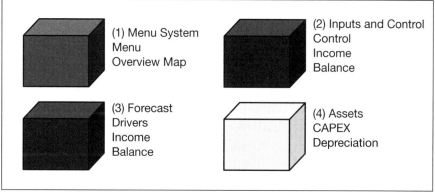

Version

Version numbers of important models should be tightly controlled by means of an individual 'owning' the file. History or Version sheets allow for notes on the changes or errors found since the reason for changes will be forgotten in 12 months' time. Figure 1.15 is a simple recording sheet for relevant information.

Version

Figure 1.15

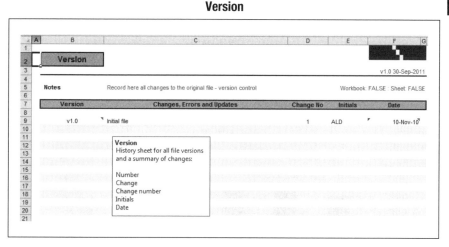

Documentation

Many models do not provide sufficient documentation to assist users. Explanation of key formulas or the structure of the application should be included with the model on a separate sheet or as a pasted Acrobat or Word object. Documentation helps with the audit process since an exterior reviewer should be able to understand the process and logic faster. Simple comments in individual files can help to explain formulas and procedures.

EXAMPLE MODELS

The example in Figure 1.16 shows the basic layout used in this book. The inputs, calculations and outputs are clearly marked and the information moves from the top to the bottom of the sheet.

Figure 1.16   **Example**

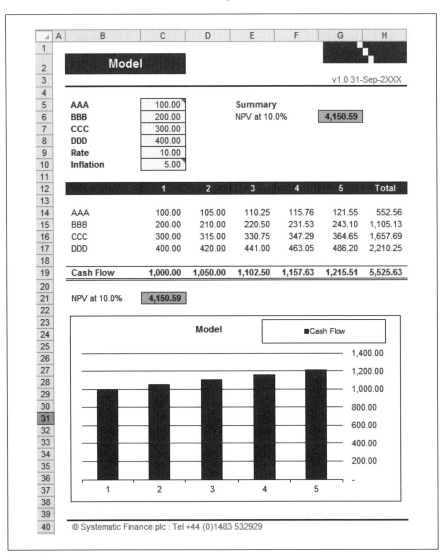

SUMMARY

This chapter details some basic rules followed by the modelling in this book. There is no single method or methodology and it is up to the modeller to develop a style that is clear and consistent and can be repeated again and again. The objective is to outline ideas for developing models with a robust structure that can be maintained without radical redesign. It is not an exhaustive list but more a statement of best practice. The next chapters start the model template and seek to put into practice the ideas in this chapter.

Functions

File: MCFM_Functions.xls

The last chapter emphasised the use of clear short formulas as part of a basic modelling standard which can be audited and understood easily. Formula constructions such as IF, IF, IF … tend to be difficult to understand and prone to simple errors. While there are around 450 functions in Excel, most of them are not applicable to cash flow modelling. The Excel file for this chapter contains lists in alphabetical and subject order together with a list of Analysis ToolPak functions to serve as an overall reference (Figure 2.1). The latter are more advanced functions which are not always available with a 'typical' installation of Office. Check for the installation of Analysis ToolPak as detailed in Appendix 1. If it is not present you will need to go to `File`, `Options`, `Add-Ins`, `Manage Add-Ins` to install the extra functions (Figure 2.2).

Finance functions

Figure 2.1

Function	Type	Analysis Toolpak	Description
EFFECT	Financial	Yes	Returns the effective annual interest rate
FV	Financial	-	Returns the future value of an investment
FVSCHEDULE	Financial	Yes	Returns the future value of an initial principal after applying a series of
INTRATE	Financial	Yes	Returns the interest rate for a fully invested security
IPMT	Financial	-	Returns the interest payment for an investment for a given period
IRR	Financial	-	Returns the internal rate of return for a series of cash flows
ISPMT	Financial	-	Calculates the interest paid during a specific period of an investment
MDURATION	Financial	Yes	Returns the Macauley modified duration for a security with an assumed
MIRR	Financial	-	Returns the internal rate of return where positive and negative cash
NOMINAL	Financial	Yes	Returns the annual nominal interest rate
NPER	Financial	-	Returns the number of periods for an investment
NPV	Financial	-	Returns the net present value of an investment based on a series of
ODDFPRICE	Financial	Yes	Returns the price per $100 face value of a security with an odd first
ODDFYIELD	Financial	Yes	Returns the yield of a security with an odd first period
ODDLPRICE	Financial	Yes	Returns the price per $100 face value of a security with an odd last
ODDLYIELD	Financial	Yes	Returns the yield of a security with an odd last period
PMT	Financial	-	Returns the periodic payment for an annuity
PPMT	Financial	-	Returns the payment on the principal for an investment for a given
PRICE	Financial	Yes	Returns the price per $100 face value of a security that pays periodic
PRICEDISC	Financial	Yes	Returns the price per $100 face value of a discounted security
PRICEMAT	Financial	Yes	Returns the price per $100 face value of a security that pays interest at
PV	Financial	-	Returns the present value of an investment
RATE	Financial	-	Returns the interest rate per period of an annuity

Add-Ins – Analysis ToolPak and Solver

Figure 2.2

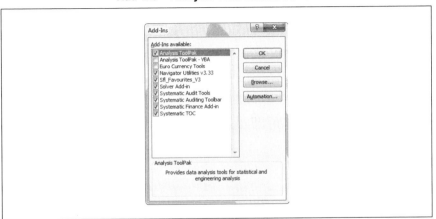

CATEGORIES

This chapter provides simple examples of most of the functions used in this book together with a note of the formulas used:

- Finance functions for time value of money, discounted cash flow and interest rates.
- Mathematics functions such INT, ROUND and MOD.
- Time functions for setting up consistent timelines.
- Lookup functions such HLOOKUP, VLOOKUP, INDEX, CHOOSE, MATCH and OFFSET.
- Logic functions such as IF, AND and OR.
- Text functions for manipulating text such as TEXT.
- Other functions such as the information functions CELL and INFO.

FINANCE

The cash flow model in this book needs to calculate the value produced or added during the forecast period together with the repayment of loans. Loans are an example of time value of money problems where you want to calculate the loan payment or find the interest rate in an existing loan. Figure 2.3 shows a loan of 1,000 over three years at a rate of 10 per cent nominal with the rentals of 95.10 payable quarterly in advance. Normally you would calculate the annuity payment required to return the desired rate; however, the rental has been entered to allow calculation of all five variables. Since the inputs are only entered to two decimal places there will be rounding errors.

The method allows you to calculate the fifth variable if you know four in the same way as a financial calculator such as an HP 12C or TI BAIIPlus. The Excel functions work in the same way:

- NPER – number of payments required to amortise the principal.
- RATE – periodic nominal interest rate inherent in the structure.
- PV – present value or initial capital.
- PMT – payment or annuity amount.
- FV – future or residual value if the payment does not amortise the full principal.

TVM functions

Figure 2.3

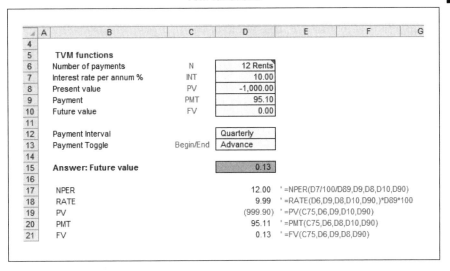

Some of the background calculations are in the workings at the bottom of the page (see Figure 2.4). The payment interval alternatives are monthly, quarterly, semi-annual and annual in a validation list box. A MATCH function finds the row number and chooses the frequency. Rather than calculating the periodic interest rate several times, the model shows the periodic rate in line 75.

Payments can be in advance or in arrears, which means that the rental is payable at the beginning or end of its period. In Excel functions, the flag '1' means in advance and '0' means in arrears.

Workings

Figure 2.4

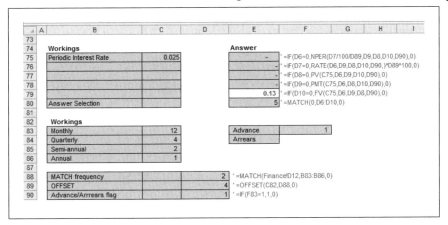

In order to complete accounting statements, loan payments need to be split between interest and principal, or in other words be amortised. Since the payment is in advance, the whole of the first payment is assumed to be principal rather than interest. The net advance after the first payment is 904.89. If you were to multiply this by the periodic nominal rate as the carrying cost of this capital for one quarter, the cost would be 22.62. Since the payment is 95.10 the principal is the difference. The principal is subtracted from the capital outstanding and the process is repeated in the next quarter. The functions IPMT and PPMT for the interest and principal will automate this process (see Figures 2.5). They take the same arguments as PMT except that there is an extra parameter for the payment number.

Figure 2.5

Amortisation

A	B	C	D	E	F	G
24	Amortisation schedule					
25				IPMT	PPMT	Balance
26			1	–	95.11	(904.89)
27			2	22.62	72.49	(832.40)
28			3	20.81	74.30	(758.10)
29			4	18.95	76.16	(681.95)
30			5	17.05	78.06	(603.89)
31			6	15.10	80.01	(523.87)
32			7	13.10	82.01	(441.86)
33			8	11.05	84.06	(357.80)
34			9	8.94	86.16	(271.63)
35			10	6.79	88.32	(183.32)
36			11	4.58	90.53	(92.79)
37			12	2.32	92.79	–
38			13			
39	Total			141.31	1,000.00	
40						
41	IPMT			–	'=IPMT($C$75,B26,$D$6,$D$8,$D$10,$D$90)	
42	PPMT			95.11	'=PPMT($C$75,B26,$D$6,$D$8,$D$10,$D$90)	

A cash flow model also has to deal with uneven cash flows and so the time value of money functions are not appropriate where there could be more than one payment or groups of payments. Here NPV for net present value and IRR for the internal rate of return are required (see Figure 2.6). These are the equivalent of PV and RATE in the time value of money functions.

The NPV function finds the present value of the outstanding cash flows at the periodic nominal rate. There are some slight rounding differences and the present value is equivalent to the net advance. The alternative is to calculate the internal rate. If you include all the cash flows the function derives the periodic nominal rate that can be multiplied by the frequency of payment.

NPV/IRR

Figure 2.6

A	B	C	D	E	F
45					
46	NPV / IRR				
47			Capital	Cash flow	Net
48	1.00		(1,000.00)	95.10	(904.90)
49	2.00			95.10	95.10
50	3.00			95.10	95.10
51	4.00			95.10	95.10
52	5.00			95.10	95.10
53	6.00			95.10	95.10
54	7.00			95.10	95.10
55	8.00			95.10	95.10
56	9.00			95.10	95.10
57	10.00			95.10	95.10
58	11.00			95.10	95.10
59	12.00			95.10	95.10
60	13.00			-	-
61	Total		(1,000.00)	1,141.20	141.20
62					
63	NPV		904.80	' =NPV(C75,F49:F60)	
64	IRR %		9.99	' =IRR(F48:F60)*D89*100	

The final financial functions are EFFECT and NOMINAL for converting between nominal and effective rates and vice versa (see Figure 2.7). The effective rate takes into account the number of compounding periods in a year. If there is one payment then the effective and nominal rates are the same. As the number of compounding periods increase, the effective rates rises relative to the nominal rate. Most Excel functions require periodic nominal rates.

The entries are the relevant rate and the number of payments per annum. Ten per cent quarterly nominal is equivalent to an effective rate of 10.38 per cent. You could also calculate this manually by future valuing 100 over four quarters at the periodic rate. The future value is 110.38 and subtracting the initial 100 leaves the effective rate of 10.38 per cent.

Effective/nominal

Figure 2.7

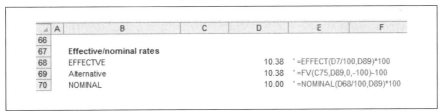

A	B	C	D	E	F
66					
67	Effective/nominal rates				
68	EFFECTVE			10.38	' =EFFECT(D7/100,D89)*100
69	Alternative			10.38	' =FV(C75,D89,0,-100)-100
70	NOMINAL			10.00	' =NOMINAL(D68/100,D89)*100

MATHEMATICS

The basic mathematics function is SUM, which can be entered with the shortcut Alt + =. SUMIF is an alternative whereby you can set a condition against a criteria range and then sum the range that meets the condition.

The example in Figure 2.8 shows criteria of 140 against the selection range column D. The sum range is in column E. This can be used for selecting only those periods during a historic or forecast period.

Figure 2.8

Mathematics functions

	Period	Cash 1	Cash 2	Total	Mask	SUMIF	MOD	CEILING	FLOOR
1		100.00	50.00	150.00	FALSE	-	1.00	4.00	-
2		200.00	60.00	260.00	FALSE	-	2.00	4.00	-
3		300.00	70.00	370.00	FALSE	-	3.00	4.00	-
4		400.00	80.00	480.00	FALSE	-	-	4.00	4.00
5		500.00	90.00	590.00	FALSE	-	1.00	8.00	4.00
6		600.00	100.00	700.00	FALSE	-	2.00	8.00	4.00
7		700.00	110.00	810.00	FALSE	-	3.00	8.00	4.00
8		800.00	120.00	920.00	FALSE	-	-	8.00	8.00
9		900.00	130.00	1,030.00	FALSE	-	1.00	12.00	8.00
10		1,000.00	140.00	1,140.00	FALSE	-	2.00	12.00	8.00
11		1,100.00	150.00	1,250.00	TRUE	1,250.00	3.00	12.00	8.00
12		1,200.00	160.00	1,360.00	TRUE	1,360.00	-	12.00	12.00
13		1,300.00	170.00	1,470.00	TRUE	1,470.00	1.00	16.00	12.00
14		1,400.00	180.00	1,580.00	TRUE	1,580.00	2.00	16.00	12.00
15		1,500.00	190.00	1,690.00	TRUE	1,690.00	3.00	16.00	12.00
16		1,600.00	200.00	1,800.00	TRUE	1,800.00	-	16.00	16.00
17		1,700.00	210.00	1,910.00	TRUE	1,910.00	1.00	20.00	16.00
18		1,800.00	220.00	2,020.00	TRUE	2,020.00	2.00	20.00	16.00
19		1,900.00	230.00	2,130.00	TRUE	2,130.00	3.00	20.00	16.00
20		2,000.00	240.00	2,240.00	TRUE	2,240.00	-	20.00	20.00
Total		21,000.00	2,900.00	23,900.00		17,450.00			

SUM	23,900.00	' =SUM(E6:E25)	
Lower Limit	140.00	140	
Criteria	>140	' =">"&C30	
SUMIF	17,450.00	' =SUMIF(D6:D25,C31,E6:E25)	
Period	4.00	4	
MOD	1.00	' =MOD(B6,$C$34)	
CEILING	4.00	' =CEILING(B6,$C$34)	
FLOOR	-	' =FLOOR(B6,$C$34)	
SUMPRODUCT	3,710,000.00	' =SUMPRODUCT(C6:C25,D6:D25)	
Array	3,710,000.00	' =SUM(C6:C25*D6:D25)	

Sometimes you may want to find period ends for tax calculations or the date for replacement of assets. For quarterly periods, you could use a formula such as:

```
=IF(Period/4 = INT(Period/4)...
```

An alternative is to use the function MOD, which calculates the modulus or remainder. In column H the period end is marked with a zero since the modulus is zero.

You may want to find the previous or next period end and the functions FLOOR and CEILING provide the last and next divisible period. During the first year the ceiling is four whereas the floor is zero.

SUMPRODUCT is also useful for weighting calculations. For example, loan amount and interest rates when you are computing the interest payable. You could multiply each one individually and then add each cell but SUMPRODUCT achieves both. An alternative would be to enter a SUM function as an array with Control + Shift + Enter in the form:

```
={SUM(C6:C25*D6:D25)}
```

The function multiplies out all the possibilities again as a compact formula. Excel then views the array as a block of cells and will not allow you to delete individual elements.

TIME

Many models use period numbers to denote time and in effect assume 360-day years and 30-day months. This only approximates time as January and February are different lengths. The Analysis ToolPak functions EDATE and EOMONTH allow a start date and future dates as multiples of an interval. EDATE advances in periodic intervals while EOMONTH shows the end of the periodic month. Figure 2.9 shows a time period starting in January 2010 with a monthly interval. Since the start date is the end of the month both functions show the same result.

Time

Figure 2.9

	B	C	D	E	F
4					
5	Start	31-Jan-12			
6	Interval	1.00			
7					
8	Period	EDATE	EOMONTH		
9					
10	0	31-Jan-12	31-Jan-12		
11	1	29-Feb-12	29-Feb-12		
12	2	31-Mar-12	31-Mar-12		
13	3	30-Apr-12	30-Apr-12		
14	4	31-May-12	31-May-12		
15	5	30-Jun-12	30-Jun-12		
16	6	31-Jul-12	31-Jul-12		
17	7	31-Aug-12	31-Aug-12		
18	8	30-Sep-12	30-Sep-12		
19	9	31-Oct-12	31-Oct-12		
20	10	30-Nov-12	30-Nov-12		
21	11	31-Dec-12	31-Dec-12		
22	12	31-Jan-13	31-Jan-13		
23	13	28-Feb-13	28-Feb-13		
24	14	31-Mar-13	31-Mar-13		
25	15	30-Apr-13	30-Apr-13		
26	16	31-May-13	31-May-13		
27	17	30-Jun-13	30-Jun-13		
28	18	31-Jul-13	31-Jul-13		
29	19	31-Aug-13	31-Aug-13		
30	20	30-Sep-13	30-Sep-13		
31					
32	EDATE	31-Jan-12	'=EDATE($C$5,$C$6*B10)		
33	EOMONTH	31-Jan-12	'=EOMONTH($C$5,$C$6*B10)		

Analysis ToolPak functions do not always translate well on non-English Excel versions and therefore you always need replacements if you think that a user with German or French Excel may access the file. The code below provides workable code to replace the functions with user-defined code:

```
Function SFLEndOfMonth(ByVal InStartdate As
Double, ByVal InMonths As Integer)

    'replaces the EOMONTH function

    SFLEndOfMonth = DateSerial(Year(InStartdate),
Month(InStartdate) + InMonths + 1, 0)
End Function

Function SFLExtendDate(ByVal InStartdate As
Double, ByVal InMonths As Integer)

    'replaces the EDATE function

    SFLExtendDate = DateSerial(Year(InStartdate
),Month(InStartdate) + InMonths, Application.
WorksheetFunction.Min(Day(InStartdate), Day(Dat
eSerial(Year(InStartdate), Month(InStartdate) +
InMonths + 1, 0))))
End Function
```

LOOKUP

Lookup functions are needed to obtain information from tables or for generating scenarios. Models need to be flexible and make choices and the data in Figure 2.10 displays the same answers using different functions. The simplest lookup function is CHOOSE, which allows you to have an index number and a series of choices. One benefit is that you do not have to declare a range and can obtain the choices from different sheets.

INDEX supports a one- or two-dimensional range and provides for an xy coordinate within the range as a row and column number. You have to provide a fixed range unless you enter a scalable range in the form:

```
=OFFSET(Sheet1!$B$2,0,0,CurrentRows(Sheet1!$B$2,1
000),CurrentCols(Sheet1!$B$2,1000))
```

This example name will expand and shrink by up to a thousand rows and columns from the starting cell B2.

Lookups

Figure 2.10

Period	1	2	3	4		CHOOSE	INDEX	OFFSET	LOOKUP
AA	100.00	200.00	300.00	400.00		300.00	300.00	300.00	300.00
BB	101.00	202.00	303.00	404.00		303.00	303.00	303.00	303.00
CC	102.00	204.00	306.00	408.00		306.00	306.00	306.00	306.00
DD	103.00	206.00	309.00	412.00		309.00	309.00	309.00	309.00
EE	104.00	208.00	312.00	416.00		312.00	312.00	312.00	312.00
FF	105.00	210.00	315.00	420.00		315.00	315.00	315.00	315.00
GG	106.00	212.00	318.00	424.00		318.00	318.00	318.00	318.00
HH	107.00	214.00	321.00	428.00		321.00	321.00	321.00	321.00
II	108.00	216.00	324.00	432.00		324.00	324.00	324.00	324.00
JJ	109.00	218.00	327.00	436.00		327.00	327.00	327.00	327.00
KK	110.00	220.00	330.00	440.00		330.00	330.00	330.00	330.00
LL	111.00	222.00	333.00	444.00		333.00	333.00	333.00	333.00
MM	112.00	224.00	336.00	448.00		336.00	336.00	336.00	336.00

Select Column   3

CHOOSE	300.00	'=CHOOSE($D$20,C6,D6,E6,F6)	
INDEX	300.00	'=INDEX(C6:F6,0,$D$20)	
OFFSET	300.00	'=OFFSET(B6,0,$D$20)	
LOOKUP	300.00	'=LOOKUP($D$20,$C$5:$F$5,C6:F6)	

OFFSET is useful where you do not want to declare a complete range and has the advantage of not requiring a range. Here you enter a starting cell and state how many rows down and how many columns across you need for the answer. If the rows and columns are negative, the movement is up and back. The example above starts at column B and selects the third column across.

LOOKUP works by entering a lookup value, which is three in Figure 2.10 above. It looks for the value across the cells C5:F5 and finds it in the third column. These two elements are locked and the formula derives the third element in the lookup answer vector, which changes as you move down the table.

LOGIC

Models need to make decisions and IF is generally one of the first functions that new users include in their spreadsheets. It tends to be overused with nested IF statements. These can be difficult to understand and audit. One method is to use AND and OR to reduce the number of IF functions required, or alternatively you could rewrite and simplify the code.

The example in Figure 2.11 displays three volumes and the code finds the volume increasing, reducing or in the middle. The first line is increasing since the last is larger than both to the left. The second is 'OK' since the last is larger than one but not the other. The last is becoming worse since the last is lower than both the first two.

AND results in true if all statements are true, whereas OR is true if any of the conditions are true. AND and OR are combined with IF in Figure 2.11 to display 'Better', 'OK' or 'Worse'

Figure 2.11

Logic

	Element	1	2	3	AND	OR
7	AA	100.00	200.00	300.00	TRUE	TRUE
8	BB	100.00	300.00	200.00	FALSE	TRUE
9	CC	300.00	200.00	100.00	FALSE	FALSE
11	AND	TRUE	'=AND(E7>D7,E7>C7)			
12	OR	TRUE	'=OR(E7>D7,E7>C7)			
13	IF	Better	'=IF(AND(E7>D7,E7>C7),"Better",IF(OR(E7>D7,E7>C7),"OK","Worse"))			
14		OK	'=IF(AND(E8>D8,E8>C8),"Better",IF(OR(E8>D8,E8>C8),"OK","Worse"))			
15		Worse	'=IF(AND(E9>D9,E9>C9),"Better",IF(OR(E9>D9,E9>C9),"OK","Worse"))			

TEXT

Often labels are not informative, e.g. tax or NPV. The model is easier to understand if labels 'cascade' or update automatically to include other information. For example, 'Tax at 25%' rather than 'Tax' will be easier for an end-user since they do not have to start looking for the tax rate. The function CONCATENATE allows you to join text stings, or alternatively you can use an ampersand:

```
=C5&" "&C6&" "&C7&" "&C8
```

Excel calculates numbers to more than ten decimal places so numbers have to be shortened to be used in text strings. Figure 2.12 uses TRUNC and ROUND to truncate the numbers to two percentage places. A better alternative is to employ the TEXT function to transform the number into text and then format it to two percentage places.

```
="Rate at "&TEXT(C13,"0.00%")
```

Text

Figure 2.12

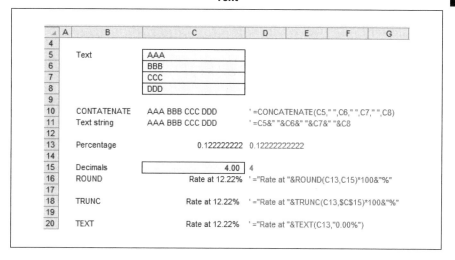

OTHER FUNCTIONS

The model needs to transpose certain information such as asset values or dates. Whilst you can use Paste Special, Formulas Transpose, this is not always the most efficient method. The array function, TRANSPOSE, uses a block of cells and is entered with Control + Shift + Enter. This action tells Excel to accept the selected block as an array (see Figure 2.13).

Transpose

Figure 2.13

	A	B	C	D	E	F	G	H
4								
5		Array	AA	BB	CC	DD		
6			11.00	22.00	33.00	44.00		
7								
8			AA	11.00		AA	11	
9			BB	22.00		BB	' =D8*2	
10			CC	33.00		CC	' =D8*3	
11			DD	44.00		DD	' =D8*4	
12								
13		TRANSPOSE	AA	11.00		' =TRANSPOSE($C$5:$F$6)		
14			BB	22.00				
15			CC	33.00				
16			DD	44.00				

CELL and INFO are useful information functions since they provide details about cells or the environment. It is useful to display the current sheet or file name on the sheet dynamically. As the file is saved with different names the information updates without further intervention. The CELL example in Figure 2.14 uses 'filename' as the parameter, while the INFO function uses 'directory'.

Figure 2.14

CELL and INFO

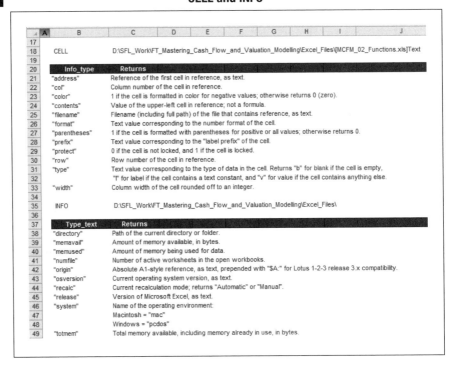

The example in Figure 2.15 extracts the file and sheet names from CELL("filename") by looking for character separators. Excel follows this syntax for cell references:

```
=[File.xls]Sheet!A1
```

The alternative is to use a user-defined function, FileSheet, with an option number:

```
Function FileSheet(No)

    Select Case No
    'Inserts the required sheet name or file name
as a function
       '1=Full name and path
       '2=Directory path
       '3=File name
       '4=Sheet name
```

```
        Case 1: FileSheet = ActiveWorkbook.FullName
        Case 2: FileSheet = ActiveWorkbook.Path
        Case 3: FileSheet = ActiveWorkbook.Name
        Case 4: FileSheet = ActiveSheet.Name
    End Select
End Function
```

Indirect addresses means that you can construct a cell reference as a text string in the above form. In the data in Figure 2.15 you want to extract the data at row 59 and column six. The function ADDRESS is one method of forming a cell reference from a sheet, row and column number in text form. INDIRECT translates the address into a cell reference and obtains the answer.

Alternatively, as shown below, you could put together a text string using R1C1 referencing rather than the more usual Excel A1 style. You can switch to this style in Excel options for normal use; however, this style is more reminiscent of early spreadsheets and most uses adopt the A1 style today.

```
="["&C67&"]"&C69&"!R"&C72&"C"&C73
```

Figure 2.15

Indirect addressing

Indirect addressing

Row / Column	3	4	5	6	7	8	9
56	226	69	285	903	929	706	938
57	513	746	650	982	180	598	170
58	508	671	374	798	49	968	151
59	184	554	33	295	33	860	950
60	283	384	678	200	170	613	544
61	448	510	999	302	66	593	703
62	633	186	483	70	83	642	449
63	626	159	436	262	584	926	812
64	136	421	454	357	305	289	181
65	798	954	192	151	574	816	917

File	MCFM_02_Functions.xls	
	'=MID(CELL("filename"),FIND("[",CELL("filename"))+1,FIND("]",CELL("filename"))-FIND("[",CELL("filename"))-1)	
Sheet	Other	
	'=RIGHT(CELL("filename",A1),LEN(CELL("filename",A1))-FIND("]",CELL("filename",A1)))	
Row	59	59
Column	6	6
ADDRESS	Other!$F$59	'=ADDRESS(C72,C73,,,C69)
INDIRECT	295.00	'=INDIRECT(C75)
String	[MCFM_02_Functions.xls]Other!R59C6	'="["&C67&"]"&C69&"!R"&C72&"C"&C73
INDIRECT	295.00	'=INDIRECT(C78,FALSE)

Excel needs to check formulas and the two methods used in the model are shown in Figure 2.16. ISERROR generates TRUE or FALSE. If there is no error, an answer is displayed or 'n/a' if the formula encounters an error. The alternative is to use IF to suppress DIV/0 errors. As part of the modelling standard, models should check themselves as much as possible and it is important to introduce checks on the code to ensure that no error messages are produced.

Figure 2.16

Error checking

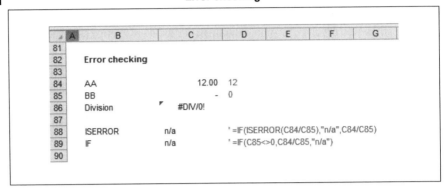

SUMMARY

This chapter provides simple examples of the main functions used in the cash flow model as a reference. Models should not use complex sets of code or nested blocks of functions as this makes models difficult to understand and increases the probability of error.

Model template

DESIGN OBJECTIVES

Chapter 1 outlined some of the common modelling errors related to layout, mixed formulas, inconsistent code etc., which often result in poorly structured models with errors or inadequate analysis. Some models seem to follow an emergent process rather than exhibit an overall plan. It is often difficult to set aside time to plan a complete model and changes to the specification and user requirements may become evident as the model progresses. Sometimes another department or client will have different objectives or provide input late in the process. For example, it is better to integrate a multi-language or currency early on in the modelling process rather than at the reporting and sign-off stage. Nevertheless, planning should be the first part of the process with clear objectives for the key outputs required.

SYSTEMATIC DESIGN METHOD

The Systematic Design Method is a collection of procedures and techniques that you can use in all types of models. The method seeks to speed up model development, reduce modelling errors and provide suitable analysis. By using the method consistently, others will understand your models quickly since all the spreadsheets will follow the same methodology. The method begins with the layout shown in Figure 3.1 which you can scale across multiple sheets as the models become more complex. The method emphasises the use of:

■ modular structure with multiple sheets for different 'chapters';
■ simple colour schemes for inputs, headers, calculations, outputs, etc.;
■ styles for inputs, outputs and other key cell types;
■ validation of key inputs to prevent inaccurate input;
■ limited names for clarity of coding;
■ specific number formats especially to highlight negative numbers and units;
■ use of form controls such as scroll bars and combo boxes for simple selection;
■ self-checks on balance sheets, loans and cash flows to improve accuracy;
■ version control on all sheets;
■ charts for model checking and presentation of results;
■ clear output reports and management summaries;
■ documentation and explanation of procedures and techniques.

Figures 3.2 and 3.3 summarise the topics covered in this book.

Figure 3.1

Layout

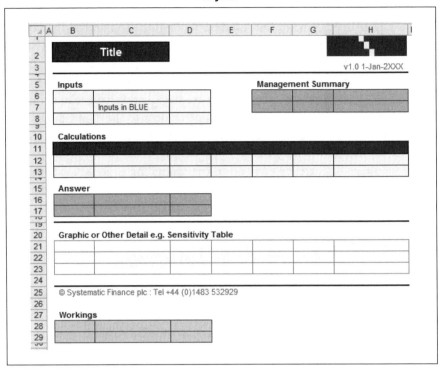

Figure 3.2

Map

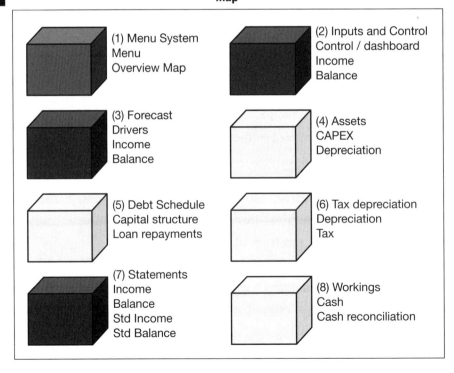

Map

Figure 3.3

(9) Cost of capital
WACC

(10) Valuation outputs
Terminal value
DCF
Returns

(11) Alternatives
Economic profit
Adjusted Present
Value

(12) Charts
Drivers
Margin

(13) Sensitivity
and returns
Sensitivity
Analysis
Returns

(14) Management
summaries
Reports
Charts

CASE OBJECTIVES

The case model spreads a set of five annual reports into an income statement and balance sheet and then treats the case as an outline acquisition. The key objective is to calculate the value of the enterprise and check the structure against basic banking covenants, such as the debt service coverage or the ratio of debt to value (leverage).

The model pays off the existing debt on inception and replaces it with a loan structure based on an enhanced share price as the existing price plus a premium. The case could be further analysed with individual forecasts of the company's divisions, operating companies or geographic split to allow forecast accounting statements to be produced for the sub-units. Key workings comprise the assets, loans, debt repayable and tax. With completed forecast statements and cash flows available to the firm, the model shows the financial benefits and allows the user to check the results against standardised or common size statements and compare them with historic and forecast ratios. With the cost of capital inputs, a free cash flow valuation is possible and the model can compare the findings against peer groups and multiples. Other modules with alternative approaches, such as economic profit and adjusted present value, are possible additions. Using a modular framework you can easily add new features to the model.

A model that produces a single answer does not produce a suitable level of analysis as you need more information for decisions. You need to understand:

- what happens to the key outputs as a variable changes or flexes;
- the relative importance of different variables, e.g. are sales more important than capital expenditure?

It is important that the model is designed from the outset to allow sensitivity and 'what-if' analysis. Some models use macros or duplicate sheets to attain some form of multiple answers, but this is inefficient, inflexible and prone to error. This model will use tables and types of scenarios to demonstrate changes in value or ability to pay.

The model needs summaries and charts for reporting since different audiences require varied levels of information. Finally, some documentation of the model would be useful in order to explain the mechanics, where to enter data, the reports available and generally how to use the model (see Figure 3.4).

Figure 3.4

Framework

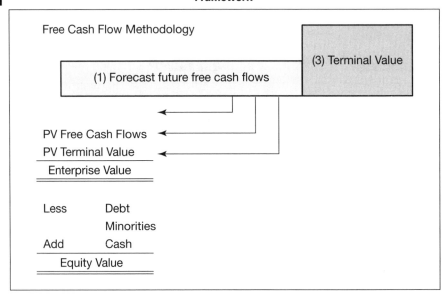

The model shown in Figure 3.4 needs to provide a range of outputs to satisfy banking covenants and valuation. It is not enough to generate a value since you need to know if it is 'enough' to satisfy the requirements of various stakeholders. The table below sets out the general values for returns and debt service:

Source and use of funds	
Equity allocation	
Goodwill calculation	
Firm and equity valuation	
Firm internal rate of return (IRR)	12.5%
Equity internal rate of return	25%
Purchase enterprise value/EBITDA	7×
Maximum senior debt/EBITDA	3×
Exit EV/EBITDA	5×
Total debt/EBITDA	4×

Enterprise value, in simple form, comprises the market value of debt and equity as opposed to an accounting value shown in annual reports. EBITDA stands for earnings before interest, tax, depreciation and amortisation. This represents the net operating profit with non-cash items such as depreciation added back to form a simple proxy to operating cash flow. It should not be confused with operating cash as it does not include changes in working capital. A company can generate a healthy EBIT but still consume cash by the inefficient management of working capital.

The model can be broken down into stages as reflected in the chapters in this book:

- Cover – front sheet with disclaimer as the first sheet any user sees on opening the model.
- Menu – basic information such as the author, version number, file name, etc.
- Map – pictorial representation of each of the modules and sheets to illustrate the model framework.
- Summary – executive management summary showing the findings against the key criteria above.
- Control – input and dashboard sheet with case information such as the dates, units, currency, loan restructuring and results against management criteria.
- Income – historic income statement for five years.
- Balance – historic balance sheet for five years.
- Forecast – calculation of key drivers such as sales growth, cost percentages, capital expenditure and other metrics needed to map the accounting statements over the forecast period.
- Sources and Uses Charts – pie charts with the sources of debt and equity and how the funds are used in the initial purchase price.
- Assets – capital expenditure profile with depreciation calculations and net book value as a workings sheet. This generates entries for the forecast income statement and balance sheet.
- Debt Schedule – drawdown of new debt together with repayment profile used to calculate the interest payable, debt payments and net debt outstanding.
- Tax Depreciation – tax depreciation and written down value using straight line or double declining method depending on the tax jurisdiction.
- Tax – taxable income adding back accounting depreciation and taking into account the tax depreciation along the lines of US or UK tax.
- Forecast Income – historic and forecast income statement in landscape mode.
- Forecast Balance – historic and forecast balance sheet on the same sheet.

- Standard Income – standardised or common size income statement with sales factored to 100 and all other lines expressed as a factor against sales. This provides a ratio to sales for every line on the income statement and is useful for highlighting revenue and costs trends.

- Standard Balance – common size balance sheet with items expressed as a factor of total assets or liabilities.

- Forecast Cash – forecast IAS cash flow working down from EBITDA, through cash from operations, investing and financing to reconcile with the balance sheet change in cash.

- Forecast OpCash – reworked cash flow statement to calculate the cash available to service debt as the starting line for the next sheet.

- Forecast DebtCash – debt waterfall sheet starting with the cash available and subtracting the interest and principal payment for each of the new debts. The net cash reconciles back to the residual cash in the balance sheet.

- Ratios – financial and debt ratios based on a ratio pyramid starting with return on equity and leading down in to return on sales, asset leverage and asset turnover.

- Charts Dashboard – single page report of important ratios charts such as return on equity, return on assets, gearing and interest cover.

- WACC – weighted average cost of capital calculation from equity, preference shares and debt for the forecast periods expressed as a historic value, forecast value and cumulative percentage.

- WACC Calculation – pictorial representation of the make-up of the cost of capital.

- Valuation – free cash valuation using the cash flow statement and cost of capital with a terminal value based on an EBITDA multiple or a growth model output.

- Economic Profit – alternative methodology showing the profit after a charge for the capital utilised and reconciled to the free cash method. This method is useful for showing the source of the value.

- APV – adjusted present value breaking up the free cash valuation into segments to demonstrate the value of cost savings or leverage as a proportion of the total.

- Sensitivity – matrices illustrating the change in outputs from alterations in key variables.

- Analysis-dynamic charts from every schedule in the model to allow a user to review any aspect of the model.

- Returns – cash flows and returns available to the different providers of capital.

- Workings – backing sheet with lists, combo box workings, dates, binary flags and counters used in all the schedules. This sheet could be hidden on any distribution of the model.
- Version Log – history sheet listing the different versions of the file to show what has changed over time.
- Styles – sheet setting out the basic styles used in the model. As described earlier, styles represent a more efficient method of formatting cells and promoting consistency of presentation.
- Audit – memo sheet to record tests carried out on the model. All models contain errors and it is a feature of best practice to show the tests carried out to prove the integrity of the model.

Each of the sheets has a reference and line number of the left-hand side as this is useful for showing references and calculations. This example shows the calculation of accounts receivable:

  Accounts receivable: FP010*FF039

The general notation used in the model is:

- SM – summary
- IN – control
- IP – input income
- IR – input balance
- SP – standard income
- SB – standard balance
- FF or F – forecast
- FP – income
- BD – assets
- TD – tax depreciation
- CS – debt schedule
- TW – tax
- FB – balance sheet
- CF – cash
- CO – forecast operating cash
- DB – debt cash
- SL – standard forecast income
- SA – standard forecast balance
- RT – ratios
- WA – WACC
- VA – valuation

- MA – market valuation
- PE – peer groups
- AP – APV
- EP – economic profit
- RE – IRR returns

TEMPLATES

The first step is to be organised and reduce the unnecessary duplication of effort: some people start with a blank spreadsheet and re-create each page again and again in every model. This leads to unnecessary duplication and potential errors. You should always use templates for sheets, workbooks, charts and basic code in order to speed up development.

Figure 3.5 shows a standard portrait schedule with precise measurements. Column A is set to two wide and not used for stylistic reasons. When the row and column headers are removed it forms a margin with row 1. Row 2 is 18.75 high rather than the standard 11.25 and the font is set to 11 points. The rest of the sheet is set to an 8 point font size with an accounting number format. The default protection for each cell is locked and hidden. Styles are in place for the sheet header, version, copyright and other cells. A red line is drawn around the edge of the spreadsheet to specify the end of the code. This is used in preference to the grey area that some developers prefer.

Figure 3.5   **Schedule**

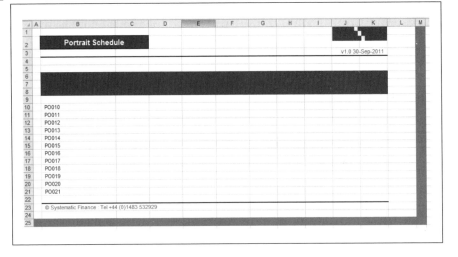

The company uses standard headers, footers and margins:

- Header: file name, sheet name, date, time.
- Left footer: company name, last saved date.
- Right footer: sheet name, page number.
- Margins: settings as in Figure 3.6.

Margins

Figure 3.6

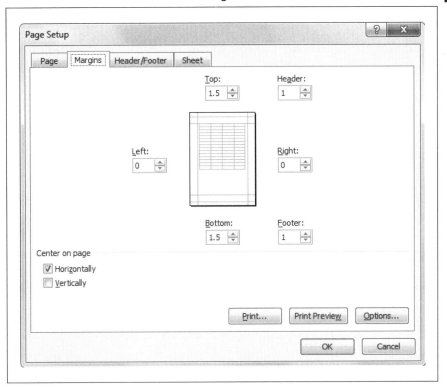

You need both landscape and portrait schedules as standards as it is quicker to right-click and copy basic sheets rather than set up the printing on every sheet. The landscape schedule needs to be wide enough for the timeline together with extra information such as units and, if necessary, narrow blank columns can also be included. You do not want to have to insert columns on 30 sheets at a later stage so it is useful to set up some 'dummy' columns now in case they are needed. In this model there are likely to be five historic periods followed by a forecast period of ten years.

You can import styles from a basic style sheet in another workbook to follow corporate colours and standards. In any case you should develop your own style sheet in corporate colours to be used on all models. It is best not to create too many styles; however, basic styles are needed for headers, headings, numbers, checks and alerts in the same way as a well-structured Word document (see Figures 3.7 and 3.8).

Figure 3.7

Style sheet

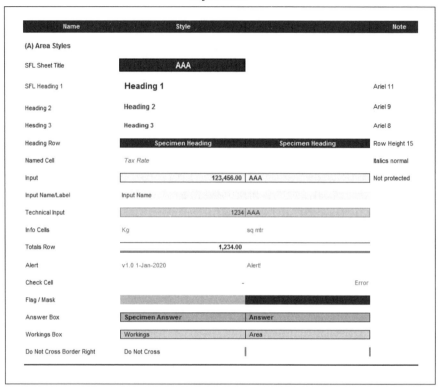

Figure 3.8

Available styles

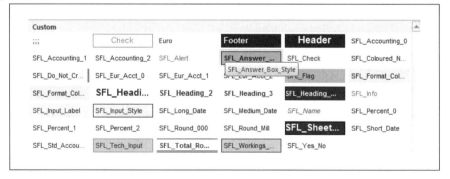

Initially, you can copy a number of sheets from initial templates by right-clicking the tab and selecting the Copy option:

- cover;

- menu;

- landscape schedule;

- portrait schedule;

- workings;

- version;

- audit;

- styles.

You can think of spreadsheet models as a book with a cover, table of contents, summary and chapters representing individual sheets. Figure 3.9 contains a specimen disclaimer and a confirmation of the product name, file name and version.

Cover

Figure 3.9

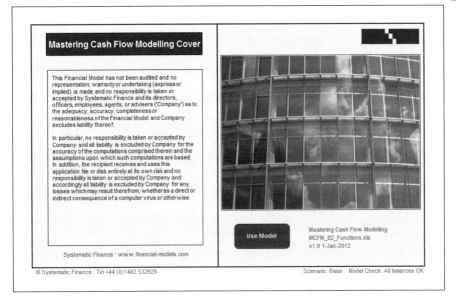

The menu sheet contains basic information about the file, such as:

- author;

- manager;

- company;

- contact details;

- file objective;

- last revision date;

- file name;
- version;
- audit status.

You can return the current file name with =CELL("Filename"), but this inserts the full path, file and sheet name. A simple way is to insert a Visual Basic function into the file:

```
Function FileSheet(No)

Select Case No
'Inserts the required sheet name or file name as
a function

'1=Full name and path
'2=Directory path
'3=File name
'4=Sheet name

Case 1: FileSheet = ActiveWorkbook.FullName
Case 2: FileSheet = ActiveWorkbook.Path
Case 3: FileSheet = ActiveWorkbook.Name
Case 4: FileSheet = ActiveSheet.Name
End Select
End Function
```

As basic inputs, it is a good idea to name these cells as this sheet can form part of an application template. The simplest method is to use 'Create from Selection' in Formulas and use the text in the left-hand column (see Figure 3.10). You can quickly apply styles to the input cells as an alternative to individual formatting.

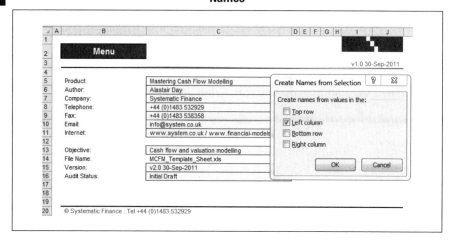

Figure 3.10   **Names**

Other standard sheets are the version and audit sheets as basic sheets for recording information (see Figures 3.11 and 3.12). It is important to note what has changed, or any errors found in the model, and to be sure that a specific version number continues to derive the same answers as earlier versions.

Version

Figure 3.11

Version	Description	Date	Change	Initials
v1.0	Initial File	30-Sep-11	1	ALD

v2.0 30-Sep-2011

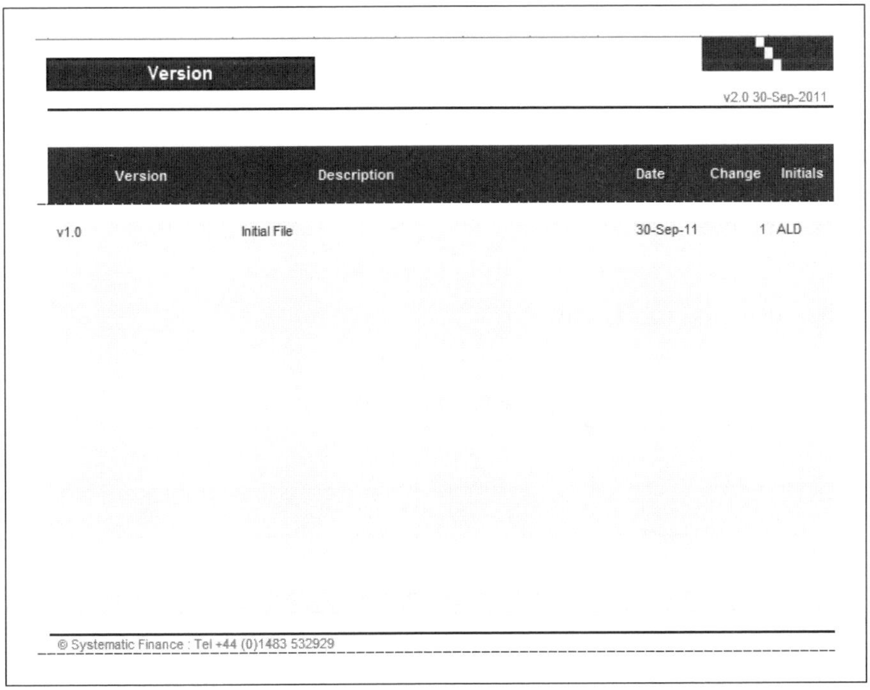

© Systematic Finance : Tel +44 (0)1483 532929

Sheets

Figure 3.12

Cover · Menu · Landscape Schedule · Portrait Schedule · Workings · Version · Audit · Styles

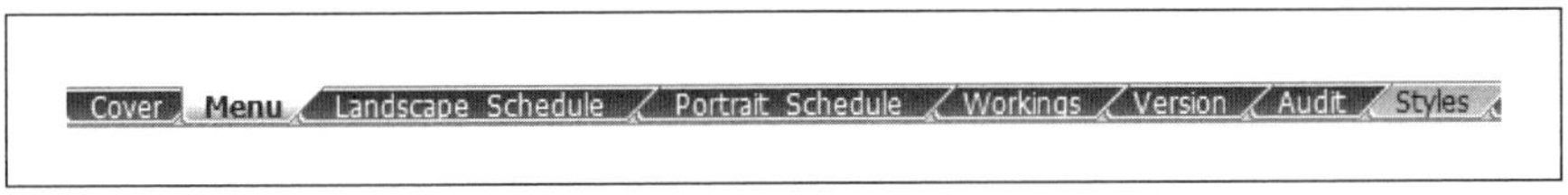

INPUT SHEET

The dashboard acts as a control or input sheet. It is important that the model follows a clear information flow from inputs through calculations to output and reports (see Figure 3.13). Anybody using the model needs to know where to enter data. Similarly, protection is difficult to complete if cells are not colour-coded and you forget to unlock the cells where you need to enter data.

You can copy a new sheet from the portrait template and the data entered on the sheet. The basic inputs are:

- client name in text form;
- revision reference;
- start date for the model used to set up timelines;
- interval in months (1,3,6,12);
- currency as a Swift code, e.g. USD;
- units, e.g. millions;
- forecast period beyond the initial historic results;
- number of ordinary shares outstanding;
- current share (stock) price;
- offer premium as a percentage of the ordinary share price;
- existing debt retired;
- fees and transaction costs relating to the restructuring;
- new debt and equity structure.

Figure 3.13　　　　　　　　　**Information flow**

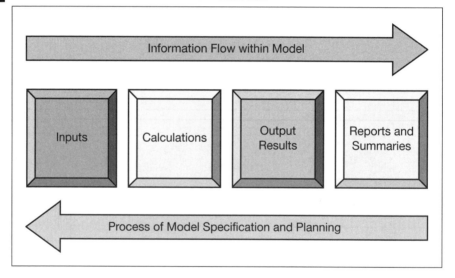

The table in Figures 3.14 and 3.15 shows the raw data with the numbers formatted with the basic styles of a two-digit accounting number, short date and percentages. The accounting format does not display negative numbers in red on most versions of Excel and so this is a simplified format to ensure that negative numbers are shown correctly. The hash means that a number is entered as applicable and a comma forms the thousand separator.

```
#,##0.00 ;[RED](#,##0.00);-;"Please enter a
number!"
```

Control inputs 1

Figure 3.14

IN005	Client Name		AAAAA
IN006	Revision reference		Rev 1-Jan-2012
IN007	Start Date		01-Jan-12
IN008	Interval		12.00
IN009	Currency		USD
IN010	Units:		Millions
IN011	Forcast Period		10.0 years
IN012			
IN013	Uses of funds		
IN014	Current stock price		1.50
IN015	Offer premium		10.00%
IN016	Offer price per share	IN014*1+IN015	1.65
IN017			
IN018	Shares outstanding (MM)		7,000.00
IN019	Equity purchase price		11,550.00
IN020			
IN021	Equity purchase price	IN019	11,550.00
IN022	Debt retired	FB057	16,776.00
IN023	Initial advisory fee		0.50%
IN024	Financing fee		1.00%
IN025	Transaction costs		292.75
IN026			
IN027	Total uses		28,618.77
IN028			
IN029	Equity allocation		
IN030	Outside equity		24.22%
IN031	Management equity A		64.95%
IN032	Management equity B		10.83%
IN033	Total Equity Allocation		100.00%

Control inputs 2

Figure 3.15

Sources of funds			%	Distribution
Existing debt	100.00%	–	–	
Senior debt A	100.00%	12,000.00	41.93%	
Senior debt B	100.00%	5,000.00	17.47%	
Junior debt C	–	2,500.00	8.74%	
Junior debt D	–	2,000.00	6.99%	
Junior debt E	–	2,000.00	6.99%	
Other	–	–	–	
Preferred stock		500.00	1.75%	
Outside equity		1,118.77	3.91%	
Management equity A		3,000.00	10.48%	
Management equity B		500.00	1.75%	

The inputs can be validated to ensure that the correct inputs are present using Data, Data Tools, Validation (see Figure 3.16). The validations are a mix of text length, whole numbers, percentages, list and custom formats. You can always use Edit, Find and Replace, Special to highlight the validated cells on a sheet where validation is only one of the search options.

Figure 3.16

Validation

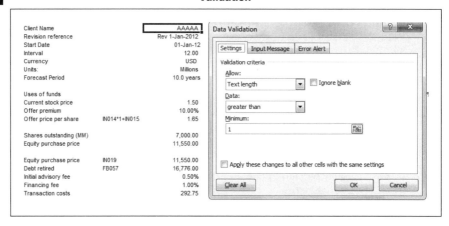

List validations are best for units and currency since these are pre-defined lists (see Figure 3.17). To save cluttering the input sheet, you can locate these lists on the workings or backing sheet. If the source appears on a different sheet, you have to name the range required for the validation to work, and these lists are therefore named SwiftList and UnitsList respectively.

Figure 3.17

List validation

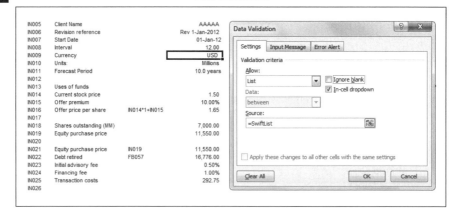

Finally, apply formatting styles to ensure that the schedule is correctly marked. The names of the new loans, their seniority and the amounts will be needed in later schedules. The principle is that these names will cascade through the model to save re-entering the names on the debt sheet, accounting statements and so on.

Figure 3.18

Colour coding

IN005	Client Name	AAAAA	
IN006	Revision reference	Rev 1-Jan-2012	
IN007	Start Date	1-January-2012	
IN008	Interval	12	
IN009	Currency	USD	
IN010	Units:	Millions	
IN011	Forecast Period	10.0 years	
IN012			
IN013	**Uses of funds**		
IN014	Current stock price		1.50
IN015	Offer premium		10.00%
IN016	Offer price per share	IN014*1+IN015	1.65
IN017			
IN018	Shares outstanding (MM)		7,000.00
IN019	**Equity purchase price**		**11,550.00**
IN020			
IN021	Equity purchase price	IN019	11,550.00
IN022	Debt retired	FB057	16,776.00
IN023	Initial advisory fee		0.5%
IN024	Financing fee		1.0%
IN025	Transaction costs		292.75
IN026	**Total uses**		**28,618.77**
IN027			
IN028	**Equity allocation**		
IN029	Outside equity		24.22%
IN030	Management equity A		64.95%
NI031	Management equity B		10.83%
NI032	**Total Equity Allocation**		**100.00%**

Sources of funds

			%	Distribution
Existing debt	Senior	–	–	
Senior debt A	Senior	12,000.00	41.93%	
Senior debt B	Senior	5,000.00	17.47%	
Junior debt C	Junior	2,500.00	8.74%	
Junior debt D	Junior	2,000.00	6.99%	
Junior debt E	Junior	2,000.00	6.99%	
Other	Junior	–	–	
Preferred stock		500.00	1.75%	
Outside equity		1,118.77	3.91%	
Management equity A		3,000.00	10.48%	
Management equity B		500.00	1.75%	
Total sources		**28,618.77**	**100.00%**	

There is a simple chart on the right of Figure 3.18 that shows the distribution of funds as an alternative to spark lines. This uses the REPT function to repeat a character:

```
REPT("¦",L15*50)
```

All schedules in the book contain a line number for reference purposes. The input sheet begins 'IN'. This is useful in explaining the source of data on other sheets such as ratios or cash flows. It allows any user to track calculations from the line references listed. This is a dynamic reference in the form:

```
="IN"&TEXT(ROW(B5),"000")
```

The TEXT function translates a number into text and formats it with leading zeroes. The formula uses an ampersand in preference to the CONCATENATE function.

TIMELINE

When models are not planned at the outset, one common mistake is to hard code time and the model to calculate it in several places. The principal aim should be to calculate time once, and once only. Other sheets can use the information on the initial timelines on all other schedules. The most important Excel functions for timelines are EDATE and EOMONTH. The first advances in whole months from a specific date and the second derives the end of the month from a multiple of months. These are Analysis ToolPak functions from the add-in, and if they are not displayed in the function list, you can install it manually at File, Options, Add-Ins.

In some parts of the world, such as Germany, these functions do not automatically translate to EDATUM and MONATSENDE and replacement Visual Basic functions are therefore provided below. To use them, you will need to ensure that macros are enabled in File, Options, Trust Center, Trust Settings, Macro Settings.

```
Function SFLEndOfMonth(ByVal InStartdate As
Double, ByVal InMonths As Integer)'replaces the
EOMONTH function

SFLEndOfMonth = DateSerial(Year(InStartdate),
Month(InStartdate) + InMonths + 1, 0)
End Function

Function SFLExtendDate(ByVal InStartdate As
Double, ByVal InMonths As Integer)'replaces the
EDATE function
```

```
SFLExtendDate = DateSerial( Year(InStartdate),
Month(InStartdate) + InMonths, Application.
WorksheetFunction.Min(Day(InStartdate),
Day(DateSerial( Year(InStartdate),
Month(InStartdate) + InMonths + 1, 0))))
End Function
```

The header for the timeline on the Workings sheet can be looked up elsewhere in the model, the objective being to provide all the counters that may be needed. There are five historic periods followed by up to ten forecast periods and these need to be clearly marked.

Timeline

Figure 3.19

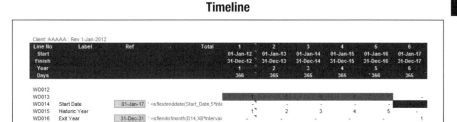

The start date is brought forward from the Control sheet and the beginning and end of each period are calculated with EOMONTH or the Visual Basic user function SFLEndofMonth (see Figures 3.19 and 3.20).

End of month

Figure 3.20

```
=cstOne
=Start_Date
=sflendofmonth(J7,Interval-cstOne)
=ROUNDUP(J6/(cstTwelve/Interval),cstZero)
=J8-J7+cstOne
```

```
=IF(J7<$D$14,cstOne,cstZero)
=IF(AND(J7>=$D$14,J7<sflendofmonth($D$14,Interval*Forecast_Period)),cstOne,cstZero)
=J9/(cstTwelve/Interval)*J13
=SUM($J$14:J14)/(cstTwelve/Interval)
```

The model uses named constants from the list in Figure 3.21 instead of typing 0 or 12. This is to confirm that no formulas are produced which mix formulas and numbers. When you audit or review the model, it is important to check that input constants have not been hard coded in formulas, thereby breaking the lines of calculation.

The binary flags denoting the historic or forecast will be important later in the model to simplify the code. Rather than using multiple IF statements, it can be more straightforward to multiply by one or zero such that there is only one logic statement to maintain. For example, the forecast period is ten years and all cash flows have to cease at the end of this period. It is therefore simpler to multiply 50 rows by the flag rather than maintaining 50 IF statements.

You can copy the formulas across the heading and the last date should be 31 December 2026 with ten forecast years.

Figure 3.21	Constant names

Constants	
cstTwelve	12
cstZero	0
cstHundred	100
cstThousand	1000
cstOne	1
cstTwo	2
cstAlmostZero	0.00000001
cstDays365	365
IRR guess	0.1
cstTen	10
cstRounding	5

SUMMARY

It is important to 'get organised' in modelling with standard procedures, templates and lots of reusable code. This chapter introduces the basic case and sets up an outline application template. Methods such as styles, colours, number formats, names and formats are important in standardising sheets and workbooks and in reducing the incidence of avoidable mistakes. The basic template consists of standard sheets for menus, schedules, timelines, version data and other backing sheets. You can save the basic application file as a template for future use. It is now ready for accepting the historic data.

Historic statements

File: MCFM_Skeleton.xls

ACCOUNTING SHEETS

The first schedules to be added to the model are the historic income and balance sheets. The analysis begins with up to five annual reports for the model company and the application needs to present them in a standardised form for further analysis. Companies vary their layout due to local accounting practices or presentation requirements and the purpose of the initial accounts is to establish a layout that can be used for other cases and in the forecast and other statements. As discussed in Chapter 3, we can consider all models to be templates or sources of reusable code.

You can copy the schedule template with a timeline and make up an historic sheet with room for five periods (see Figure 4.1). The client name and units can be added to all the sheets using the named references:

```
="Client: "&Client_Name&" : " &Revision_reference
="Units: "&Currency&" "&Units
```

Schedule

Figure 4.1

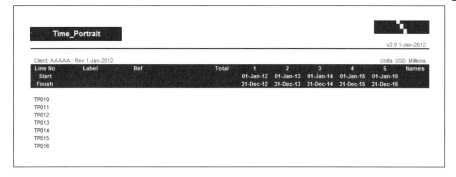

You can copy this schedule twice for the income and balance sheets. The balance sheet needs three extra columns for adjustments. Using the template ensures that all the columns and starting line numbers will be the same across all schedules.

INCOME STATEMENT

You could sit down with the annual reports and go through each one to extract the income statement, balance sheet and detail from the notes. Luckily this has been done for you and the basic numbers are set out in Figure 4.2. This is the Income Statement in a numbers-only format with costs shown as negative numbers. Styles mean that you can quickly complete the rest of the sheet using input and totals styles. In this form, the sub-totals are not clear and the model is not usable.

Figure 4.2

Initial Income Statement

Line No	Label	Ref		Total	1	2	3	4	5	Names
Start					01-Jan-12	01-Jan-13	01-Jan-14	01-Jan-15	01-Jan-16	
Finish					31-Dec-12	31-Dec-13	31-Dec-14	31-Dec-15	31-Dec-16	
IP010	Revenue	USD Millions			33,974.00	39,454.00	42,641.00	47,298.00	54,327.00	
IP011	Cost of sales				(27,594.00)	(31,911.00)	(33,952.00)	(37,412.00)	(43,147.00)	
IP012	Gross profit				6,380.00	7,543.00	8,689.00	9,886.00	11,180.00	
IP013										
IP014	Operating expenses									
IP015	Distribution costs				(3,698.00)	(4,454.00)	(4,280.00)	(5,105.00)	(5,562.00)	
IP016	Administrative expenses				-	-	(907.00)	(1,027.00)	(1,248.00)	
IP017	Depreciation				(654.00)	(758.00)	(785.00)	(876.00)	(1,011.00)	
IP018	Amortisation				(79.00)	(51.00)	(69.00)	(87.00)	(153.00)	
IP019	Other				-	-	-	-	-	
IP020	Subtotal costs				(4,431.00)	(5,263.00)	(6,041.00)	(7,095.00)	(7,974.00)	
IP021										
IP022	Operating profit (EBIT)				1,949.00	2,280.00	2,648.00	2,791.00	3,206.00	
IP023										
IP024	Fees write-off				-	-	-	-	-	
IP025	New goodwill				-	-	-	-	-	
IP026	Subtotal				-	-	-	-	-	
IP027										
IP028	Operating profit (EBIT post-transaction)				1,949.00	2,280.00	2,648.00	2,791.00	3,206.00	

Client: AAAAA : Rev 1-Jan-2012 — Units: USD Millions

With the input and totals formats the sheet is clearer with the gross margin and operating profit enclosed in borders. Any user needs to know where to enter data. All the inputs have a value or zero since blanks can cause problems at a later stage in the model when you are calculating ratios or other formulas involving division. You can validate the inputs cells with a custom validation such as:

```
=ISNUMBER(J10)
```

This formula generates TRUE or FALSE and, if false, triggers the Validation dialog box.

The income statement follows a standard format (see Figures 4.3 and 4.4):

Revenue
    Less costs of goods sold
= *Gross profit*
    Less administration, depreciation and transaction costs
= *Operating profit*
    Less finance costs and share of associates
= *Profit before tax*
    Less income tax and discontinued operations
= *Profit for the year*
    Less dividends and minorities
= *Net profit or retained earnings*

Gross profit

Figure 4.3

Client: AAAAA : Rev 1-Jan-2012   Units: USD Millions

Line No Start Finish	Label	Ref	Total	1 01-Jan-12 31-Dec-12	2 01-Jan-13 31-Dec-13	3 01-Jan-14 31-Dec-14	4 01-Jan-15 31-Dec-15	5 01-Jan-16 31-Dec-16	Names
IP010	Revenue	USD Millions		33,974.00	39,454.00	42,641.00	47,298.00	54,327.00	
IP011	Cost of sales			(27,594.00)	(31,911.00)	(33,952.00)	(37,412.00)	(43,147.00)	
IP012	Gross profit			6,380.00	7,543.00	8,689.00	9,886.00	11,180.00	
IP013									
IP014	Operating expenses								
IP015	Distribution costs			(3,696.00)	(4,454.00)	(4,280.00)	(5,105.00)	(5,562.00)	
IP016	Administrative expenses			-	-	(907.00)	(1,027.00)	(1,248.00)	
IP017	Depreciation			(654.00)	(758.00)	(785.00)	(876.00)	(1,011.00)	
IP018	Amortisation			(79.00)	(51.00)	(69.00)	(87.00)	(153.00)	
IP019	Other			-	-	-	-	-	
IP020	Subtotal costs			(4,431.00)	(5,263.00)	(6,041.00)	(7,095.00)	(7,974.00)	
IP021									
IP022	Operating profit (EBIT)			1,949.00	2,280.00	2,648.00	2,791.00	3,206.00	
IP023									
IP024	Fees write-off			-	-	-	-	-	
IP025	New goodwill			-	-	-	-	-	
IP026	Subtotal			-	-	-	-	-	
IP027									
IP028	Operating profit (EBIT post-transaction)			1,949.00	2,280.00	2,648.00	2,791.00	3,206.00	

Net profit

Figure 4.4

Client: AAAAA : Rev 1-Jan-2012   Units: USD Millions

Line No Start Finish	Label	Ref	Total	1 01-Jan-12 31-Dec-12	2 01-Jan-13 31-Dec-13	3 01-Jan-14 31-Dec-14	4 01-Jan-15 31-Dec-15	5 01-Jan-16 31-Dec-16	Names
IP027									
IP028	Operating profit (EBIT post-transaction)			1,949.00	2,280.00	2,648.00	2,791.00	3,206.00	
IP029									
IP030	Finance income			99.00	114.00	90.00	187.00	116.00	
IP031	Finance costs								
IP032	Existing debt			(269.00)	(241.00)	(216.00)	(250.00)	(478.00)	
IP033	Senior debt A			-	-	-	-	-	
IP034	Senior debt B			-	-	-	-	-	
IP035	Other long-term			-	-	-	-	-	
IP036	Senior subordinated			-	-	-	-	-	
IP037	Junior subordinated			-	-	-	-	-	
IP038	Other			-	82.00	131.00	75.00	110.00	
IP039	Preference shares			-	-	-	-	-	
IP040	Total finance costs			(269.00)	(159.00)	(85.00)	(175.00)	(368.00)	
IP041									
IP042	Share of profit of associates			3.00	4.00	5.00	6.00	7.00	
IP043	Gain (loss) on assets			12.00	11.00	10.00	9.00	8.00	
IP044	Profit before tax			1,794.00	2,250.00	2,668.00	2,818.00	2,969.00	
IP045									
IP046	Income tax expenses			(410.00)	(583.00)	(754.00)	(673.00)	(788.00)	
IP047	Profit from continuing operations			1,384.00	1,667.00	1,914.00	2,145.00	2,181.00	
IP048									
IP049	Discontinued operations			23.00	45.00	67.00	89.00	99.00	
IP050	Profit for the year			1,407.00	1,712.00	1,981.00	2,234.00	2,280.00	
IP051									
IP052	Dividends			(590.00)	(612.00)	(542.00)	(605.00)	(662.00)	
IP053	Minority interest			1.00	2.00	3.00	-	(5.00)	
IP054									
IP055	Net profit			818.00	1,102.00	1,442.00	1,629.00	1,613.00	

BALANCE SHEET

The formatted balance sheet uses the same standard methodology as the Income Statement (see Figures 4.5 and 4.6). The format is:

Current assets
> *Accounts receivable (debtors)*
> *Inventories*
> *Prepayments and other current assets*

Non-current assets
> Land, buildings and equipment less depreciation
> Intangibles and other non-current assets
= Total assets

Current liabilities
> Overdraft
> Current portion of long-term debts
> Accounts payable (creditors)
> Dividends payable
> Income tax payable

Non-current liabilities
> Deferred taxes
> Minority interests
> Long-term debt
> = Short- and long-term liabilities

Shareholders' funds
> Ordinary shares
> Preference shares
> Retained earnings
= Shareholders' equity

Figure 4.5 **Assets**

Client: AAAAA : Rev 1-Jan-2012

Line No Start Finish	Label	Ref	Total	1 01-Jan-12 31-Dec-12	2 01-Jan-13 31-Dec-13	3 01-Jan-14 31-Dec-14	4 01-Jan-15 31-Dec-15	5 01-Jan-16 31-Dec-16
IB010	**Current assets**							
IB011	Cash & marketable securities	USD Millions		1,146.00	1,395.00	1,042.00	2,148.00	2,509.00
IB012	Accounts receivable			597.00	648.00	783.00	801.00	1,245.00
IB013	Inventories			1,306.00	1,464.00	1,911.00	2,420.00	2,669.00
IB014	Prepaid expenses			48.00	86.00	128.00	298.00	400.00
IB015	Prepaid income taxes			-	-	8.00	6.00	9.00
IB016	Other current assets 1			136.00	141.00	168.00	212.00	323.00
IB017	Other current assets 2			224.00	17.00	128.00	107.00	382.00
IB018	Other current assets 3			-	-	-	-	-
IB019	**Total current assets**			3,457.00	3,751.00	4,168.00	5,992.00	7,537.00
IB020								
IB021	**Non-current assets**							
IB022	Land and buildings			14,970.00	15,563.00	16,540.00	19,210.00	22,921.00
IB023	Net property, plant & equipment			4,859.00	4,707.00	5,389.00	6,340.00	7,495.00
IB024	Depreciation			(4,334.00)	(4,388.00)	(4,953.00)	(5,763.00)	(6,692.00)
IB025	**Net land, property, plant & equipment**			15,495.00	15,882.00	16,976.00	19,787.00	23,724.00
IB026								
IB027	Investments			414.00	1,225.00	864.00	1,116.00	1,860.00
IB028	Intangibles			-	-	-	-	-
IB029	Other asssets			-	-	-	-	-
IB030	Transaction costs			-	-	-	-	-
IB031	New goodwill			1,044.00	1,525.00	2,045.00	2,336.00	4,027.00
IB032	Other non-current assets 1			-	-	-	216.00	1,470.00
IB033	Other non-current assets 2			-	180.00	754.00	717.00	1,897.00
IB034	Other non-current assets 3			-	-	-	-	1,000.00
IB035	**Total non-current assets**			16,953.00	18,812.00	20,639.00	24,172.00	33,978.00
IB036								
IB037	**Total assets**			20,410.00	22,563.00	24,807.00	30,164.00	41,515.00

The balance sheet needs to be checked to ensure that assets less liabilities equal zero. In particular, the adjustments have to equal zero. Models should check their own content as much as possible and you could use an area on the Workings sheet to bring together all the checks. When the sum of all the checks is equal to zero, the model must balance. Other examples of checks are cash flow statements reconciling to the change in bank on the balance sheet or confirming that loans totally amortise during the forecast period.

Liabilities

Figure 4.6

Line No	Label	Ref	Total	1	2	3	4	5
Start				01-Jan-12	01-Jan-13	01-Jan-14	01-Jan-15	01-Jan-16
Finish				31-Dec-12	31-Dec-13	31-Dec-14	31-Dec-15	31-Dec-16
IB039	**Current liabilities**							
IB040	Overdraft			471.00	1,252.00	1,139.00	1,913.00	4,012.00
IB041	Current portion long-term debt (CPLTD)			6.00	662.00	502.00	626.00	71.00
IB042	Accounts payable			2,819.00	2,832.00	3,317.00	3,936.00	4,748.00
IB043	Accrued expenses			660.00	693.00	1,062.00	1,187.00	1,294.00
IB044	Dividend payable			416.00	6.00	7.00	-	-
IB045	Income tax payable			442.00	480.00	203.00	324.00	362.00
IB046	Other current liabilities 1			1,258.00	1,336.00	1,329.00	1,714.00	2,480.00
IB047	Other current liabilities 2			-	286.00	593.00	563.00	535.00
IB048	Other current liabilities 3			-	-	-	-	-
IB049	**Total current liabilities**			**6,072.00**	**7,547.00**	**8,152.00**	**10,263.00**	**13,502.00**
IB050								
IB051	**Deferred taxes**							
IB052	Other deferred liability 1			750.00	320.00	535.00	802.00	696.00
IB053	Other deferred liability 2			-	5.00	975.00	861.00	1,639.00
IB054	Minority Interest			51.00	63.00	65.00	87.00	47.00
IB055								
IB056	**Long term debt**							
IB057	Existing debt			4,531.00	4,036.00	4,545.00	6,294.00	12,693.00
IB058	Senior debt A			-	-	-	-	-
IB059	Senior debt B			-	-	-	-	-
IB060	Junior debt C			-	1,212.00	29.00	42.00	-
IB061	Junior debt D			-	-	-	-	-
IB062	Junior debt E			-	-	-	-	-
IB063	Other			-	-	-	-	-
IB064	**Total long term debt**			**4,531.00**	**5,248.00**	**4,574.00**	**6,336.00**	**12,693.00**
IB065								
IB066	**Short and long term liabilities**			**11,404.00**	**13,183.00**	**14,301.00**	**18,349.00**	**28,577.00**
IB067								
IB068	**Shareholders' equity**							
IB069	Common stock			389.00	395.00	397.00	393.00	395.00
IB070	Preferred stock			3,744.00	4,028.00	4,416.00	4,551.00	4,678.00
IB071	Retained earnings			4,873.00	4,957.00	5,693.00	6,871.00	7,865.00
IB072	**Shareholders equity**			**9,006.00**	**9,380.00**	**10,506.00**	**11,815.00**	**12,938.00**
IB073								
IB074	**Total liabilities + shareholders equity**			**20,410.00**	**22,563.00**	**24,807.00**	**30,164.00**	**41,515.00**

Client: AAAAA : Rev 1-Jan-2012

CheckSum: Balance Sheet   -   -   -   -   -

ADJUSTMENTS

The case restructures the original balance sheet using the existing cash to pay off current debts. Following the design method, you want to make it clear what you are changing rather than using complex formulas (see Figures 4.7 and 4.8). The items amended are:

- cash;
- overdraft;
- current portion of long-term debt;

- existing debt;
- ordinary shares;
- preference shares;
- retained earnings.

The model needs to restructure the balance with the new debt and share capital. There are senior and junior debts totalling 23,500.00 and share capital of 5,118.77. The transaction costs are derived from the percentages on the Control sheet. Goodwill is:

Equity price	*11,550.00*
Shareholders equity	*(12,938.00)*
Existing cash	*2,509.00*
Goodwill	*1,121.00*

The new debt has been entered as all long term since there is not enough information to calculate the current portion. The forecast section will set out the loan amortisation to allow the computation of the capital payable in the next accounting period.

Figure 4.7 **Asset adjustments**

Client: AAAAA : Rev 1-Jan-2012							Units: USI
Line No	Label	Ref	5	1	2	3	Total
Start			01-Jan-16				
Finish			31-Dec-16				
IB010	**Current assets**						
IB011	Cash & marketable securities		2,509.00	(2,509.00)	–		–
IB012	Accounts receivable		1,245.00	–	–		1,245.00
IB013	Inventories		2,669.00	–	–		2,669.00
IB014	Prepaid expenses		400.00	–	–		400.00
IB015	Prepaid income taxes		9.00	–	–		9.00
IB016	Other current assets 1		323.00	–	–		323.00
IB017	Other current assets 2		382.00	–	–		382.00
IB018	Other current assets 3		–	–	–		–
IB019	**Total current assets**		7,537.00	(2,509.00)	–	–	5,028.00
IB020							
IB021	**Non-current assets**						
IB022	Land and buildings		22,921.00	–	–		22,921.00
IB023	Net property, plant & equipment		7,495.00	–	–		7,495.00
IB024	Depreciation		(6,692.00)	–	–		(6,692.00)
IB025	Net land, property, plant & equipm		23,724.00	–	–		23,724.00
IB026							
IB027	Investments		1,860.00	–	–		1,860.00
IB028	Intangibles		–	–	–		–
IB029	Other asssets		–	–	–		–
IB030	Transaction costs		–	–	–	292.75	292.75
IB031	New goodwill		4,027.00	–	–	1,121.00	5,148.00
IB032	Other non-current assets 1		1,470.00	–	–		1,470.00
IB033	Other non-current assets 2		1,897.00	–	–		1,897.00
IB034	Other non-current assets 3		1,000.00	–	–		1,000.00
IB035	**Total non-current assets**		33,978.00	–	–	1,413.75	35,391.75
IB036							
IB037	**Total assets**		41,515.00	(2,509.00)	–	1,413.75	40,419.75

Liabilities adjustments

Figure 4.8

Line No / Start / Finish	Label	Ref	5 01-Jan-16 31-Dec-16	1	2	3	Total
IB039	**Current liabilities**						
IB040	Overdraft		4,012.00	(4,012.00)	-		-
IB041	Current portion long-term debt (CPLTD)		71.00	(71.00)	-		-
IB042	Accounts payable		4,748.00	-	-		4,748.00
IB043	Accrued expenses		1,294.00	-	-		1,294.00
IB044	Dividend payable		-	-	-		-
IB045	Income tax payable		362.00	-	-		362.00
IB046	Other current liabilities 1		2,480.00	-	-		2,480.00
IB047	Other current liabilities 2		535.00	-	-		535.00
IB048	Other current liabilities 3		-	-	-		-
IB049	**Total current liabilities**		**13,502.00**	**(4,083.00)**	**-**	**-**	**9,419.00**
IB050							
IB051	**Deferred taxes**						
IB052	Other deferred liability 1		696.00	-	-		696.00
IB053	Other deferred liability 2		1,639.00	-	-		1,639.00
IB054	Minority Interest		47.00	-	-		47.00
IB055							
IB056	**Long term debt**						
IB057	Existing debt		12,693.00	(12,693.00)	-		-
IB058	Senior debt A		-	-	-	12,000.00	12,000.00
IB059	Senior debt B		-	-	-	5,000.00	5,000.00
IB060	Junior debt C		-	-	-	2,500.00	2,500.00
IB061	Junior debt D		-	-	-	2,000.00	2,000.00
IB062	Junior debt E		-	-	-	2,000.00	2,000.00
IB063	Other		-	-	-	-	-
IB064	**Total long term debt**		**12,693.00**	**(12,693.00)**	**-**	**23,500.00**	**23,500.00**
IB065							
IB066	**Short and long term liabilities**		**28,577.00**	**(16,776.00)**	**-**	**23,500.00**	**35,301.00**
IB067							
IB068	**Shareholders' equity**						
IB069	Common stock (shares)		395.00	(395.00)	-	4,618.77	4,618.77
IB070	Preferred stock (shares)		4,678.00	(4,678.00)	-	500.00	500.00
IB071	Retained earnings		7,865.00	(7,865.00)	-		-
IB072	**Shareholders equity**		**12,938.00**	**(12,938.00)**	**-**	**5,118.77**	**5,118.77**
IB073							
IB074	**Total liabilities + shareholders equ**		**41,515.00**	**(29,714.00)**	**-**	**28,618.77**	**40,419.77**
	CheckSum: Balance Sheet		-	27,205.00	-	(27,205.00)	-

Client: AAAAA : Rev 1-Jan-2012 Units: USl

SUMMARY

This chapter enters the basic accounting information and shows how this process is quicker using the application template and cell styles started in the last chapter. The principle of setting out each schedule using the same method ensures a consistent look and feel to the model. With the balance sheet revised, the next stage in the model is to review the figures and produce a forecast set of accounting statements.

Sales forecast

FORECASTING OBJECTIVES

With the historic statements in place, the model needs to generate expectations of future performance and provide forecasted statements and cash flows. Forecasting is not a precise science and models should allow the user to analyse different economic and strategic outcomes. Cash flows form the basis of credit and valuation models since you are interested in real cash rather than accounting profit. The various stakeholders, such as potential investors and lenders as well as suppliers, customers and the government, will have different interests and priorities. For example:

- Investors need to assess value and consider whether assets are over- or undervalued. Future cash flows and their likelihood are one method of quantifying potential gains and risk.
- Bankers and lenders must consider the ability to pay and the impact of strategic and economic downturns in the company's fortunes.
- Competitors and other organisations need to assess the company's financial strength and ability to grow and compete with them.

Forecasts should identify a range of scenarios rather than single points and Chapter 15 will outline key techniques for examining sensitivity and 'what-if' analysis. A forecast that creates a single-point outcome is not helpful for analysis purposes, since there are internal and external factors which will all have an effect on the company. 'Business as usual' may ignore the impact of economic cycles, competitor reaction or the effect of changes in management strategy.

Examples of external factors include:

- economic cycles and the starting point for the forecast;
- political change such as taxes and restrictions;
- technological advances;
- social factors such as changing life styles and attitudes.

These factors are often referred to as STEP, PEST or STEEPV, depending on which exterior factors you put into the equation. Figure 5.1 shows some examples of factors which may be beyond the management's control and potentially hard to forecast.

Figure 5.1

STEP analysis

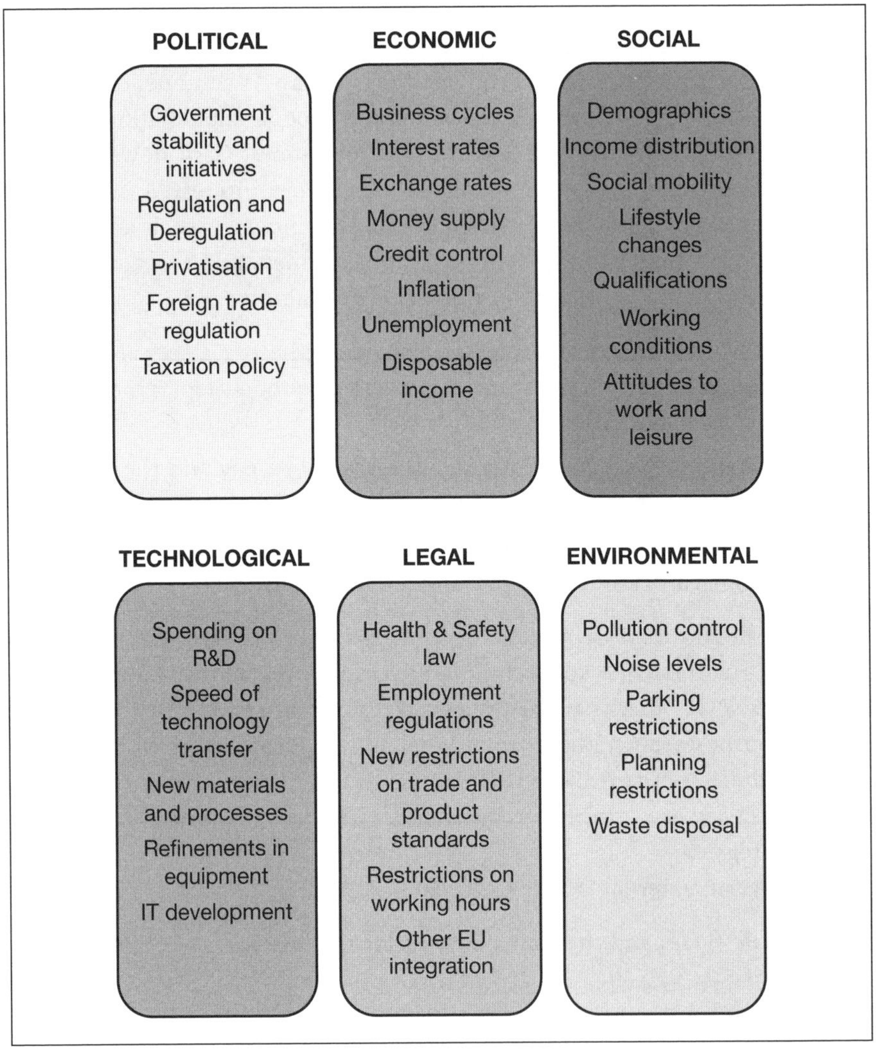

POLITICAL	ECONOMIC	SOCIAL
Government stability and initiatives Regulation and Deregulation Privatisation Foreign trade regulation Taxation policy	Business cycles Interest rates Exchange rates Money supply Credit control Inflation Unemployment Disposable income	Demographics Income distribution Social mobility Lifestyle changes Qualifications Working conditions Attitudes to work and leisure

TECHNOLOGICAL	LEGAL	ENVIRONMENTAL
Spending on R&D Speed of technology transfer New materials and processes Refinements in equipment IT development	Health & Safety law Employment regulations New restrictions on trade and product standards Restrictions on working hours Other EU integration	Pollution control Noise levels Parking restrictions Planning restrictions Waste disposal

The timed forecast period should encompass at least one business cycle in order to include the effect of the outside environment, and a common modelling mistake is to choose too short a time period. In addition, the effect of competitors should be considered as the company does not operate in a vacuum with complete freedom over its actions. You could treat the market as good, neutral or bad and the management strategy in response could form the basis of a series of modelling scenarios. Banks and funders will concentrate on the term of their loans but potential investors will look at future cash flows as the basis for generating value.

This model does not take into account inflation as a separate item and assumes that nominal rather than real figures are shown. Inflation has been historically low for the past two decades and forecasts for fewer than

15 or 20 years tend to ignore its effect. The previous accounts are shown as nominal figures, so we assume that inflation is low and can be ignored. All statements must be consistent. Similarly, this model uses one currency. If there were more than one currency, then you would need to choose whether to forecast in the local currency and then translate the final figures or translate the historic figures and produce all successive statements in the international currency. It is usually simplest to convert the accounting statements into the international currency rather than translate the final figures. For example, a Russian banking model would start in roubles and be translated into US dollars or euros for funding purposes.

You also need to be aware of the limitations of financial information in annual accounts and look carefully at the methodology. The accounting numbers should not be accepted without some investigation of the methodology. Here are some examples:

- Lack of uniformity in the preparation of accounting statements between countries and continents over disclosures, corporate legislation and local practice.

- Historical information which is backward rather than forward looking – although you often assume that an historical trend will continue.

- Changes in the external environment after the accounts date are not included, e.g. natural disasters.

- A single estimate of the balance sheet, but adjustments could have been made either side of this date.

- Ratios may not be useful in isolation and only show a relative position.

- Comparisons with other companies are difficult due to the split of industries, divisions or geography.

- Diversified companies can be hard to analyse and understand as they buy and sell subsidiaries on a regular basis.

- Window dressing (creative accounting) such as capitalising costs results in increased short-term profits and typically future liabilities on the balance sheet.

- Differences in the interpretation of accounting standards and approach which lead to inconsistencies in the presentation of information.

METHOD

The modelling forecast splits into several phases discussed in the next few chapters:

- sales and costs on the income statement;
- assets and depreciation;

- debt, interest payable and split between current and long-term portion of debt;
- tax and tax depreciation;
- balance sheet current asset and liabilities;
- cash reconciliation to the balance sheet;
- model checks to ensure that everything balances.

Each stage requires a number of assumptions with varying levels of detail and estimation. Whilst assumptions represent the best estimate, there are always unexpected events, such as economic crises or natural disasters, and therefore the model should be flexible enough to portray the downside and extreme cases. As the timeframe of the forecast increases, there is more uncertainty and the ability to forecast reduces. Assumptions possess varying levels of significance and it is imperative to try to understand both the quality and quantity of the downside cases. Alternatively, you want to discover the key success factors that are critical to performance. Two key questions to ask are:

- What is the impact of changing variable X or Y?
- Is X more important than Y or Z?

Another performance model is the 'E's model, which is useful here for comparison purposes:

- Economy – how well you buy in the means of production such as labour and materials.
- Efficiency – how well you turn the materials into finished saleable product.
- Effectiveness – how well the firm meets the targets of the key stakeholders.
- Ethics – how well the company performs as a 'corporate individual'.

At each stage there needs to be a 'sanity' test to review the figures for reasonableness. If the company has grown at 2 per cent for the last five years, you will need to explain how a 10 per cent growth can be realised and what strategy will bring this about. Similarly, there are a number of factors that cannot be estimated directly, such as political influence or management competence, and you will have to be mindful that the model is a simplification that cannot take into account all the relationships and complexity of the real world.

SALES

Sales usually drive the forecast since costs, investment and loans depend on the level of sales and sales volumes. Companies usually comprise different divisions, product areas or geographic regions as detailed in the first sections of most annual reports. There should be a review of the business of the previous 12 months. Most companies report by division and provide sales, cost and capital expenditure details, which are useful in determining the relevant contribution, profit margin and capital investment requirements of the different parts of the business (see Figure 5.2). There are many distortions, such as mid-year acquisitions, disposals, one-off windfall gains or losses, but the objective should be to understand and include the sustainable operations in the forecast. Nevertheless, an examination of all the divisions will yield a single sales growth and cost percentage to be used as a starting point in the model. You may want to change or flex this at a later stage, but you need a starting point in the model.

Example of divisional analysis

Figure 5.2

Line	Item	SGD '000,000	Reference	Dec-13	Dec-14	Dec-15	Dec-16	Dec-17
DV10	Sales by Division							
DV11	AA			8,824.8	9,916.8	9,228.8	11,397.2	12,702.9
DV12	BB			895.3	958.1	868.7	975.7	932.0
DV13	CC			835.6	878.1	678.7	807.5	959.1
DV14	DD			287.3	292.7	266.2	256.6	241.1
DV15	Intergroup			(1,460.2)	(1,530.7)	(1,280.5)	(1,424.1)	(1,494.0)
DV16	Subtotal Continuing Operations			9,382.8	10,515.0	9,761.9	12,012.9	13,341.1
DV17	Discontinued Operations							
DV18	n/a			-	-	-	-	-
DV19	n/a			-	-	-	-	-
DV20	Total			9,382.8	10,515.0	9,761.9	12,012.9	13,341.1
DV21								
DV22	% Change in Sales							
DV23	AA				12.37%	(6.94%)	23.50%	11.46%
DV24	BB				7.01%	(9.33%)	12.32%	(4.48%)
DV25	CC				5.09%	(22.71%)	18.98%	18.77%
DV26	DD				1.88%	(9.05%)	(3.61%)	(6.04%)
DV27	Intergroup				(4.83%)	16.35%	(11.21%)	(4.91%)
DV28	Subtotal Continuing Operations				12.07%	(7.16%)	23.06%	11.06%
DV29	Discontinued Operations							
DV30	n/a							
DV31	n/a							
DV32	Total				12.07%	(7.16%)	23.06%	11.06%

Divisional and product analysis will identify the core activities, which should contribute to future sales. Discontinued operations may have value, but their contribution will not form part of the potential sales. The potential sales may be a function of the macro environment, but internal factors such as the management and their strategy will determine the actual performance.

Regarding the external environment, there are forecasts available from central government or international banks and other organisations. These may assist with understanding the potential growth rates over the following periods. In mature industries, companies can only grow faster than the market by acquiring market share through superior products, techniques, innovation or acquisition.

You should also consider other factors, such as:

■ Has anything changed since the last annual report date which would affect the numbers?

■ Has there been a change in management?

■ Has the strategy changed?

■ Have raw material and other costs changed or become more volatile?

■ Has there been any competitor action which could erode margins and profits?

■ Are there any capacity or other constraints?

This is not an exhaustive list, but you should always be wary of accepting forecast data at face value without exposing it to scrutiny. It is too easy in Excel to create grids of numbers without understanding the background or challenging their basis. The Porter strategy model (Figure 5.3) may represent a sound basis for comparing the company's ability to sustain a 'competitive

| Figure 5.3 | Porter model |

SUPPLIER POWER

See buyers

THREAT OF ENTRY

Economies of scale

Absolute cost advantages

Capital requirements

Product differentiation

Government and legal barriers

Retaliation by established producers

RIVALRY AMONG EXISTING FIRMS

Concentration

Diversity of competitors

Product differentiation

Excess capacity and exit barriers

Cost conditions

THREAT OF SUBSTITUTES

Buyer propensity to substitute

Relative price/performance of substitutes

BUYER POWER

PRICE SENSITIVITY

Cost of product relative to total costs

Product differentiation

Competition between buyers

BARGAINING POWER

Size and concentration of buyers relative to suppliers

Buyers' switching costs

Buyers' information

Buyers' ability to backwards integrate

advantage' and achieve a performance above the sector norm. Each year some companies improve, whilst others decline or become insolvent, so you have to view the performance against the industry and market. Comparison with peer groups can also be useful in building up a market picture.

The model in Figure 5.3 shows the potential forces acting on the company, which vary by industry type:

- Supplier power – forcing higher input prices.
- Threat of entry – governed by the cost of entry into the sector.
- Threat of substitutes – removing a need for the company's products.
- Buyer power – forcing down prices or imposing constraints.
- Rivalry in the sector – either a limited number of companies control competition and therefore increase margins, or there are a number of players but no single firm has a critical mass that allows it to control the market.

COMMON SIZE ANALYSIS

Common size analysis or standard statements can also be useful in uncovering trends (see Figures 5.4 and 5.5). This would take a long time with a pocket calculator but of course is very quick to set up in Excel. The method consists of making every line in the income statement a percentage of sales and then converting it to a factor. Thus, sales are 100 in each year and every other line is a factor of sales, which allows you to more easily spot any trends.

The formula using the named constant CstHundred is:

```
=Income!J10/Income!J$10*cstHundred
```

It is sometimes easier to list a series of constants on the Workings sheet as named cells. For example, if you have a constant for 365 days it would be easy to switch a model to a 360-day banking year by changing the value rather than updating every formula. Examples of constants are:

cstTwelve	12.00
cstZero	–
cstHundred	100.00
cstThousand	1,000.00
cstOne	1.00
cstTwo	2.00
cstAlmostZero	0.00000001
cstDays365	365.00
IRR guess rate	10.00%
cstTen	10.00
cstRounding	5.00

To speed up the process, you can:

- Copy the existing income statement (right-click the tab and make a copy).
- Copy the formula down.
- Format using styles such as the row total style.
- Use label numbers on the left-hand side.
- Use negative costs where applicable.

In Figure 5.4, it is clear that the company is maintaining its margins and controlling its costs effectively. These figures provide a starting point for the forecast, which will need to be checked against past performance.

Figure 5.4

Standardised sales and costs

Line No	Label	Ref	Units	Total	1 01-Jan-12 31-Dec-12	2 01-Jan-13 31-Dec-13	3 01-Jan-14 31-Dec-14	4 01-Jan-15 31-Dec-15	5 01-Jan-16 31-Dec-16
	Model Check: All balances OK								
SP010	Revenue		USD Millions		100.0	100.0	100.0	100.0	100.0
SP011	Cost of sales				(81.2)	(80.9)	(79.6)	(79.1)	(79.4)
SP012	Gross profit				18.8	19.1	20.4	20.9	20.6
SP013									
SP014	Operating expenses				-	-	-	-	-
SP015	Distribution costs				(10.9)	(11.3)	(10.0)	(10.8)	(10.2)
SP016	Administrative expenses				-	-	(2.1)	(2.2)	(2.3)
SP017	Depreciation				(1.9)	(1.9)	(1.8)	(1.9)	(1.9)
SP018	Amortisation				(0.2)	(0.1)	(0.2)	(0.2)	(0.3)
SP019	Other				-	-	-	-	-
SP020	Subtotal costs				(13.0)	(13.3)	(14.2)	(15.0)	(14.7)
SP021					-	-	-	-	-
SP022	Operating profit (EBIT)				5.7	5.8	6.2	5.9	5.9

Figure 5.5

Standardised profit

Line No	Label	Ref	Units	Total	1 01-Jan-12 31-Dec-12	2 01-Jan-13 31-Dec-13	3 01-Jan-14 31-Dec-14	4 01-Jan-15 31-Dec-15	5 01-Jan-16 31-Dec-16
SP027									
SP028	Operating profit (EBIT post-transaction)				5.7	5.8	6.2	5.9	5.9
SP029									
SP030	Finance income				0.3	0.3	0.2	0.4	0.2
SP031	Finance costs				-	-	-	-	-
SP032	Existing debt				(0.8)	(0.6)	(0.5)	(0.5)	(0.9)
SP033	Senior debt A				-	-	-	-	-
SP034	Senior debt B				-	-	-	-	-
SP035	Junior debt C				-	-	-	-	-
SP036	Junior debt D				-	-	-	-	-
SP037	Junior debt E				-	-	-	-	-
SP038	Other				-	0.2	0.3	0.2	0.2
SP039	Preference shares				-	-	-	-	-
SP040	Total finance costs				(0.8)	(0.4)	(0.2)	(0.4)	(0.7)
SP041									
SP042	Share of profit of associates				0.0	0.0	0.0	0.0	0.0
SP043	Gain (loss) on assets				0.0	0.0	0.0	0.0	0.0
SP044	Profit before tax				5.3	5.7	6.3	6.0	5.5
SP045									
SP046	Income tax expenses				(1.2)	(1.5)	(1.8)	(1.4)	(1.5)
SP047	Profit for the year				4.1	4.2	4.5	4.5	4.0
SP048									
SP049	Discontinued operations				0.1	0.1	0.2	0.2	0.2
SP050	Profit for the year				4.1	4.3	4.6	4.7	4.2
SP051									
SP052	Dividends				(1.7)	(1.6)	(1.3)	(1.3)	(1.2)
SP053	Minority interest				0.0	0.0	0.0	-	(0.0)
SP054									
SP055	Net profit				2.4	2.8	3.4	3.4	3.0

Similarly, the net profit is static although there has been a fall in the last year, which appears to have been caused by higher funding costs. Further examination will reveal trends – you can use F11 or Alt + F1 to draw charts to show the patterns more clearly.

You can apply the same procedure to the balance sheet and make each line item a percentage of total assets or liabilities expressed as a factor (see Figures 5.6 and 5.7). This time an ISERROR function is included to default to zero in the event of a divide by zero or other error:

```
=IF(ISERROR(Balance!J11/Balance!J$37*cstHundred),
0,Balance!J11/Balance!J$37*cstHundred)
```

Standardised assets

Figure 5.6

Line No	Label	Ref	Units	Total	1 01-Jan-12 31-Dec-12	2 01-Jan-13 31-Dec-13	3 01-Jan-14 31-Dec-14	4 01-Jan-15 31-Dec-15	5 01-Jan-16 31-Dec-16
	Model Check: All balances OK								
SB010	**Current assets**								
SB011	Cash & marketable securities		USD Millions		5.6	6.2	4.2	7.1	6.0
SB012	Accounts receivable				2.9	2.9	3.2	2.7	3.0
SB013	Inventories				6.4	6.5	7.7	8.0	6.4
SB014	Prepaid expenses				0.2	0.4	0.5	1.0	1.0
SB015	Prepaid income taxes				-	-	0.0	0.0	0.0
SB016	Other current assets 1				0.7	0.6	0.7	0.7	0.8
SB017	Other current assets 2				1.1	0.1	0.5	0.4	0.9
SB018	Other current assets 3				-	-	-	-	-
SB019	**Total current assets**				16.9	16.6	16.8	19.9	18.2
SB020					-	-	-	-	-
SB021	**Non-current assets**								
SB022	Land and buildings				73.3	69.0	66.7	63.7	55.2
SB023	Net property, plant & equipment				23.8	20.9	21.7	21.0	18.1
SB024	Depreciation				(21.2)	(19.4)	(20.0)	(19.1)	(16.1)
SB025	**Net land, property, plant & equipment**				75.9	70.4	68.4	65.6	57.1
SB026									
SB027	Investments				2.0	5.4	3.5	3.7	4.5
SB028	Intangibles				-	-	-	-	-
SB029	Other asssets				-	-	-	-	-
SB030	Transaction costs				-	-	-	-	-
SB031	New goodwill				5.1	6.8	8.2	7.7	9.7
SB032	Other non-current assets 1				-	-	-	0.7	3.5
SB033	Other non-current assets 2				-	0.8	3.0	2.4	4.6
SB034	Other non-current assets 3				-	-	-	-	2.4
SB035	**Total non-current assets**				83.1	83.4	83.2	80.1	81.8
SB036					-	-	-	-	-
SB037	**Total assets**				100.0	100.0	100.0	100.0	100.0

Standardised liabilities

Figure 5.7

Line No.	Label	Ref	Units	Total	1 01-Jan-12 31-Dec-12	2 01-Jan-13 31-Dec-13	3 01-Jan-14 31-Dec-14	4 01-Jan-15 31-Dec-15	5 01-Jan-16 31-Dec-16
SB039	**Current liabilities**								
SB040	Overdraft				2.3	5.5	4.6	6.3	9.7
SB041	Current portion long-term debt (CPLTD)				0.0	2.9	2.0	2.1	0.2
SB042	Accounts payable				13.8	12.6	13.4	13.0	11.4
SB043	Accrued expenses				3.2	3.1	4.3	3.9	3.1
SB044	Dividend payable				2.0	0.0	0.0	-	-
SB045	Income tax payable				2.2	2.1	0.8	1.1	0.9
SB046	Other current liabilities 1				6.2	5.9	5.4	5.7	6.0
SB047	Other current liabilities 2				-	1.3	2.4	1.9	1.3
SB048	Other current liabilities 3				-	-	-	-	-
SB049	**Total current liabilities**				29.8	33.4	32.9	34.0	32.5
SB050					-	-	-	-	-
SB051	Deferred taxes				-	-	-	-	-
SB052	Other deferred liability 1				3.7	1.4	2.2	2.7	1.7
SB053	Other deferred liability 2				-	0.0	3.9	2.9	3.9
SB054	Minority Interest				0.2	0.3	0.3	0.3	0.1
SB055					-	-	-	-	-
SB056	**Long term debt**				-	-	-	-	-
SB057	Existing debt				22.2	17.9	18.3	20.9	30.6
SB058	Senior debt A				-	-	-	-	-
SB059	Senior debt B				-	-	-	-	-
SB060	Junior debt C				-	5.4	0.1	0.1	-
SB061	Junior debt D				-	-	-	-	-
SB062	Junior debt E				-	-	-	-	-
SB063	Other				-	-	-	-	-
SB064	**Total long term debt**				22.2	23.3	18.4	21.0	30.6
SB065					-	-	-	-	-
SB066	**Short and long term liabilities**				55.9	58.4	57.6	60.8	68.8
SB067					-	-	-	-	-
SB068	**Shareholders' equity**				-	-	-	-	-
SB069	Common stock (shares)				1.9	1.8	1.6	1.3	1.0
SB070	Preferred stock (shares)				18.3	17.9	17.8	15.1	11.3
SB071	Retained earnings				23.9	22.0	22.9	22.8	18.9
SB072	**Shareholders equity**				44.1	41.6	42.4	39.2	31.2

FORECAST SHEET

Copy a further template for the forecast since you need to be able to list the key drivers for the income and balance sheet on a single control page. You can also calculate the historic performance for each factor and use it as a basis for the future. The historic performance is set out below. The sales growth is derived from:

(This year – Last year) / Last year

```
=(Income!K10-Income!J10)/Income!J10
```

Cost of sales and other costs are a percentage of sales such that sales drive the forecast. There is not enough information to split between fixed and variable costs, so a simple percentage is used in Figure 5.8. Dividends will be a percentage of the post-tax profit while tax will be levied on the pre-tax profit. Discontinued operations are simply a number since there is no logical link between sales and this factor. The forecast percentages and numbers are the same for each of the ten periods since this makes the model easier to check. It is easier to use simple numbers on the initial case and then further refine them when there is some confirmation that the model is working correctly.

| Figure 5.8 | | | Forecast percentages | | | | | | | |

Line No	Label	Ref.	Total	1	2	3	4	5	6
Start				01-Jan-12	01-Jan-13	01-Jan-14	01-Jan-15	01-Jan-16	01-Jan-17
Finish				31-Dec-12	31-Dec-13	31-Dec-14	31-Dec-15	31-Dec-16	31-Dec-17
	(1) Income statement								
F012	Sales growth	IP010	USD Millions		16.13%	8.08%	10.92%	14.86%	10.00%
F013	Cost of sales / sales	IP011		(81.22%)	(80.88%)	(79.62%)	(79.10%)	(79.42%)	(79.50%)
F014									
F015	Operating expenses / sal	IP014							
F016	Distribution costs	IP015		(10.88%)	(11.29%)	(10.04%)	(10.79%)	(10.24%)	(10.00%)
F017	Administrative expenses	IP016		-	-	(2.13%)	(2.17%)	(2.30%)	(2.00%)
F018	Depreciation	IP017		(1.93%)	(1.92%)	(1.84%)	(1.85%)	(1.86%)	
F019	Amortisation	IP018		(0.23%)	(0.13%)	(0.16%)	(0.18%)	(0.28%)	-
F020	Other	IP019		-	-	-	-	-	
F021	Minorities	IP053							
F022	Dividends	IP052		(41.93%)	(35.75%)	(27.36%)	(27.08%)	(29.04%)	(30.00%)
F023									
F024	Other								
F025	Share of profit of associa	IP042		3.00	4.00	5.00	6.00	7.00	5.00
F026	Gain (loss) on assets	IP043		12.00	11.00	10.00	9.00	8.00	10.00
F027									
F028	Tax rates								
F029	Marginal tax rate	IP046		22.85%	25.91%	28.26%	23.88%	26.54%	25.00%
F030	Effective tax rate								25.00%
F031									
F032	Discontinued operations								
F033	Discontinued operations	IP049		23.00	45.00	67.00	89.00	99.00	-

You can then start to build up an income statement on another copied sheet, leaving blanks for depreciation, finance income and interest costs. Further workings will be needed on the Assets, Tax and Debt sheets to calculate these figures. The rule in modelling is to keep the code as simple as possible: when it becomes complicated, you should break out onto a separate worksheet in order to build up blocks of auditable code.

Work down the sheet inserting the tax, discontinued items and dividends. Figure 5.9 shows a specimen income statement. The periods 1 to 5 and the labels can be linked to the historic income statement. The bar in the centre is part of the style guide to denote a changing formula across the line. This is to show that the quasi rule of inconsistent formulas is no longer valid, but also to warn a future developer not to drag right across the forecast formula.

In order to check the code graphically, you can select, for example, the Gross Profit and then press F11 or Alt + F1 to draw a quick chart (see Figure 5.10). F11 places the chart on a new chart sheet while Alt + F1 positions the object on the current sheet. You can also use Control to select multiple lines and labels to save using the full Chart Wizard. The shortcuts will create your default chart and then you can amend or further refine the presentation (Figure 5.11).

Forecast income

Figure 5.9

Line No	Label	Ref	5	6	7	8	9	10	11
Start			01-Jan-16	01-Jan-17	01-Jan-18	01-Jan-19	01-Jan-20	01-Jan-21	01-Jan-22
Finish			31-Dec-16	31-Dec-17	31-Dec-18	31-Dec-19	31-Dec-20	31-Dec-21	31-Dec-22
FP010	Revenue	IP010	54,327.00	59,759.70	65,735.67	72,309.24	79,540.16	87,494.18	96,243.59
FP011	Cost of sales	IP011	(43,147.00)	(47,508.96)	(52,259.86)	(57,485.84)	(63,234.43)	(69,557.87)	(76,513.66)
FP012	Gross profit	IP012	11,180.00	12,250.74	13,475.81	14,823.39	16,305.73	17,936.31	19,729.94
FP013									
FP014	Operating expenses	IP014							
FP015	Distribution costs	IP015	(5,562.00)	(5,975.97)	(6,573.57)	(7,230.92)	(7,954.02)	(8,749.42)	(9,624.36)
FP016	Administrative expenses	IP016	(1,248.00)	(1,195.19)	(1,314.71)	(1,446.18)	(1,590.80)	(1,749.88)	(1,924.87)
FP017	Depreciation	IP017	(1,011.00)						
FP018	Amortisation	IP018	(153.00)	-	-	-	-	-	-
FP019	Other	IP019	-	-	-	-	-	-	-
FP020	Subtotal costs	IP020	(7,974.00)	(7,171.16)	(7,888.28)	(8,677.11)	(9,544.82)	(10,499.30)	(11,549.23)
FP021									
FP022	Operating profit (EBIT	IP022	3,206.00	5,079.57	5,587.53	6,146.29	6,760.91	7,437.01	8,180.71
FP023									
FP024	Fees write-off	IP024	-						
FP025	New goodwill	IP025	-						
FP026	Subtotal	IP026	-	-	-	-	-	-	-
FP027									
FP028	Operating profit (EBIT	IP028	3,206.00	5,079.57	5,587.53	6,146.29	6,760.91	7,437.01	8,180.71

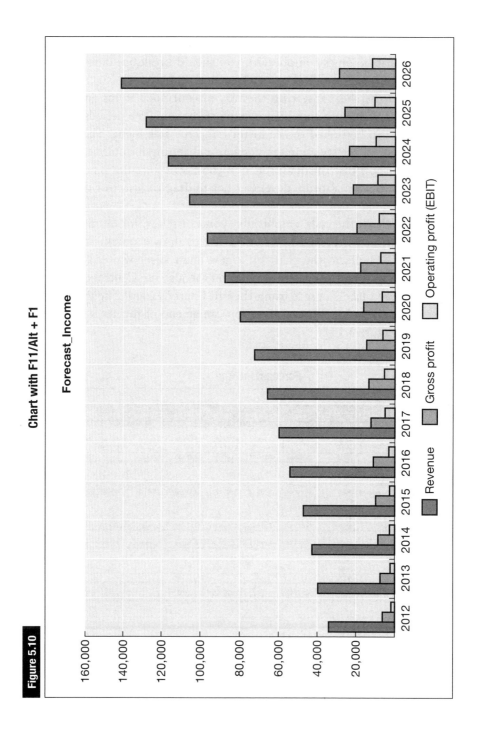

Figure 5.10

Forecast profit

Figure 5.11

Line No	Label	Ref	5	6	7	8	9	10	11
Start			01-Jan-16	01-Jan-17	01-Jan-18	01-Jan-19	01-Jan-20	01-Jan-21	01-Jan-22
Finish			31-Dec-16	31-Dec-17	31-Dec-18	31-Dec-19	31-Dec-20	31-Dec-21	31-Dec-22
FP027									
FP028	Operating profit (EBIT	IP028	3,206.00	5,079.57	5,587.53	6,146.29	6,760.91	7,437.01	8,180.71
FP029									
FP030	Finance income	IP030	116.00	-	-	-	-	-	-
FP031	Finance costs	IP031							
FP032	Existing debt	IP032	(478.00)						
FP033	Senior debt A	IP033	-						
FP034	Senior debt B	IP034	-						
FP035	Junior debt C	IP035	-						
FP036	Junior debt D	IP036	-						
FP037	Junior debt E	IP037	-						
FP038	Other	IP038	110.00						
FP039	Preference shares	IP039	-						
FP040	Total finance costs	-	(368.00)	-	-	-	-	-	-
FP041									
FP042	Share of profit of associ	IP042	7.00	5.00	5.00	5.00	5.00	5.00	5.00
FP043	Gain (loss) on assets	IP043	8.00	10.00	10.00	10.00	10.00	10.00	10.00
FP044	Profit before tax	IP044	2,969.00	5,094.57	5,602.53	6,161.29	6,775.91	7,452.01	8,195.71
FP045									
FP046	Income tax expenses	IP046	(788.00)						
FP047	Profit from continuing	IP047	2,181.00	5,094.57	5,602.53	6,161.29	6,775.91	7,452.01	8,195.71
FP048									
FP049	Discontinued operations	IP049	99.00	-	-	-	-	-	-
FP050	Profit for the year	IP050	2,280.00	5,094.57	5,602.53	6,161.29	6,775.91	7,452.01	8,195.71
FP051									
FP052	Dividends	IP052	(662.00)	(1,528.37)	(1,680.76)	(1,848.39)	(2,032.77)	(2,235.60)	(2,458.71)
FP053	Minority interest	IP053	(5.00)	-	-	-	-	-	-
FP054									
FP055	Net profit	IP055	1,613.00	3,566.20	3,921.77	4,312.90	4,743.14	5,216.40	5,736.99

SUMMARY

This chapter commences the forecasting process using key drivers and discusses the care that is needed in the choice of inputs together with continuous questioning of the results. Thorough analysis of the strategy, markets, management and future trends are required and the model has to be flexible enough to accept changes that will cascade through the rest of the model. You can identify factors that you will want to vary on future scenarios with the proviso that the forecast has to be reasonable and achievable by the management team in the forecast economic climate. By using efficiency measures such as copying templates and styles you can rapidly code an initial forecast and income statement sheet. The next stage is to add assets, loans and tax before bringing it all together on the forecast balance sheet.

6

Assets

FIXED ASSETS

This chapter shows how to build asset tables as defined working areas to provide the inputs to income statements and balance sheets. The fixed assets bear a relationship to sales since on-going investment is essential to produce future profits and cash flows. This is not necessarily a linear relationship, but it may be stable if the pattern of sales and costs do not change markedly over time. In a simple model, fixed assets could be related in a fixed assets turnover ratio derived from sales/fixed assets. The control sheet contains a schedule of asset purchases and this schedule seeks to derive the entries for historic and future capital expenditure.

Asset values can be problematic as most countries adhere to historical accounting. Land purchased 50 years ago may be understated or the firm may have revalued property in the interim. Looking at peer group companies with different accounting conventions can result in distortions in value. Similarly, in times of economic depression, capacity could be available without investing in new equipment. At this stage the model seeks to compute the accounting values, and any adjustments to market values can be made later.

The Forecast sheet needs more variables as below, split between:

■ existing assets with balances from the restructured historic sheets;

■ new land;

■ new equipment;

■ new IT.

The other information in the forecast sheet details the spending pattern, which for simplicity we will assume expends the same amount in each period. The model also needs to know the depreciation period for each class of asset and the method. The depreciation method is a list and best handled by a simple list validation.

EXCEL FUNCTIONS

Excel contains several functions for calculating depreciation:

■ SLN – straight line to zero or a salvage value as the most common accounting depreciation method.

■ SYD – sum of digits (rule of 78) as an approximation to amortisation which is often still used to allocate interest in a loan over individual periods.

■ DB – simple declining balance as used in some tax depreciation methods.

■ DDB – double declining balance.

■ VDB – declining balance followed by a switch to straight line when it is more beneficial. The US tax depreciation system, the Modified Accelerated Cost Recovery System (MACRS), is built on this method.

This model chooses between straight line and sum of digits for the accounting depreciation and between straight line and declining balance for the tax depreciation (see Figure 6.1). It assumes that accounting depreciation will be added back to taxable profits and tax depreciation subtracted as in the UK or US. A further sheet reconciles the tax and calculates the income statement tax payable.

Figure 6.1 **Depreciation methods**

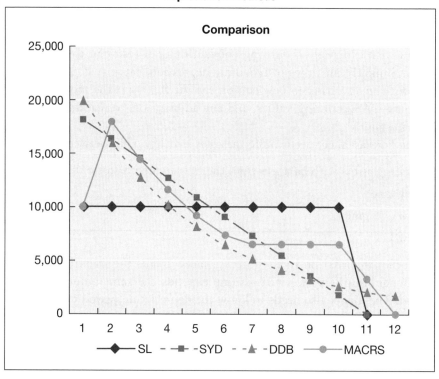

The straight line method assumes equal depreciation in each of the periods and, for simplicity, no salvage value is included. The sum of digits or rule of 78 method approximates to an amortisation curve and is based on the formula:

Total factor = [n * (n + 1)]/2, where n is equal to the number of periods

An example would be (12 * 13)/2 = 78 for a 12 quarter period. The first period is then calculated as 12/78 multiplied by the capital value and the second period is 11/78. The sum of digits method is often used for splitting interest on loans, hire purchase or lease purchase contracts in order to book more interest in early periods. This method becomes inaccurate if there are gap periods or structured payments as it does not take into account the time value of money.

The declining balance method is used in UK tax depreciation in the form of writing down allowances. The standard rate is 20 per cent, where the charge is 20 per cent of the previous capital balance. This means that the charge is high in the early periods and then becomes even smaller. It is asymptotic in that it never actually touches zero, although it becomes mathematically very close. The Excel function requires a factor for the input and this is currently 200 in the UK. DDB represents a double declining balance method.

The US tax system is based on a declining balance method with a choice to switch to straight line when it is beneficial to do so. While you may switch to straight line, you cannot switch back to declining balance at a later stage. This provides a method for eradicating the 'tail' found in the declining balance method. The US tax depreciation system, called the Modified Accelerated Cost Recovery System (MACRS), is based on this method, and was introduced in 1993 to replace the Accelerated Cost Recovery System dating from 1981 (see table below). The cost of the asset is expensed over a defined period called the recovery or class life. The life depends on the type of asset.

MACRS class	Property
3 years	Certain special manufacturing tools
5 years	Cars, light trucks, computers and certain special manufacturing equipment
7 years	Most industrial equipment, office equipment and fixtures
10 years	Longer-life industrial equipment
27.5 years	Residential rental real property
39 years	Non-residential real property including commercial and industrial buildings

The method uses a 200 per cent declining balance method. An example is an asset costing 100,000 with a five-year life: the first period is 200/5 = 40 per cent or 40,000. There is a further rule in that the first year is halved to stop people claiming a full year's depreciation for an asset that may have been acquired on the last day of the tax year. The actual charge is therefore 20,000. In the next year, you bring forward (80*2)/5 = 32,000. A full table of percentages is shown on the next page.

US MACRS percentages						
Recovery year	3-year property	5-year property	7-year property	10-year property	15-year property	20-year property
1	33.33	20.00	14.29	10.00	5.00	3.750
2	44.45	32.00	24.49	18.00	9.50	7.219
3	14.81 *	19.20	17.49	14.40	8.55	6.677
4	7.41	11.52 *	12.49	11.52	7.70	6.177
5		11.52	8.93 *	9.22	6.93	5.713
6		5.76	8.92	7.37	6.23	5.285
7			8.93	6.55 *	5.90 *	4.888
8			4.46	6.55	5.90	4.522
9				6.56	5.91	4.462 *
10				6.55	5.90	4.461
11				3.28	5.91	4.462
12					5.90	4.461
13					5.91	4.462
14					5.90	4.461
15					5.91	4.462
16					2.95	4.461
17						4.462
18						4.461
19						4.462
20						4.461
21						2.231

*Indicates where the switch to straight line depreciation occurs.

The variables on the Forecast sheet detail the amounts, methodology and spending pattern while the tax depreciation includes the writing down method and percentage. If straight line is chosen then you need to input the number of years. Enter the data as in Figure 6.2 since the Assets schedule will need to refer back to the control sheet with all the forecast variables.

Inputs

Figure 6.2

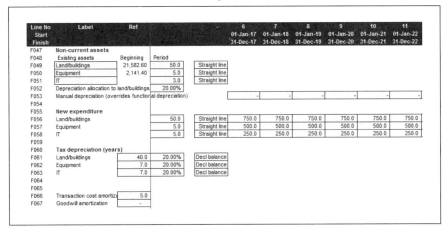

EXISTING ASSETS

To start this schedule, copy a template sheet in landscape form with all the dates and layout elements. The sections you need on the new sheet are:

- existing assets;
- depreciation for new assets by category;
- written down value.

You need the depreciation for the income statement and the written down values will be added to the balance sheet fixed assets (see Figure 6.3).

Existing assets

Figure 6.3

The current written down value can be gained from the historic adjusted balance sheet and the depreciation period can be gained from the Forecast sheet. The model needs to check that it does not calculate beyond the depreciation period using the formula:

```
O12: =-ABS(IF(Assets!O$6<=$K12,
   IF(Forecast!$H49=cstZero, SLN($J12,cstZero,$K12),
   SYD($J12,cstZero,$K12,Assets!O$10)),cstZero))
```

The first method used is straight line and the second is sum of digits with the inputs to the SYD function as shown in Figure 6.4.

Figure 6.4

Sum of digits

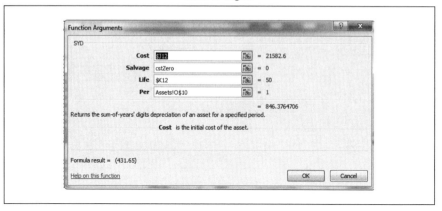

The model is using the straight line method so it simply divides the capital by the number of years since there is no salvage value (see Figure 6.5).

Figure 6.5

Existing depreciation

Line No	Label	Ref	6	7	8	9	10
Start			01-Jan-17	01-Jan-18	01-Jan-19	01-Jan-20	01-Jan-
Finish			31-Dec-17	31-Dec-18	31-Dec-19	31-Dec-20	31-Dec-
BD010	(A) Depreciation		1	2	3	4	
BD011	Existing equipment						
BD012	Land/buildings	F049	(431.65)	(431.65)	(431.65)	(431.65)	(431.
BD013	Equipment	F050	(428.28)	(428.28)	(428.28)	(428.28)	(428.
BD014	IT						
BD015	Total		(859.93)	(859.93)	(859.93)	(859.93)	(859.

NEW ASSET DEPRECIATION

New assets are divided between land and buildings, equipment and IT to allow for different depreciation periods. There is also planned expenditure in each period so the model has to compute the depreciation for each asset in each year. This means that you have one set of assets in year 1 and two in year 2 and so on until the end of the writing-down period for each asset. Depending on the depreciation periods, the assets will start to be written-down to zero during the forecast period.

First, you need the asset values and years down the left-hand side in order to form an efficient lookup to compare the periods and decide if a calculation is applicable. You can use the TRANSPOSE function as an array. Here you enter the function in the first cell, drag down to the end of the sequence and, while they are still selected, enter them with Control + Shift + Enter.

```
L19: =TRANSPOSE(-ABS(Forecast!$O$56:$X$56))
```

You can also transpose the dates in row 7 and format them so that only the year shows. This is a custom number format using 'yyyy' to suppress the months and days.

The formula needs to start at the current year number and continue for the depreciation period before suppressing the value to zero. For a calculation to be possible the year number along the top of the table first must be greater than the numerical year down the left-hand side. Second, the year must be less than the year number plus the relevant depreciation period. Third, the method is either straight line or sum of digits. This is summarised in the formula below where certain rows and columns are locked to allow for copying down and across:

```
O19: =IF(AND(YEAR(Assets!O$7)>=YEAR
($N19), YEAR(Assets!O$7)<YEAR($N19)
+$E$18), IF(Forecast!$H$56=cstZero,
SLN($L19,cstZero,$E$18), SYD($L19,cstZero,$E$18,
Assets!O$10-$M19)),cstZero)
```

You can also transpose the dates in row 7 and format them so that only the year shows, as in Figure 6.6 below.

Table set-up

Figure 6.6

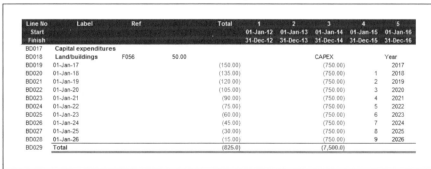

Line No	Label	Ref		Total	1	2	3	4	5
Start					01-Jan-12	01-Jan-13	01-Jan-14	01-Jan-15	01-Jan-16
Finish					31-Dec-12	31-Dec-13	31-Dec-14	31-Dec-15	31-Dec-16
BD017	Capital expenditures								
BD018	Land/buildings	F056		50.00			CAPEX		Year
BD019	01-Jan-17				(150.00)		(750.00)		2017
BD020	01-Jan-18				(135.00)		(750.00)	1	2018
BD021	01-Jan-19				(120.00)		(750.00)	2	2019
BD022	01-Jan-20				(105.00)		(750.00)	3	2020
BD023	01-Jan-21				(90.00)		(750.00)	4	2021
BD024	01-Jan-22				(75.00)		(750.00)	5	2022
BD025	01-Jan-23				(60.00)		(750.00)	6	2023
BD026	01-Jan-24				(45.00)		(750.00)	7	2024
BD027	01-Jan-25				(30.00)		(750.00)	8	2025
BD028	01-Jan-26				(15.00)		(750.00)	9	2026
BD029	Total				(825.0)		(7,500.0)		

Figure 6.7

Depreciation sequence

Line No Start Finish	Label	Ref	6 01-Jan-17 31-Dec-17	7 01-Jan-18 31-Dec-18	8 01-Jan-19 31-Dec-19	9 01-Jan-20 31-Dec-20	10 01-Jan-21 31-Dec-21
BD016							
BD017	Capital expenditures						
BD018	Land/buildings	F056					
BD019	01-Jan-17		(15.00)	(15.00)	(15.00)	(15.00)	(15.00)
BD020	01-Jan-18		-	(15.00)	(15.00)	(15.00)	(15.00)
BD021	01-Jan-19		-	-	(15.00)	(15.00)	(15.00)
BD022	01-Jan-20		-	-	-	(15.00)	(15.00)
BD023	01-Jan-21		-	-	-	-	(15.00)
BD024	01-Jan-22		-	-	-	-	-
BD025	01-Jan-23		-	-	-	-	-
BD026	01-Jan-24		-	-	-	-	-
BD027	01-Jan-25		-	-	-	-	-
BD028	01-Jan-26		-	-	-	-	-
BD029	Total		(15.00)	(30.00)	(45.00)	(60.00)	(75.00)

You can copy the formula across and down as the row and columns are locked so that they pick up the relevant data. The formula results in a distinctive triangular pattern as the model adds new expenditure in each year (see Figure 6.7). The total in row 29 shows the annual total for that asset type.

You can repeat the table for the equipment and IT categories. Whereas the land and buildings are depreciated over 40 years, equipment will be fully depreciated over the period down to zero. The model uses three years for IT equipment, which results in a 'self-checking' pattern as shown in Figure 6.8.

Figure 6.8

IT depreciation

Line No Start Finish	Label	Ref	6 01-Jan-17 31-Dec-17	7 01-Jan-18 31-Dec-18	8 01-Jan-19 31-Dec-19	9 01-Jan-20 31-Dec-20	10 01-Jan-21 31-Dec-21
BD044	IT	F058					
BD045	01-Jan-17		(83.33)	(83.33)	(83.33)	-	-
BD046	01-Jan-18		-	(83.33)	(83.33)	(83.33)	-
BD047	01-Jan-19		-	-	(83.33)	(83.33)	(83.33)
BD048	01-Jan-20		-	-	-	(83.33)	(83.33)
BD049	01-Jan-21		-	-	-	-	(83.33)
BD050	01-Jan-22		-	-	-	-	-
BD051	01-Jan-23		-	-	-	-	-
BD052	01-Jan-24		-	-	-	-	-
BD053	01-Jan-25		-	-	-	-	-
BD054	01-Jan-26		-	-	-	-	-
BD055	Total		(83.33)	(166.67)	(250.00)	(250.00)	(250.00)
BD056							
BD057	Total calculated book depreciation		(1,058.27)	(1,256.60)	(1,454.93)	(1,569.93)	(1,684.93)
BD058							
BD059	Manually input book depreciation		-	-	-	-	-
BD060							
BD061	Book depreciation		(1,058.27)	(1,256.60)	(1,454.93)	(1,569.93)	(1,684.93)

WRITTEN DOWN VALUE

The written down value is simply the original value plus the cumulative depreciation from the table in Figure 6.8 above (see Figure 6.9). Again you lock the column to only allow you to copy down and across in one action. These values will be used in the forecast balance sheet as fixed assets.

```
O71: =IF(O19<>cstZero,-$L19+SUM($O19:O19),cstZero)
```

Written down value

Figure 6.9

Line No	Label	Ref	6	7	8	9	10
Start			01-Jan-17	01-Jan-18	01-Jan-19	01-Jan-20	01-Jan-21
Finish			31-Dec-17	31-Dec-18	31-Dec-19	31-Dec-20	31-Dec-21
BD068	New equipment		22,864.07	22,004.14	21,144.20	20,284.27	19,424.34
BD069							
BD070	Land/buildings						
BD071	01-Jan-17		735.00	720.00	705.00	690.00	675.00
BD072	01-Jan-18		-	735.00	720.00	705.00	690.00
BD073	01-Jan-19		-	-	735.00	720.00	705.00
BD074	01-Jan-20		-	-	-	735.00	720.00
BD075	01-Jan-21		-	-	-	-	735.00
BD076	01-Jan-22		-	-	-	-	-
BD077	01-Jan-23		-	-	-	-	-
BD078	01-Jan-24		-	-	-	-	-
BD079	01-Jan-25		-	-	-	-	-
BD080	01-Jan-26		-	-	-	-	-
BD081	Total		735.00	1,455.00	2,160.00	2,850.00	3,525.00
BD082							
BD083	Equipment						
BD084	01-Jan-17		400.00	300.00	200.00	100.00	-
BD085	01-Jan-18		-	400.00	300.00	200.00	100.00
BD086	01-Jan-19		-	-	400.00	300.00	200.00
BD087	01-Jan-20		-	-	-	400.00	300.00
BD088	01-Jan-21		-	-	-	-	400.00
BD089	01-Jan-22		-	-	-	-	-
BD090	01-Jan-23		-	-	-	-	-
BD091	01-Jan-24		-	-	-	-	-
BD092	01-Jan-25		-	-	-	-	-
BD093	01-Jan-26		-	-	-	-	-
BD094	Total		400.00	700.00	900.00	1,000.00	1,000.00
BD095							

ASSET SUMMARY

It is useful to summarise the net values in case they are needed later in the model or for checking purposes. You can also include a facility on the Forecast sheet to capitalise and write down the initial transaction expenses of 292.80 over an extended period (see Figure 6.10). The period is five years on the Control sheet, which equates to 58.55 per annum.

Figure 6.10

Summary

Line No	Label	Ref	6	7	8	9	10
Start			01-Jan-17	01-Jan-18	01-Jan-19	01-Jan-20	01-Jan-21
Finish			31-Dec-17	31-Dec-18	31-Dec-19	31-Dec-20	31-Dec-21
BD095							
BD096	IT						
BD097	01-Jan-17		166.67	83.33	-	-	-
BD098	01-Jan-18		-	166.67	83.33	-	-
BD099	01-Jan-19		-	-	166.67	83.33	-
BD100	01-Jan-20		-	-	-	166.67	83.33
BD101	01-Jan-21		-	-	-	-	166.67
BD102	01-Jan-22		-	-	-	-	-
BD103	01-Jan-23		-	-	-	-	-
BD104	01-Jan-24		-	-	-	-	-
BD105	01-Jan-25		-	-	-	-	-
BD106	01-Jan-26		-	-	-	-	-
BD107	Total		166.67	250.00	250.00	250.00	250.00
BD108							
BD109	NBV summary						
BD110	Land/buildings		21,885.95	22,174.30	22,447.64	22,705.99	22,949.34
BD111	Equipment		2,113.12	1,984.84	1,756.56	1,428.28	1,000.00
BD112	IT		166.67	250.00	250.00	250.00	250.00
BD113	Total		24,165.73	24,409.14	24,454.20	24,384.27	24,199.34
BD114							
BD115	Amortization						
BD116	Transaction Cost Amorti:	292.8	(58.55)	(58.55)	(58.55)	(58.55)	(58.55)
BD117							
BD118	Goodwill Amortization	5,148.0	-	-	-	-	-

TAX DEPRECIATION

The tax depreciation layout is the same as the accounting depreciation so you can right-click the tab and make a copy of the Depreciation sheet. Rename it Tax_Deprn. In the UK and USA accounting depreciation is added back to profit and replaced with tax depreciation and therefore the model will need both forms of depreciation to calculate tax correctly. The model chooses tax depreciation between straight line and declining balance in this model as set up in the Forecast sheet. Update the formula for the existing assets:

```
O12: =-IF(Tax_Deprn!O$10<=$K12, IF(Forecast!$H$61=0,
SLN($J12,$L12,$K12), DDB($J12,cstZero,$K12,O$10,
Forecast!$E61*10)),cstZero)
```

The choice of function is between SLN and DDB and again you obtain the distinctive self-checking pattern of code. You could also check the pattern by comparing the amounts against a chart. Again bring the numbers forward at the bottom of the sheet to calculate the tax depreciated totals (see Figure 6.11).

Tax schedule

Figure 6.11

Line No	Label	Ref		Total	1	2	3	4	5
Start					01-Jan-12	01-Jan-13	01-Jan-14	01-Jan-15	01-Jan-16
Finish					31-Dec-12	31-Dec-13	31-Dec-14	31-Dec-15	31-Dec-16
TD010	(A) Depreciation								
TD011	Existing equipment			Check	Beginning	Period	Salvage		
TD012	Land/buildings	BD012	USD Millions	(8,660.30)	21,582.60	40.00	-		2017
TD013	Equipment	BD013		(1,857.00)	2,141.40	7.00	-		2017
TD014	IT	BD014							
TD015	Total				23,724.00				
TD016									
TD017	Capital expenditures								
TD018	Land/buildings	F056	40.00				CAPEX		Year
TD019	01-Jan-17			(300.95)			(750.00)		2017
TD020	01-Jan-18			(277.31)			(750.00)	1.00	2018
TD021	01-Jan-19			(252.43)			(750.00)	2.00	2019
TD022	01-Jan-20			(226.25)			(750.00)	3.00	2020
TD023	01-Jan-21			(198.68)			(750.00)	4.00	2021
TD024	01-Jan-22			(169.66)			(750.00)	5.00	2022
TD025	01-Jan-23			(139.12)			(750.00)	6.00	2023
TD026	01-Jan-24			(106.97)			(750.00)	7.00	2024
TD027	01-Jan-25			(73.13)			(750.00)	8.00	2025
TD028	01-Jan-26			(37.50)			(750.00)	9.00	2026
TD029	Total			(1,782.00)			(7,500.00)		
TD030									
TD031	Equipment	F057	7.00				CAPEX		Year
TD032	01-Jan-17			(500.00)			(500.00)		2017
TD033	01-Jan-18			(500.00)			(500.00)	1.00	2018
TD034	01-Jan-19			(500.00)			(500.00)	2.00	2019
TD035	01-Jan-20			(452.57)			(500.00)	3.00	2020
TD036	01-Jan-21			(433.59)			(500.00)	4.00	2021
TD037	01-Jan-22			(407.03)			(500.00)	5.00	2022
TD038	01-Jan-23			(295.88)			(400.00)	6.00	2023
TD039	01-Jan-24			(190.67)			(300.00)	7.00	2024
TD040	01-Jan-25			(97.96)			(200.00)	8.00	2025
TD041	01-Jan-26			(28.57)			(100.00)	9.00	2026
TD042	Total			(3,406.27)			(4,000.00)		

The new assets (see Figure 6.12) follow the same method with a straight line or declining balance:

```
O19: =IF(AND(YEAR(Tax_Deprn!O$7)>=YEAR($N19),
YEAR(Tax_Deprn!O$7)< YEAR($N19)+$E$18),
IF(Forecast!$H$62=0,$L19/$E$18,-DDB(ABS($L19),
cstZero,$E$18,O$10-$M19,Forecast!$E$61*10)),cstZero)
```

Figure 6.12

Existing and new assets

Line No	Label		5	6	7	8	9	10
Start			01-Jan-16	01-Jan-17	01-Jan-18	01-Jan-19	01-Jan-20	01-Jan-21
Finish			31-Dec-16	31-Dec-17	31-Dec-18	31-Dec-19	31-Dec-20	31-Dec-21
TD010	**(A) Depreciation**		1	2	3	4	5	
TD011	**Existing equipment**							
TD012	Land/buildings	2017	(1,079.13)	(1,025.17)	(973.91)	(925.22)	(878.96)	
TD013	Equipment	2017	(611.83)	(437.02)	(312.16)	(222.97)	(159.26)	
TD014	IT							
TD015	Total		(1,690.96)	(1,462.19)	(1,286.07)	(1,148.19)	(1,038.22)	
TD016								
TD017	**Capital expenditures**							
TD018	**Land/buildings**	Year						
TD019	01-Jan-17	2017	(37.50)	(35.63)	(33.84)	(32.15)	(30.54)	
TD020	01-Jan-18	2018	-	(37.50)	(35.63)	(33.84)	(32.15)	
TD021	01-Jan-19	2019	-	-	(37.50)	(35.63)	(33.84)	
TD022	01-Jan-20	2020	-	-	-	(37.50)	(35.63)	
TD023	01-Jan-21	2021	-	-	-	-	(37.50)	
TD024	01-Jan-22	2022	-	-	-	-	-	
TD025	01-Jan-23	2023	-	-	-	-	-	
TD026	01-Jan-24	2024	-	-	-	-	-	
TD027	01-Jan-25	2025	-	-	-	-	-	
TD028	01-Jan-26	2026	-	-	-	-	-	
TD029	Total		(37.50)	(73.13)	(106.97)	(139.12)	(169.66)	
TD030								
TD031	**Equipment**	Year						
TD032	01-Jan-17	2017	(142.86)	(102.04)	(72.89)	(52.06)	(37.19)	
TD033	01-Jan-18	2018	-	(142.86)	(102.04)	(72.89)	(52.06)	
TD034	01-Jan-19	2019	-	-	(142.86)	(102.04)	(72.89)	
TD035	01-Jan-20	2020	-	-	-	(142.86)	(102.04)	
TD036	01-Jan-21	2021	-	-	-	-	(142.86)	
TD037	01-Jan-22	2022	-	-	-	-	-	
TD038	01-Jan-23	2023	-	-	-	-	-	
TD039	01-Jan-24	2024	-	-	-	-	-	
TD040	01-Jan-25	2025	-	-	-	-	-	
TD041	01-Jan-26	2026	-	-	-	-	-	
TD042	Total		(142.86)	(244.90)	(317.78)	(369.85)	(407.03)	

SUMMARY

The Assets sheet is essentially a workings sheet to generate data for the forecast accounting statements. The data for the existing assets, spend, timing and method can be translated into depreciation per period, gross and written down value. The same method is useful for the tax depreciation and it is straightforward to use the Assets sheet as a template for tax depreciation. Again, the design method of utilising standard schedules and styles means that this schedule can be completed quickly in an auditable form.

Debt

DEBT SCHEDULE

The Asset schedule generates key numbers, such as depreciation and fixed assets, ready for feeding into the forecast balance sheet. The design method ensures that there are blocks of auditable code on separate sheets and workings are separated on to individual schedules. It is better to set out a progression of workings rather than attempt to achieve the same answers with complex code. The next stage is to calculate the entries for the new debt entered on the Control and Forecast sheets. Figures 7.1 and 7.2 are extracts from the two input sheets where you need to know the split of debt, the term, interest rates and the intended capital repayment pattern.

Control

Figure 7.1

Sources of funds			%
Existing debt	Senior	-	-
Senior debt A	Senior	12,000.00	41.93%
Senior debt B	Senior	5,000.00	17.47%
Junior debt C	Junior	2,500.00	8.74%
Junior debt D	Junior	2,000.00	6.99%
Junior debt E	Junior	2,000.00	6.99%
Other	Junior	-	-
Preferred stock		500.00	1.75%
Outside equity		1,118.77	3.91%
Management equity A		3,000.00	10.48%
Management equity B		500.00	1.75%
Total sources		28,618.77	100.00%

Interest rates

Figure 7.2

Line No	Label	Ref	6 01-Jan-17 31-Dec-17	7 01-Jan-18 31-Dec-18	8 01-Jan-19 31-Dec-19	9 01-Jan-20 31-Dec-20	10 01-Jan-21 31-Dec-21
F089							
F090	Debt						
F091	Senior debt A	IB058	10.00%	10.00%	10.00%	10.00%	10.00%
F092	Senior debt B	IB059	10.00%	10.00%	10.00%	10.00%	10.00%
F093	Junior debt C	IB060	10.00%	10.00%	10.00%	10.00%	10.00%
F094	Junior debt D	IB061	10.00%	10.00%	10.00%	10.00%	10.00%
F095	Junior debt E	IB062	20.00%	20.00%	20.00%	20.00%	20.00%
F096	Other	IB063	20.00%	20.00%	20.00%	20.00%	20.00%
F097							
F098	Debt interest rates						
F099	Finance income	IP030	0.50%	0.50%	0.50%	0.50%	0.50%
F100	Existing debt	IP032	5.00%	5.00%	5.00%	5.00%	5.00%
F101	Senior debt A	IP033	4.50%	4.50%	4.50%	4.50%	4.50%
F102	Senior debt B	IP034	5.00%	5.00%	5.00%	5.00%	5.00%
F103	Junior debt C	IP035	6.00%	6.00%	6.00%	6.00%	6.00%
F104	Junior debt D	IP036	6.25%	6.25%	6.25%	6.25%	6.25%
F105	Junior debt E	IP037	6.50%	6.50%	6.50%	6.50%	6.50%
F106	Other	IP038	6.75%	6.75%	6.75%	6.75%	6.75%
F107	Preferred stock coupon		5.00%	5.00%	5.00%	5.00%	5.00%
F108	Preferred stock par value		100.00	100.00	100.00	100.00	100.00

The debt is divided into senior and junior debt so that you can change the structure easily. In a later section, the model calculates the cover figures against tranche of debt. This means working out the cash available to settle that portion of the debt and the cash required by the funder.

The full inputs needed are:

- loan name to be repeated on other schedules;
- capital amount per tranche;
- loan seniority: senior or junior;
- method of interest calculation as a percentage payable on the balance outstanding or using an Excel function such as PPMT and IPMT;
- annual percentage capital repayment used in manual calculations;
- loan term for Excel functions;
- interest rate charged.

REQUIRED ENTRIES

The lists on the Workings sheet need to be checked to ensure that the correct choices are available on the Forecast sheet. A drop-down list with a formatted number is easier for a user than having to remember that an IPMT function is equal to one and manual write-downs are entered as zero. A one or zero can be used to select the method required. The list must be a named range and it is useful to replace the ones and zeros with more meaningful descriptions, as shown in Figure 7.3. The code for this is:

```
Number format: "Manual";-1;"Function"
```

| Figure 7.3 | | Lists |

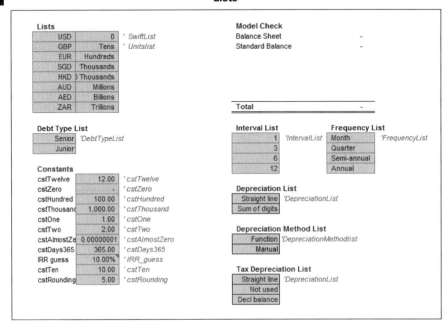

You can then copy the template sheet with the dates twice to form a starting point for the Debt schedule and the Forecast sheet. Again, this ensures a consistent 'look and feel' to the model. You need to calculate the written down loan value, the interest payable and the split of loan payable between current and long-term debt.

The loan write down depends on the method. It is either the previous balance less an input percentage for that period or based on:

```
O11: =IF(Forecast!$I91=cstOne,N11-
Control!$K15*Forecast!O91, N11-
PPMT(Forecast!$O$101,Debt_
Schedule!O$9,Forecast!$J$91,-Debt_
Schedule!$N11,cstZero))
```

The PPMT function requires the same entries as a PMT function together with an extra input for the period number (see Figure 7.4). This amortises the capital at the fixed interest rate over the term to a balance of zero (see Figure 7.5).

PPMT function

Figure 7.4

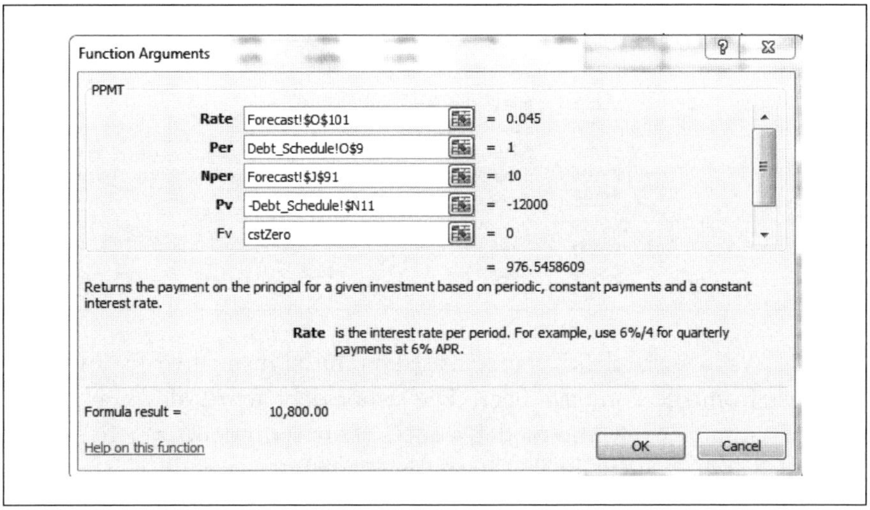

Figure 7.5

Debt entries

Line No Start Finish	Label	Ref
CS010	Existing debt	IN014
CS011	Senior debt A	IN015
CS012	Senior debt B	IN016
CS013	Junior debt C	IN017
CS014	Junior debt D	IN018
CS015	Junior debt E	IN019
CS016	Other	IN020
CS017	Preferred stock	IN021
CS018	Shareholders equity	FB065+FB067
CS019	Book capitalization	Sum
CS020		
CS021	Total debt	FB059
CS022		
CS023	Book equity	FB067
CS024		
CS025	Current portion long term debt	
CS026	Existing debt	CS010
CS027	Senior debt A	CS011
CS028	Senior debt B	CS012
CS029	Junior debt C	CS013
CS030	Junior debt D	CS014
CS031	Junior debt E	CS015
CS032	Other	CS016
CS033	Total	
CS034		
CS035	Interest rates	
CS036	Existing debt	F100
CS037	Senior debt A	F101
CS038	Senior debt B	F102
CS039	Junior debt C	F103
CS040	Junior debt D	F104
CS041	Junior debt E	F105
CS042	Other	F106

Figure 7.6 shows the debt balances based on initial manual write down percentages from the Forecast sheet. The senior debt writes down at 10 per cent per annum while the model reduces short-term debt over five years. The balance sheet entry for the current portion of long-term debt represents the difference between the two years:

```
O28:  =O11-P11
```

Debt balances

Figure 7.6

Line No	Label	Ref	5	6	7	8	9
Start			01-Jan-16	01-Jan-17	01-Jan-18	01-Jan-19	01-Jan-20
Finish			31-Dec-16	31-Dec-17	31-Dec-18	31-Dec-19	31-Dec-20
				1	2	3	4
CS010	Existing debt	IN014	-	-	-	-	-
CS011	Senior debt A	IN015	12,000.00	10,800.00	9,600.00	8,400.00	7,200.00
CS012	Senior debt B	IN016	5,000.00	4,500.00	4,000.00	3,500.00	3,000.00
CS013	Junior debt C	IN017	2,500.00	2,250.00	2,000.00	1,750.00	1,500.00
CS014	Junior debt D	IN018	2,000.00	1,800.00	1,600.00	1,400.00	1,200.00
CS015	Junior debt E	IN019	2,000.00	1,600.00	1,200.00	800.00	400.00
CS016	Other	IN020	-	-	-	-	-
CS017	Preferred stock	IN021	500.00	-	-	-	-
CS018	Shareholders equity	FB065+FB06˙	5,118.77	-	-	-	-
CS019	**Book capitalization**	Sum	29,118.77	20,950.00	18,400.00	15,850.00	13,300.00
CS020							
CS021	Total debt	FB059		18,400.00	15,850.00	13,300.00	10,750.00
CS022							
CS023	Book equity	FB067		-	-	-	-
CS024							
CS025	Current portion long term debt						
CS026	Existing debt	CS010					
CS027	Senior debt A	CS011	1,200.00	1,200.00	1,200.00	1,200.00	1,200.00
CS028	Senior debt B	CS012	500.00	500.00	500.00	500.00	500.00
CS029	Junior debt C	CS013	250.00	250.00	250.00	250.00	250.00
CS030	Junior debt D	CS014	200.00	200.00	200.00	200.00	200.00
CS031	Junior debt E	CS015	400.00	400.00	400.00	400.00	400.00
CS032	Other	CS016	-	-	-	-	-
CS033	Total		2,550.00	2,550.00	2,550.00	2,550.00	2,550.00

INTEREST RATES

The annual interest rates are set out on the Forecast sheet. The model assumes that with the manual method, you hold the capital for the year and pay interest on the balance. The calculation is therefore the capital outstanding multiplied by the relevant interest rate.

If the annuity functions are selected, you can use an IPMT function to derive the interest payable (see Figure 7.7):

```
O46: =IF(Forecast!$I91=cstOne,-
N11*O37, -IPMT(Forecast!$O$101,Debt_
Schedule!O$9,Forecast!$J$91,-Debt_
Schedule!$N11,cstZero))
```

Figure 7.7

Interest payable

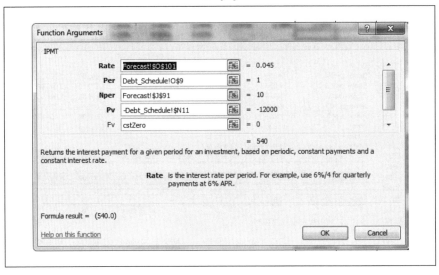

The interest payable is then available for the income statement together with the balance sheet entries of current and long-term debt.

FORECAST INCOME STATEMENT

You can add the interest payable to the income statement at line 32 (Figure 7.8). This will change depending on the loan written down method chosen.

Figure 7.8

Forecast interest

=Workings!B6	=Workings!C6	=Workings!D6	=Workings!O6	=Workings!P6
=Workings!B7			=Workings!O7	=Workings!P7
=Workings!B8			=Workings!O8	=Workings!P8
="FP"&TEXT(ROW(A31=Income!C31	=Income!B31			
="FP"&TEXT(ROW(A32=Income!C32	=Income!B32	=Debt_Schedule!O45	=Debt_Schedule!P45
="FP"&TEXT(ROW(A33=Income!C33	=Income!B33	=Debt_Schedule!O46	=Debt_Schedule!P46
="FP"&TEXT(ROW(A34=Income!C34	=Income!B34	=Debt_Schedule!O47	=Debt_Schedule!P47
="FP"&TEXT(ROW(A35=Income!C35	=Income!B35	=Debt_Schedule!O48	=Debt_Schedule!P48
="FP"&TEXT(ROW(A36=Income!C36	=Income!B36	=Debt_Schedule!O49	=Debt_Schedule!P49
="FP"&TEXT(ROW(A37=Income!C37	=Income!B37	=Debt_Schedule!O50	=Debt_Schedule!P50
="FP"&TEXT(ROW(A38=Income!C38	=Income!B38	=Debt_Schedule!O51	=Debt_Schedule!P51
="FP"&TEXT(ROW(A39=Income!C39	=Income!B39		
="FP"&TEXT(ROW(A40=Income!C40	=SUM(D30:D38)	=SUM(O31:O39)	=SUM(P31:P39)
="FP"&TEXT(ROW(A41			
="FP"&TEXT(ROW(A42=Income!C42	=Income!B42	=Forecast!O25	=Forecast!P25
="FP"&TEXT(ROW(A43=Income!C43	=Income!B43	=Forecast!O26	=Forecast!P26
="FP"&TEXT(ROW(A44=Income!C44	=Income!B44	=O28+O30+O40+O42+O43	=P28+P30+P40+P42+P43

FORECAST BALANCE SHEET

The blank template sheet brings forward the standard header and line numbers. You can populate the sheet with the line descriptions from the historic income statement (see Figure 7.9). The model needs to bring forward the historic entries and the next chapter will map out the forecast entries from the Forecast, Assets and Debt sheets.

Assets

Figure 7.9

Line No Start Finish	Label	Ref		Total	1 01-Jan-12 31-Dec-12	2 01-Jan-13 31-Dec-13
FB010	Current assets					
FB011	Cash & marketable securities	FB087	USD Millions		1,146.0	1,395.0
FB012	Accounts receivable	FP010*F039			597.0	648.0
FB013	Inventories	FP010*F040			1,306.0	1,464.0
FB014	Prepaid expenses	FP010*F041			48.0	86.0
FB015	Prepaid income taxes	FP010*F042			-	-
FB016	Other current assets 1	FP010*F043			136.0	141.0
FB017	Other current assets 2	FP010*F044			224.0	17.0
FB018	Other current assets 3	FP010*F045			-	-
FB019	Total current assets				3,457.0	3,751.0
FB021	Non-current assets					
FB022	Net land, property, plant & equipment	BD113			15,495.0	15,882.0
FB023	Investments	FP010*F070			414.0	1,225.0
FB024	Intangibles	FP010*F071			-	-
FB025	Other asssets	FP010*F071			-	-
FB026	Transaction costs	FP010+BD116			-	-
FB027	New goodwill	FP010+BD118			1,044.0	1,525.0
FB028	Other non-current assets 1	FP010*F073			-	-
FB029	Other non-current assets 2	FP010*F074			-	180.0
FB030	Other non-current assets 3	FP010*F075			-	-
FB031	Total non-current assets				16,953.0	18,812.0
FB033	Total assets				20,410.0	22,563.0

The schedule matches the line numbers in the historic sheets, as it is important that all calculations line up to avoid simple mistakes. The self-check is also present to prove that this statement contains no errors by ensuring that assets equal liabilities (see Figure 7.10).

Figure 7.10

Liabilities

Line No	Label	Ref	Total	1	2
Start				01-Jan-12	01-Jan-13
Finish				31-Dec-12	31-Dec-13
FB035	Current liabilities				
FB036	Overdraft	FB088		471.0	1,252.0
FB037	Current portion long-term debt (CPLTI	CS026.CS032		6.0	662.0
FB038	Accounts payable	FP010*F078		2,819.0	2,832.0
FB039	Accrued expenses	FP010*F079		660.0	693.0
FB040	Dividend payable	FP010*F080		416.0	6.0
FB041	Income tax payable	FP010*F081		442.0	480.0
FB042	Other current liabilities 1	FP010*F082		1,258.0	1,336.0
FB043	Other current liabilities 2	FP010*F083		-	286.0
FB044	Other current liabilities 3	FP010*F084		-	-
FB045	**Total current liabilities**			6,072.0	7,547.0
FB047	Deferred taxes			-	-
FB048	Other deferred liability 1	FP010*F086		750.0	320.0
FB049	Other deferred liability 2	FP010*F087		-	5.0
FB050	Minority Interest	FP010*F088		51.0	63.0
FB051					
FB052	Long term debt				
FB053	Existing debt	CS010		4,531.0	4,036.0
FB054	Senior debt A	CS011		-	-
FB055	Senior debt B	CS012		-	-
FB056	Junior debt C	CS013		-	1,212.0
FB057	Junior debt D	CS014		-	-
FB058	Junior debt E	CS015		-	-
FB059	Other	CS016		-	-
FB060	**Total long term debt**			4,531.0	5,248.0
				-	-
FB062	**Short and long term liabilities**			11,404.0	13,183.0
FB064	Shareholders' equity				
FB065	Common stock (shares)	FB065		389.0	395.0
FB066	Preferred stock (shares)	FB066		3,744.0	4,028.0
FB067	Retained earnings	FB067+FP055		4,873.0	4,957.0
FB068	**Shareholders equity**			9,006.0	9,380.0
FB070	**Total liabilities + shareholders equity**			20,410.0	22,563.0
FB072	CheckSum: Balance Sheet	FB033-FB070	No Errors	-	-

The next stage is to populate the forecast balance sheet with known entries. You can find the asset values and goodwill on the Assets sheet (Figure 7.11) together with the debt entries on the Debt sheet (Figure 7.12). The debt will need to be split between the current portion and long-term debt. The next chapter will map out the other balance sheet entries.

Assets entries

Figure 7.11

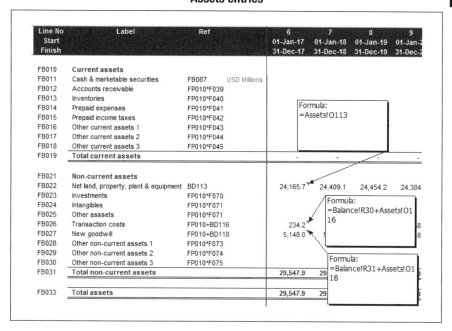

Line No Start Finish	Label	Ref		6 01-Jan-17 31-Dec-17	7 01-Jan-18 31-Dec-18	8 01-Jan-19 31-Dec-19	9 01-Jan-2 31-Dec-2
FB010	Current assets						
FB011	Cash & marketable securities	FB087	USD Millions				
FB012	Accounts receivable	FP010*F039					
FB013	Inventories	FP010*F040					
FB014	Prepaid expenses	FP010*F041		Formula:			
FB015	Prepaid income taxes	FP010*F042		=Assets!O113			
FB016	Other current assets 1	FP010*F043					
FB017	Other current assets 2	FP010*F044					
FB018	Other current assets 3	FP010*F045					
FB019	Total current assets			-	-	-	-
FB021	Non-current assets						
FB022	Net land, property, plant & equipment	BD113		24,165.7	24,409.1	24,454.2	24,384
FB023	Investments	FP010*F070		Formula:			
FB024	Intangibles	FP010*F071		=Balance!R30+Assets!O1			
FB025	Other asssets	FP010*F071		16			
FB026	Transaction costs	FP010+BD116		234.2			8
FB027	New goodwill	FP010+BD118		5,148.0	5		8
FB028	Other non-current assets 1	FP010*F073					
FB029	Other non-current assets 2	FP010*F074		Formula:			
FB030	Other non-current assets 3	FP010*F075		=Balance!R31+Assets!O1			
FB031	Total non-current assets			29,547.9	29	18	
FB033	Total assets			29,547.9	29		

Liabilities entries

Figure 7.12

Line No Start Finish	Label	Ref	6 01-Jan-17 31-Dec-17	7 01-Jan-18 31-Dec-18	8 01-Jan-19 31-Dec-19
FB035	Current liabilities				
FB036	Overdraft	FB088			
FB037	Current portion long-term debt (CPLTI	CS026.CS032	2,550.0	2,550.0	2,550.0
FB038	Accounts payable	FP010*F078			
FB039	Accrued expenses	FP010*F079	Formula:		
FB040	Dividend payable	FP010*F080	=Debt_Schedule!O33		
FB041	Income tax payable	FP010*F081			
FB042	Other current liabilities 1	FP010*F082			
FB043	Other current liabilities 2	FP010*F083			
FB044	Other current liabilities 3	FP010*F084			
FB045	Total current liabilities		2,550.0	2,550.0	2,550.0
FB047	Deferred taxes		Formula:		
FB048	Other deferred liability 1	FP010*F086	=Debt_Schedule!O10		
FB049	Other deferred liability 2	FP010*F087			
FB050	Minority Interest	FP010*F088			
FB051					
FB052	Long term debt				
FB053	Existing debt	CS010	-		
FB054	Senior debt A	CS011	9,600.0	8,400.0	7,200.0
FB055	Senior debt B	CS012	4,000.0	3,500.0	3,000.0
FB056	Junior debt C	CS013	2,000.0	1,750.0	1,500.0
FB057	Junior debt D	CS014	1,600.0	1,400.0	1,200.0
FB058	Junior debt E	CS015	1,200.0	800.0	400.0
FB059	Other	CS016	-	-	-
FB060	Total long term debt		18,400.0	15,850.0	13,300.0
FB062	Short and long term liabilities		20,950.0	18,400.0	15,850.0

SUMMARY

The design method requires simple formulas and separate workings areas for each category and this chapter sets out the debt calculations such as the interest payable, and current and long-term debt. The write down options are an annual percentage or calculations using the built-in Excel amortisation functions. The model maps the entries to the forecast income statement and balance sheet.

Balance sheet

This chapter brings together information from the Forecast sheet together with the workings on the Assets and Debt sheets to complete the accounting statements. The information should flow logically through the model and where possible all information should be sourced from a sheet to the left of the current sheet. The intention is to avoid long formulas and show the mapping of the information onto the forecast sheets. Information can then 'cascade' or flow through the model.

The previous sheets together with the forecast percentages will derive the accounting entries except for cash. Cash and marketable or short-term debt securities will act as a 'plug' to the balance sheet (see Figure 8.1). If you plot all the assets and liabilities except cash or short-term debt, you will have a positive or a debt balance. If the liabilities are greater than assets, then you must have a cash-balancing item. If the values are the other way around, then you have a current liability. You can also calculate the amount of debt directly and this should equal the 'plug' number.

Balance sheet structure

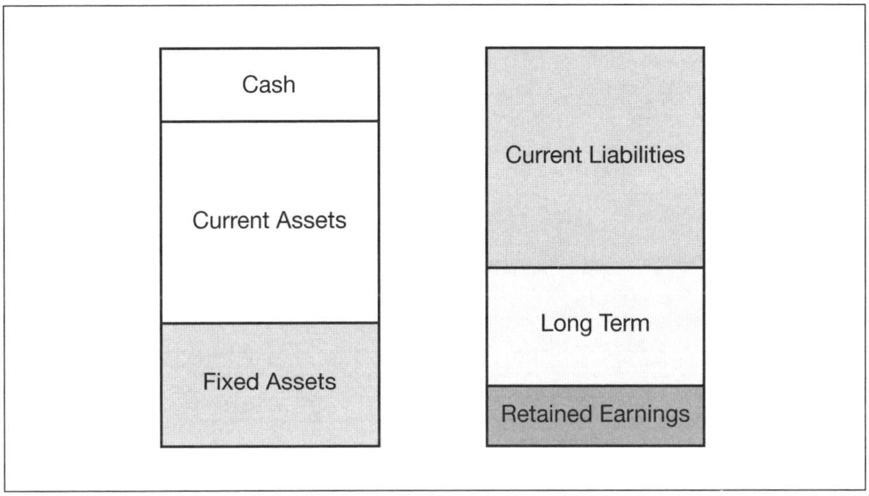

Figure 8.1

CURRENT ASSETS

The first stage is to map the variables from the Forecast sheet. Either you can calculate the percentages of sales or costs, or alternatively use hard numbers if there does not appear to be a firm relationship. On the Forecast sheet, you set out the numbers and percentages to be used:

■ accounts receivable – percentage of sales;

■ inventory – percentage of cost of sales;

■ other current assets – percentage of sales.

```
Accounts receivable 012: =Forecast_
Income!O$10*Forecast!O39/cstDays365
Inventories 013: =-Forecast_
Income!O$11*Forecast!O40/cstDays365
Prepaid expenses 014: =Forecast_
Income!O$10*Forecast!O41
```

cstDays365 is a constant in the model. It is used here since you may wish to switch the model into a 360-day banking year without changing individual formulas. The Ref column in Figure 8.2 shows the formula references.

Assets

Line No Start Finish	Label	Ref		6 01-Jan-17 31-Dec-17	7 01-Jan-18 31-Dec-18	8 01-Jan-19 31-Dec-19
FB010	Current assets					
FB011	Cash & marketable securities	FB087	USD Millions			
FB012	Accounts receivable	FP010*F039		5,730.4	6,303.4	6,933.8
FB013	Inventories	FP010*F040		2,603.2	2,863.6	3,149.9
FB014	Prepaid expenses	FP010*F041		149.4	164.3	180.8
FB015	Prepaid income taxes	FP010*F042		-	-	-
FB016	Other current assets 1	FP010*F043		1,195.2	1,314.7	1,446.2
FB017	Other current assets 2	FP010*F044		-	-	-
FB018	Other current assets 3	FP010*F045		-	-	-
FB019	Total current assets			9,678.2	10,646.0	11,710.6
FB021	Non-current assets					
FB022	Net land, property, plant & equipment	BD113		24,165.7	24,409.1	24,454.2
FB023	Investments	FP010*F070		1,792.8	1,972.1	2,169.3
FB024	Intangibles	FP010*F071		-	-	-
FB025	Other asssets	FP010*F072		-	-	-
FB026	Transaction costs	IB030+BD116		234.2	175.7	117.1
FB027	New goodwill	IB031+BD118		5,148.0	5,148.0	5,148.0
FB028	Other non-current assets 1	FP010*F073		1,195.2	1,314.7	1,446.2
FB029	Other non-current assets 2	FP010*F074		1,792.8	1,972.1	2,169.3
FB030	Other non-current assets 3	FP010*F075		-	-	-
FB031	Total non-current assets			34,328.7	34,991.6	35,504.0
FB033	Total assets			44,006.9	45,637.7	47,214.7

NON-CURRENT ASSETS

The entries for property, plant and equipment together with transaction costs and goodwill were completed in the last chapter. There are forecast percentages for the other items as a percentage of sales expressed in days. Line 10 of the Income Statement gives the total of all the sales components:

```
Investments 023: =Forecast_
Income!O$10*Forecast!O70
```

You should also ensure that depreciation, goodwill and any fees written down are added to the Income Statement in lines 17, 24 and 25.

CURRENT LIABILITIES

The overdraft is a 'plug' item to be calculated later. The current portion of long-term debt comes from the Debt sheet. You can enter the other current liabilities as a percentage of the cost of sales expressed as days. These are in the same order on the Forecast sheet (see Figure 8.3).

```
Accounts payable O38: =-Forecast_
Income!O$11*Forecast!O78/cstDays365
```

Liabilities

Figure 8.3

Line No Start Finish	Label	Ref	6 01-Jan-17 31-Dec-17	7 01-Jan-18 31-Dec-18	8 01-Jan-19 31-Dec-19
FB035	Current liabilities				
FB036	Overdraft	FB088			
FB037	Current portion long-term debt (CPLTD)	CS026.CS032	2,550.0	2,550.0	2,550.0
FB038	Accounts payable	FP011*F078	3,904.8	4,295.3	4,724.9
FB039	Accrued expenses	FP011*F079	1,195.2	1,314.7	1,446.2
FB040	Dividend payable	FP011*F080	-	-	-
FB041	Income tax payable	FP011*F081	298.8	328.7	361.5
FB042	Other current liabilities 1	FP011*F082	2,390.4	2,629.4	2,892.4
FB043	Other current liabilities 2	FP011*F083	597.6	657.4	723.1
FB044	Other current liabilities 3	FP011*F084	4,780.8	5,258.9	5,784.7
FB045	Total current liabilities		15,717.6	17,034.4	18,482.8
FB047	Deferred taxes				
FB048	Other deferred liability 1	FP010*F086	597.6	657.4	723.1
FB049	Other deferred liability 2	FP010*F087	1,792.8	1,972.1	2,169.3
FB050	Minority Interest	FP010*F088	-	-	-
FB051					
FB052	Long term debt				
FB053	Existing debt	CS010	-		
FB054	Senior debt A	CS011	9,600.0	8,400.0	7,200.0
FB055	Senior debt B	CS012	4,000.0	3,500.0	3,000.0
FB056	Junior debt C	CS013	2,000.0	1,750.0	1,500.0
FB057	Junior debt D	CS014	1,600.0	1,400.0	1,200.0
FB058	Junior debt E	CS015	1,200.0	800.0	400.0
FB059	Other	CS016	-	-	-
FB060	Total long term debt		18,400.0	15,850.0	13,300.0
FB062	Short and long term liabilities		36,508.0	35,513.8	34,675.2

LONG-TERM LIABILITIES AND SHAREHOLDERS' FUNDS

Deferred taxes are derived in the next section. Other deferred liabilities can be expressed as a percentage of sales. Long-term debt is located on the Debt sheet where the long-term liability is the total less the repayment due within 12 months.

| Figure 8.4 | | Shareholders' funds | | | | |

| Line No | Label | Ref | 6 | 7 | 8 |
| Start | | | 01-Jan-17 | 01-Jan-18 | 01-Jan-19 |
Finish			31-Dec-17	31-Dec-18	31-Dec-19
FB062	Short and long term liabilities		36,508.0	35,513.8	34,675.2
FB064	Shareholders' equity				
FB065	Common stock (shares)	IN022+IN023+IN024	4,618.8	4,618.8	4,618.8
FB066	Preferred stock (shares)	IN021	500.0	500.0	500.0
FB067	Retained earnings	FB067+FP055	2,729.7	5,907.7	9,569.6
FB068	Shareholders equity		7,848.5	11,026.5	14,688.4
FB070	Total liabilities + shareholders equity		44,356.5	46,540.3	49,363.6
FB072	CheckSum: Balance Sheet	FB033-FB070	(349.5)	(902.6)	(2,148.9)

The Control sheet sets out the combination of common shares made up of outside and management equity (see Figure 8.4). There is also an entry for preferred stock. The model adds the retained earnings left on the Income Statement to the balance of retained earnings on the Balance sheet. This number will change as you insert tax on the Income Statement.

| Figure 8.5 | | Share capital | |

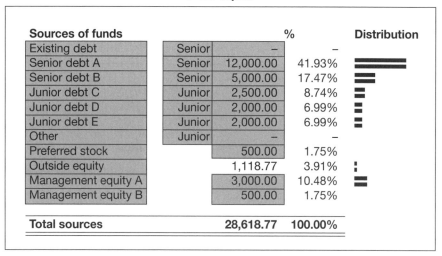

Sources of funds			%	Distribution
Existing debt	Senior	–	–	
Senior debt A	Senior	12,000.00	41.93%	
Senior debt B	Senior	5,000.00	17.47%	
Junior debt C	Junior	2,500.00	8.74%	
Junior debt D	Junior	2,000.00	6.99%	
Junior debt E	Junior	2,000.00	6.99%	
Other	Junior	–	–	
Preferred stock		500.00	1.75%	
Outside equity		1,118.77	3.91%	
Management equity A		3,000.00	10.48%	
Management equity B		500.00	1.75%	
Total sources		28,618.77	100.00%	

The Distribution chart in Figure 8.5 uses the REPT function to place a chart in cells rather than using a chart object:

```
=REPT("¦",L15*50)
```

TAX

The model needs an entry for tax in the Income Statement and Balance sheet. You need a further copy of the landscape template sheet with the timeline for the tax workings (see Figure 8.6).

Tax workings

Figure 8.6

Line No Start Finish	Label	Ref		6 01-Jan-17 31-Dec-17	7 01-Jan-18 31-Dec-18	8 01-Jan-19 31-Dec-19
TW010	Net income before taxes	FP044	USD Millions	3,056.56	3,528.56	4,054.35
TW011						
TW012	Book depreciation	BD061		1,058.27	1,256.60	1,454.93
TW013	Tax depreciation	TD057		(1,942.74)	(1,902.67)	(1,869.72)
TW014						
TW015	Goodwill impairment	BD118		-	-	-
TW016						
TW017	Pre net operating profit/(loss)			2,172.08	2,882.49	3,639.56
TW018						
TW019	Net operating loss used	MIN(TW017,TW029)		-	-	-
TW020	Net operating loss carry forward					
TW021						
TW022	Current taxable Income			2,172.08	2,882.49	3,639.56
TW023						
TW024	Current tax expense	TW022*F029		(543.02)	(720.62)	(909.89)
TW025						
TW026	Total book tax	(TW010+TW015)+(TW012.TW014)*F029		(543.02)	(720.62)	(909.89)
TW027	Deferred taxes	TW026-TW024		-	-	-
TW028						
TW029	Beginning net operating losses	TW033		-	-	-
TW030	Current net operating loss	TW017		-	-	-
TW031	Net operating loss c/f utilized	TW019		-	-	-
TW032						
TW033	Ending net operating losses	TW029+TW030-TW031		-	-	-

Earlier chapters calculated the accounting and tax depreciation. Under this tax system, you add back accounting depreciation and replace it with the standardised tax depreciation. This is to offer a common method of depreciation for tax purposes. Accounting depreciation normally uses straight line depreciation while tax is based on a declining balance method.

The model calculates tax on the adjusted profit with the tax rate from the Forecast sheet. The model can carry forward any losses from previous years and take this into account on the tax payable and deferred. You can enter the tax payable in the Income Statement and the deferred tax on the Balance sheet.

BALANCING ITEM

Similarly, you need to bring forward items for a workings area at the bottom of the Balance sheet. This is to show clearly the derivation of cash and short-term debt (see Figure 8.7).

Figure 8.7 — **Cash workings**

Line No	Label	Ref	6 01-Jan-17 31-Dec-17	7 01-Jan-18 31-Dec-18	8 01-Jan-19 31-Dec-19
Start Finish					
FB072	CheckSum: Balance Sheet	FB033-FB070	-	-	-
	© Systematic Finance : Tel +44 (0)1483 532929				
FB077	**Workings**				
FB078	Current assets (no cash)	FB012.FB018	9,678.2	10,646.0	11,710.6
FB079	Fixed assets	FB031	34,328.7	34,991.6	35,504.0
FB080	Total assets	Sum	44,006.9	45,637.7	47,214.7
FB081					
FB082	Current liabilities	FB037.FB044	15,717.6	17,034.4	18,482.8
FB083	Tax and long term debt	FB047.FB050+FB060	20,790.4	18,479.4	16,192.4
FB084	Net worth	FB068	6,878.2	8,827.5	10,994.6
FB085		Sum	43,386.2	44,341.3	45,669.8
FB086					
FB087	Cash	FB085-FB080	-	-	-
FB088	Debt	FB080-FB085	620.7	1,296.4	1,544.9
FB089	Check		-	-	-
FB090					
FB091	**Alerts**				
FB092	Check cash - debt				
FB093	Difference to workings below	No Errors			
FB094					
FB095	Capital structure debt		20,950.0	18,400.0	15,850.0
FB096	Balance sheet debt (LT+CPLTD)		20,950.0	18,400.0	15,850.0
FB097	Difference	No Errors	-	-	-
FB098					
FB099	Current portion long-term debt (CPLTD)		2,550.0	2,550.0	2,550.0
FB100	Diffference	No Errors	-	-	-

The workings area brings forward the current and non-current assets without cash on one side and the liabilities without short-term overdraft debt on the other side. There are two IF statements to derive cash or short-term debt:

```
Cash O87:  =IF(O80>=O85,cstZero,O85-O80)
Debt O88:  =IF(O80>O85,O80-O85,cstZero)
```

These items link to the Balance sheet at lines 11 and 36. The Balance sheet should then balance with zero errors at the bottom. Any errors can be traced back to the individual sheets.

The income tax expense adjusts the profit after tax and the dividends payable. The retained earnings feed through to shareholders' funds and adjust the amount of short-term debt required. Figures 8.8–8.10 show the completed financial statements.

Complete income statement

Figure 8.8

Line No Start Finish	Label	Ref	6 01-Jan-17 31-Dec-17	7 01-Jan-18 31-Dec-18	8 01-Jan-19 31-Dec-19
FP022	Operating profit (EBIT	IP022	4,021.31	4,330.93	4,691.35
FP023					
FP024	Fees write-off	IP024	(58.55)	(58.55)	(58.55)
FP025	New goodwill	IP025	-	-	-
FP026	Subtotal	IP026	(58.55)	(58.55)	(58.55)
FP027					
FP028	Operating profit (EBIT	IP028	3,962.76	4,272.38	4,632.80
FP029					
FP030	Finance income	IP030	298.80	328.68	361.55
FP031	Finance costs	IP031	-	(31.03)	(64.82)
FP032	Existing debt	IP032	-	-	-
FP033	Senior debt A	IP033	(540.00)	(486.00)	(432.00)
FP034	Senior debt B	IP034	(250.00)	(225.00)	(200.00)
FP035	Junior debt C	IP035	(150.00)	(135.00)	(120.00)
FP036	Junior debt D	IP036	(125.00)	(112.50)	(100.00)
FP037	Junior debt E	IP037	(130.00)	(104.00)	(78.00)
FP038	Other	IP038	-	-	-
FP039	Preference shares	IP039	(25.00)	(25.00)	(25.00)
FP040	Total finance costs	-	(1,220.00)	(1,118.53)	(1,019.82)
FP041					
FP042	Share of profit of associ	IP042	5.00	5.00	5.00
FP043	Gain (loss) on assets	IP043	10.00	10.00	10.00
FP044	Profit before tax	IP044	3,056.56	3,497.53	3,989.53
FP045					
FP046	Income tax expenses	IP046	(543.02)	(712.87)	(893.69)
FP047	Profit from continuing	IP047	2,513.54	2,784.66	3,095.84
FP048					
FP049	Discontinued operations	IP049	-	-	-
FP050	Profit for the year	IP050	2,513.54	2,784.66	3,095.84
FP051					
FP052	Dividends	IP052	(754.06)	(835.40)	(928.75)
FP053	Minority interest	IP053	-	-	-
FP054					
FP055	Net profit	IP055	1,759.48	1,949.26	2,167.09

SUMMARY

After calculating the debt and assets, you can map out the other entries into the Income Statement and Balance sheet. Cash and short-term debt cannot be directly calculated and these are used as a 'plug' or balancing item to ensure that assets equal liabilities. A further check line at the bottom of the Balance sheet ensures that the two sides are equal. With a functioning balance and income statement, the next chapters produce a cash flow and ratios.

Figure 8.9

Complete assets

Line No / Start / Finish	Label	Ref		6 / 01-Jan-17 / 31-Dec-17	7 / 01-Jan-18 / 31-Dec-18	8 / 01-Jan-19 / 31-Dec-19
FB010	Current assets					
FB011	Cash & marketable securities	FB087	USD Millions	-	-	-
FB012	Accounts receivable	FP010*F039		5,730.4	6,303.4	6,933.8
FB013	Inventories	FP010*F040		2,603.2	2,863.6	3,149.9
FB014	Prepaid expenses	FP010*F041		149.4	164.3	180.8
FB015	Prepaid income taxes	FP010*F042		-	-	-
FB016	Other current assets 1	FP010*F043		1,195.2	1,314.7	1,446.2
FB017	Other current assets 2	FP010*F044		-	-	-
FB018	Other current assets 3	FP010*F045		-	-	-
FB019	Total current assets			9,678.2	10,646.0	11,710.6
FB021	Non-current assets					
FB022	Net land, property, plant & equipment	BD113		24,165.7	24,409.1	24,454.2
FB023	Investments	FP010*F070		1,792.8	1,972.1	2,169.3
FB024	Intangibles	FP010*F071		-	-	-
FB025	Other asssets	FP010*F072		-	-	-
FB026	Transaction costs	IB030+BD116		234.2	175.7	117.1
FB027	New goodwill	IB031+BD118		5,148.0	5,148.0	5,148.0
FB028	Other non-current assets 1	FP010*F073		1,195.2	1,314.7	1,446.2
FB029	Other non-current assets 2	FP010*F074		1,792.8	1,972.1	2,169.3
FB030	Other non-current assets 3	FP010*F075		-	-	-
FB031	Total non-current assets			34,328.7	34,991.6	35,504.0
FB033	Total assets			44,006.9	45,637.7	47,214.7

Figure 8.10

Complete liabilities

Client: AAAAA : Rev 1-Jan-2012

Line No / Start / Finish	Label	Ref	6 / 01-Jan-17 / 31-Dec-17	7 / 01-Jan-18 / 31-Dec-18	8 / 01-Jan-19 / 31-Dec-19
FB035	Current liabilities				
FB036	Overdraft	FB088	620.7	1,296.4	1,544.9
FB037	Current portion long-term debt (CPLTD)	CS026.CS032	2,550.0	2,550.0	2,550.0
FB038	Accounts payable	FP011*F078	3,904.8	4,295.3	4,724.9
FB039	Accrued expenses	FP011*F079	1,195.2	1,314.7	1,446.2
FB040	Dividend payable	FP011*F080	-	-	-
FB041	Income tax payable	FP011*F081	298.8	328.7	361.5
FB042	Other current liabilities 1	FP011*F082	2,390.4	2,629.4	2,892.4
FB043	Other current liabilities 2	FP011*F083	597.6	657.4	723.1
FB044	Other current liabilities 3	FP011*F084	4,780.8	5,258.9	5,784.7
FB045	Total current liabilities		16,338.3	18,330.7	20,027.7
FB047	Deferred taxes		-	-	-
FB048	Other deferred liability 1	FP010*F086	597.6	657.4	723.1
FB049	Other deferred liability 2	FP010*F087	1,792.8	1,972.1	2,169.3
FB050	Minority Interest	FP010*F088	-	-	-
FB051					
FB052	Long term debt				
FB053	Existing debt	CS010	-		
FB054	Senior debt A	CS011	9,600.0	8,400.0	7,200.0
FB055	Senior debt B	CS012	4,000.0	3,500.0	3,000.0
FB056	Junior debt C	CS013	2,000.0	1,750.0	1,500.0
FB057	Junior debt D	CS014	1,600.0	1,400.0	1,200.0
FB058	Junior debt E	CS015	1,200.0	800.0	400.0
FB059	Other	CS016	-	-	-
FB060	Total long term debt		18,400.0	15,850.0	13,300.0
FB062	Short and long term liabilities		37,128.7	36,810.2	36,220.1
FB064	Shareholders' equity				
FB065	Common stock (shares)	IN022+IN023+IN024	4,618.8	4,618.8	4,618.8
FB066	Preferred stock (shares)	IN021	500.0	500.0	500.0
FB067	Retained earnings	FB067+FP055	1,759.5	3,708.7	5,875.8
FB068	Shareholders equity		6,878.2	8,827.5	10,994.6
FB070	Total liabilities + shareholders equity		44,006.9	45,637.7	47,214.7

9

Cash flow

OUTLINE

The forecast model provides a trial balance in the form of an Income Statement and Balance sheet; however, this tells you nothing about the amount of cash produced or the company's ability to meet its future financial obligations. You need to understand the ability to pay as a company risks going out of business if it does not generate sufficient cash. A company could raise capital in the form of further borrowing, but cash flow in the longer term has to be sufficient to meet all obligations.

Cash flow statements are required in most annual reports in order to show clearly the sources and uses of cash. The objectives are:

■ To identify the sources and uses of cash as opposed to revenue and cost which are defined by accounting regulations and conventions.

■ To separate the sources and uses of cash arising from the main operations as opposed to peripheral activities or 'on–off' transactions such as government grants.

■ To calculate the level of cash flow for comparison purposes, for example the cash produced by operations or the cash before funding.

The cash flow starts with the operating profit before tax and adds back non-cash items to form the earnings before interest, tax, depreciation and amortisation (EBITDA) (see Figure 9.1). Further items are either a number from the Income Statement or a change in balance during the year on the Balance sheet. Debtor side increases will reduce the amount of cash while the credit side increases increase the amount of cash. For modelling purposes, it is best to structure the formulas so that an increase automatically produces a positive or negative number:

■ Debtors: last year – this year.

■ Creditors: this year – last year.

Figure 9.2 shows the main headings to derive cash from operations as the main trading cash line. This is one of the important lines for analysing an ability to pay since this does not include ancillary sources. Using cash from operations, the company has to invest in new equipment and service investments. After financing there may be a shortfall or positive balance before the introduction of new funding in the form of loans, bonds and share capital.

You may need a reconciliation item since the amount added to retained earnings on the Balance sheet may not be the same as the retained earnings on the Income Statement. If you do not include a reconciliation item, you may encounter errors. This is due to issues such as:

■ prior year P&L adjustment;

■ shares issued and share issue premium;

- shares issued for scrip dividends;
- shares repurchased;
- preference shares issued;
- goodwill written off and written back;
- foreign exchange translation;
- revaluation for the year;
- transfer to/from reserves.

After adding or subtracting the reconciliation items, the model should indicate the net increase or decrease in cash and cash equivalents. This must be the same as the difference in cash on the Balance sheet and the model should self-check with an error message if it fails to balance.

Figure 9.1   **Cash flow**

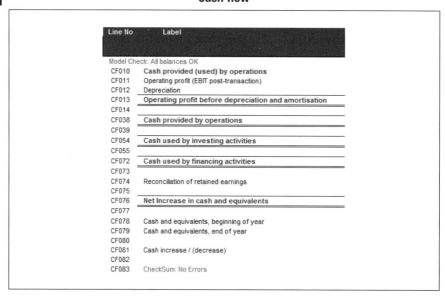

Figure 9.2   **Sources and uses**

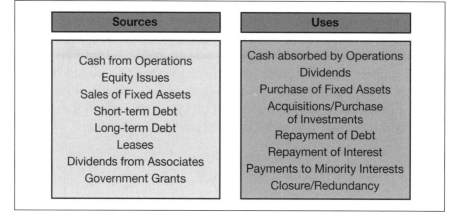

You can copy a template landscape schedule three times and rename them:

- Forecast_Cash – international cash statement.
- Forecast_OpCash – cash available for debt service.
- Forecast_DebtCash – cash waterfall of debt servicing and reconciliation back to balance sheet cash.

CASH FLOW STATEMENT

The cash flow statements must conform to the design method by using the same columns and units. If you use positive costs in a model or fail to keep to the same columns, you will find it hard to reconcile a cash statement and make it balance. The statement starts with the net operating profit plus the non-operating items such as depreciation and amortisation (earnings before interest, tax, depreciation and amortisation). Since accounting depreciation methodology varies between countries, this strips out the main distorting effect encountered when comparing international companies.

The next step is make adjustments for working capital, dividends and interest. This includes the items shown in Figure 9.3. To ensure that you have extracted all the items you could print a copy of the Income Statement and Balance sheet and tick each item as you use it or alternatively use colour coding. You have to include all items below operating profit on the Income Statement and all entries on the Balance sheet except cash.

Cash from operations

Figure 9.3

Line No	Label	Ref		Total	1 01-Jan-12 31-Dec-12	2 01-Jan-13 31-Dec-13
Start						
Finish						
CF010	Cash provided (used) by operations					
CF011	Operating profit (EBIT post-transaction)	FP028	USD Millions		1,949.00	2,280.00
CF012	Depreciation	IP017+FP018			733.00	809.00
CF013	Operating profit before depreciation and amortisation				2,682.00	3,089.00
CF014						
CF015	Accounts receivable	FB012				(51.00)
CF016	Inventories	FB013				(158.00)
CF017	Prepaid expenses	FB014				(38.00)
CF018	Prepaid income taxes	FB015				-
CF019	Other current assets 1	FB016				(5.00)
CF020	Other current assets 2	FB017				207.00
CF021	Other current assets 3	FB018				-
CF022	Accounts payable	FB038				13.00
CF023	Accrued expenses	FB039				33.00
CF024	Dividend payable	FB040				(410.00)
CF025	Income tax payable	FB041				38.00
CF026	Other current liabilities 1	FB042				78.00
CF027	Other current liabilities 2	FB043				286.00
CF028	Other current liabilities 3	FB044				-
CF029	Income tax expenses	FP046				(583.00)
CF030	Finance costs	FP031				-
CF031	Existing debt	FP032				(241.00)
CF032	Senior debt A	FP033				-
CF033	Senior debt B	FP034				-
CF034	Junior debt C	FP035				-
CF035	Junior debt D	FP036				-
CF036	Junior debt E	FP037				-
CF037	Other	FP038				82.00
CF038	Cash provided by operations					2,340.00

After cash from operations, you need to list the investments and assets. Again, these entries are a line item on the Income Statement or a change in balance on the Balance sheet as shown by the references in Figure 9.4.

Figure 9.4

Cash used by investing and financing activities

Line No	Label	Ref	Total	1	2
Start				01-Jan-12	01-Jan-13
Finish				31-Dec-12	31-Dec-13
CF038	Cash provided by operations				2,340.00
CF039					
CF040	Cash provided (used) by investing activities				
CF041	Net land, property, plant & equipment	FB022			(1,196.00)
CF042	Investments	FB023			(811.00)
CF043	Intangibles	FB024			-
CF044	Other asssets	FB025			-
CF045	Transaction costs	FB026			-
CF046	New goodwill	FB027			(481.00)
CF047	Other non-current assets 1	FB028			-
CF048	Other non-current assets 2	FB029			(180.00)
CF049	Other non-current assets 3	FB030			-
CF050	Share of profit of associates	FP042			4.00
CF051	Gain (loss) on assets	FP043			11.00
CF052	Discontinued operations	FP049			45.00
CF053	Finance income	FP030			114.00
CF054	Cash used by investing activities				(2,494.00)
CF055					
CF056	Cash provided (used) by financing activities				
CF057	Overdraft debt	FB036			781.00
CF058	Current portion long-term debt (CPLTD)	FB037			656.00
CF059	Existing debt	FB053			(495.00)
CF060	Senior debt A	FB054			-
CF061	Senior debt B	FB055			-
CF062	Junior debt C	FB056			1,212.00
CF063	Junior debt D	FB057			-
CF064	Junior debt E	FB058			-
CF065	Common stock (shares)	FB065			6.00
CF066	Preferred stock (shares)	FB066			284.00
CF067	Dividends	FP052			(612.00)
CF068	Deferred taxes	FB047			-
CF069	Other deferred liability 1	FB048			(430.00)
CF070	Other deferred liability 2	FB049			5.00
CF071	Minority Interest	FB050			14.00
CF072	Cash used by financing activities				1,421.00

The financing activities include the new debt together with the overdraft debt formed as a balancing item. The current portion of long-term debt is the difference between the start and end of the year. Other items in this section include ordinary and preferred shares, minorities, dividends and deferred liabilities.

Cash increase

Figure 9.5

Line No Start Finish	Label	Ref	Total	1 01-Jan-12 31-Dec-12	2 01-Jan-13 31-Dec-13
CF072	Cash used by financing activities				1,421.00
CF073					
CF074	Reconciliation of retained earnings	FB067-FP055			(1,018.00)
CF075					
CF076	Net Increase in cash and equivalents				249.00
CF077					
CF078	Cash and equivalents, beginning of year	CF079			1,146.00
CF079	Cash and equivalents, end of year	FB011		1,146.00	1,395.00
CF080					
CF081	Cash increase / (decrease)				249.00
CF082					
CF083	CheckSum: No Errors				-

You can calculate the reconciliation as the difference between the retained earnings on the income and balance sheets, as in Figure 9.5:

```
K74: =Forecast_Balance!K67-Forecast_Balance!J67-
Forecast_Income!K55
```

After the reconciliation item, you can bring forward the starting and finishing cash balance and compare it to the finishing value on the cash flow statement. A check should be present to ensure that the statement balances and throws up any unknown errors. The completed forecast cash flow with all the categories completed is shown in Figures 9.6–9.8.

Forecast cash from operations

Figure 9.6

Line No Start Finish	Label	Ref	6 01-Jan-17 31-Dec-17	7 01-Jan-18 31-Dec-18	8 01-Jan-19 31-Dec-19
CF010	Cash provided (used) by operations				
CF011	Operating profit (EBIT post-transaction)	FP028	3,962.76	4,272.38	4,632.80
CF012	Depreciation	IP017+FP018	1,058.27	1,256.60	1,454.93
CF013	Operating profit before depreciation and amortis		5,021.02	5,528.98	6,087.74
CF014					
CF015	Accounts receivable	FB012	(4,485.38)	(573.04)	(630.34)
CF016	Inventories	FB013	65.77	(260.32)	(286.36)
CF017	Prepaid expenses	FB014	250.60	(14.94)	(16.43)
CF018	Prepaid income taxes	FB015	9.00	-	-
CF019	Other current assets 1	FB016	(872.19)	(119.52)	(131.47)
CF020	Other current assets 2	FB017	382.00	-	-
CF021	Other current assets 3	FB018	-	-	-
CF022	Accounts payable	FB038	(843.15)	390.48	429.53
CF023	Accrued expenses	FB039	(98.81)	119.52	131.47
CF024	Dividend payable	FB040	-	-	-
CF025	Income tax payable	FB041	(63.20)	29.88	32.87
CF026	Other current liabilities 1	FB042	(89.61)	239.04	262.94
CF027	Other current liabilities 2	FB043	62.60	59.76	65.74
CF028	Other current liabilities 3	FB044	4,780.78	478.08	525.89
CF029	Income tax expenses	FP046	(543.02)	(712.87)	(893.69)
CF030	Finance costs	FP031	-	(31.03)	(64.82)
CF031	Existing debt	FP032	-	-	-
CF032	Senior debt A	FP033	(540.00)	(486.00)	(432.00)
CF033	Senior debt B	FP034	(250.00)	(225.00)	(200.00)
CF034	Junior debt C	FP035	(150.00)	(135.00)	(120.00)
CF035	Junior debt D	FP036	(125.00)	(112.50)	(100.00)
CF036	Junior debt E	FP037	(130.00)	(104.00)	(78.00)
CF037	Other	FP038	-	-	-
CF038	Cash provided by operations		2,381.40	4,071.52	4,583.06

Figure 9.7

Forecast cash used in investing and financing

Line No Start Finish	Label	Ref	6 01-Jan-17 31-Dec-17	7 01-Jan-18 31-Dec-18	8 01-Jan-19 31-Dec-19
CF038	Cash provided by operations		2,381.40	4,071.52	4,583.06
CF039					
CF040	Cash provided (used) by investing activities				
CF041	Net land, property, plant & equipment	FB022	(1,500.00)	(1,500.00)	(1,500.00)
CF042	Investments	FB023	67.21	(179.28)	(197.21)
CF043	Intangibles	FB024	-	-	-
CF044	Other asssets	FB025	-	-	-
CF045	Transaction costs	FB026	58.55	58.55	58.55
CF046	New goodwill	FB027	-	-	-
CF047	Other non-current assets 1	FB028	274.81	(119.52)	(131.47)
CF048	Other non-current assets 2	FB029	104.21	(179.28)	(197.21)
CF049	Other non-current assets 3	FB030	1,000.00	-	-
CF050	Share of profit of associates	FP042	5.00	5.00	5.00
CF051	Gain (loss) on assets	FP043	10.00	10.00	10.00
CF052	Discontinued operations	FP049	-	-	-
CF053	Finance income	FP030	298.80	328.68	361.55
CF054	Cash used by investing activities		318.57	(1,575.85)	(1,590.79)
CF055					
CF056	Cash provided (used) by financing activities				
CF057	Overdraft debt	FB036	620.69	675.69	248.54
CF058	Current portion long-term debt (CPLTD)	FB037	2,550.00	-	-
CF059	Existing debt	FB053	-	-	-
CF060	Senior debt A	FB054	(2,400.00)	(1,200.00)	(1,200.00)
CF061	Senior debt B	FB055	(1,000.00)	(500.00)	(500.00)
CF062	Junior debt C	FB056	(500.00)	(250.00)	(250.00)
CF063	Junior debt D	FB057	(400.00)	(200.00)	(200.00)
CF064	Junior debt E	FB058	(800.00)	(400.00)	(400.00)
CF065	Common stock (shares)	FB065	-	-	-
CF066	Preferred stock (shares)	FB066	(25.00)	(25.00)	(25.00)
CF067	Dividends	FP052	(754.06)	(835.40)	(928.75)
CF068	Deferred taxes	FB047	-	-	-
CF069	Other deferred liability 1	FB048	(98.40)	59.76	65.74
CF070	Other deferred liability 2	FB049	153.79	179.28	197.21
CF071	Minority Interest	FB050	(47.00)	-	-
CF072	Cash used by financing activities		(2,699.99)	(2,495.67)	(2,992.27)

Figure 9.8

Forecast reconciliation

Line No Start Finish	Label	Ref	6 01-Jan-17 31-Dec-17	7 01-Jan-18 31-Dec-18	8 01-Jan-19 31-Dec-19
CF072	Cash used by financing activities		(2,699.99)	(2,495.67)	(2,992.27)
CF073					
CF074	Reconciliation of retained earnings	FB067-FP05	-	-	-
CF075					
CF076	Net Increase in cash and equivalents		(0.01)	(0.00)	0.00
CF077					
CF078	Cash and equivalents, beginning of year	CF079	-	-	-
CF079	Cash and equivalents, end of year	FB011	-	-	-
CF080					
CF081	Cash increase / (decrease)		-	-	-
CF082					
CF083	CheckSum: No Errors		-	-	-

CASH FOR DEBT SERVICE

For debt service, you need to understand what cash is available to each provider of share capital or loans. Debt service coverage allows you to review the number of times the amounts are covered against the cash flow available to that provider. To achieve this, you need to rework the cash flow statement into sections to form a waterfall of cash. These are the sections:

- Forecast_OpCash – operating cash available for debt service.
- Forecast_DebtCash – debt waterfall to show the cash available to settle each form of debt.

The EBITDA figure is the same as in the cash flow statement followed by the changes in working capital with the servicing of finance omitted. Income tax remains in the schedule as you are trying to find the cash available to service finance. Most lines in the schedule are the same as in the cash flow statement and this schedule represents a reworking of the figures to show more clearly the cash available to different groups (see Figure 9.9).

Operating cash

Figure 9.9

Line No	Label	Ref	6	7	8
Start			01-Jan-17	01-Jan-18	01-Jan-19
Finish			31-Dec-17	31-Dec-18	31-Dec-19
CF010	Cash provided (used) by operations				
CF011	Operating profit (EBIT po	FP028 USD Millions	3,962.76	4,272.38	4,632.80
CF012	Depreciation	FP017+FP018	1,058.27	1,256.60	1,454.93
CF013	Operating profit before depreciation and amo₁		5,021.02	5,528.98	6,087.74
CF014					
CF015	Accounts receivable	FB012	(4,485.38)	(573.04)	(630.34)
CF016	Inventories	FB013	65.77	(260.32)	(286.36)
CF017	Prepaid expenses	FB014	250.60	(14.94)	(16.43)
CF018	Prepaid income taxes	FB015	9.00	-	-
CF019	Other current assets 1	FB016	(872.19)	(119.52)	(131.47)
CF020	Other current assets 2	FB017	382.00	-	-
CF021	Other current assets 3	FB018	-	-	-
CF022	Accounts payable	FB038	(843.15)	390.48	429.53
CF023	Accrued expenses	FB039	(98.81)	119.52	131.47
CF024	Income tax payable	FB041	(63.20)	29.88	32.87
CF025	Other current liabilities 1	FB042	(89.61)	239.04	262.94
CF026	Other current liabilities 2	FB043	62.60	59.76	65.74
CF027	Other current liabilities 3	FB044	4,780.78	478.08	525.89
CF028	Income tax expenses	FP046	(543.02)	(712.87)	(893.69)
CF029	Operating cash		3,576.40	5,165.06	5,577.88
CF030					
CF031	Cash provided (used) by investing activities				
CF032	Net land, property, plant	FB022	(1,500.00)	(1,500.00)	(1,500.00)
CF033	Investments	FB023	67.21	(179.28)	(197.21)
CF034	Intangibles	FB024	-	-	-
CF035	Other asssets	FB025	-	-	-
CF036	Transaction costs	FB026	58.55	58.55	58.55
CF037	New goodwill	FB027	-	-	-
CF038	Other non-current asset	FB028	274.81	(119.52)	(131.47)
CF039	Other non-current asset	FB029	104.21	(179.28)	(197.21)
CF040	Other non-current asset	FB030	1,000.00	-	-
CF041	Share of profit of associ	FP042	5.00	5.00	5.00
CF042	Gain (loss) on assets	FP043	10.00	10.00	10.00
CF043	Discontinued operations	FP049	-	-	-
CF044	Cash used by investing activities		19.77	(1,904.53)	(1,952.34)
CF045					
CF046	Net Increase in cash and equivalents		3,596.17	3,260.53	3,625.55

The investing activities are the same as in the previous section except that it excludes non-trading finance income as this fits into the next schedule. The sum at line 46 represents the amount of cash available to service debt, which is sometimes known as cash flow available for debt service (CFADS). Like EBITDA and cash from operations, this is an important measure for determining the ability to pay and service debt.

CASH WATERFALL

The cash waterfall picks up the CFADS line and starts with these totals labelled as Cash for retirement of the senior debt. You can use text strings in the labels to pick up the name of the loan automatically:

```
C10:  ="Cash For retirement of "&Forecast_
Balance!$C$54
```

For each block the entries (see Figure 9.10) are:

- Cash – amount brought forward from the previous section.
- Percentage repaid – the percentage on the Forecast sheet for the manual repayment.
- Mandatory repayment – difference between the year end balances on the Debt schedule. This takes account of repayments using Excel functions.
- Interest – as calculated on the Debt sheet.
- Total retired – addition of the principal and interest.
- Cover – cash brought forward divided by the total repayable. You need a MIN function to find the low point during the model period rather than an average. Turns are marked with an 'x' in the number format:

```
Format:  _-*  #,##0.00x_-;[Red](#,##0.00x);_-*
"-"??_-;_-@_-
```

Debts repayable

Figure 9.10

Line No Start Finish	Label	Ref	6 01-Jan-17 31-Dec-17	7 01-Jan-18 31-Dec-18	8 01-Jan-19 31-Dec-19
DB010	Cash For retirement of Senior debt A	CF046	3,596.17	3,260.53	3,625.55
DB011	Percentage repaid		10.0%	10.0%	10.0%
DB012	Senior debt A mandatory repayment	CS011	(1,200.00)	(1,200.00)	(1,200.00)
DB013	Interest	CS046	(540.00)	(486.00)	(432.00)
DB014	Senior debt A retired		(1,740.00)	(1,686.00)	(1,632.00)
DB015	Minimum Cover	DB010/DB013	2.07x	1.93x	2.22x
DB016					
DB017	Cash for retirement of Senior debt B	DB010+DB014	1,856.17	1,574.53	1,993.55
DB018	Percentage repaid		10.0%	10.0%	10.0%
DB019	Senior debt B mandatory repayment	CS012	(500.00)	(500.00)	(500.00)
DB020	Interest	CS047	(250.00)	(225.00)	(200.00)
DB021	Senior debt B retired		(750.00)	(725.00)	(700.00)
DB022	Minimum Cover	DB017/DB020	2.47x	2.17x	2.85x
DB023					
DB024	Cash for retirement of Junior debt C	DB017+DB021	1,106.17	849.53	1,293.55
DB025	Percentage repaid		10.0%	10.0%	10.0%
DB026	Junior debt C mandatory repayment	CS013	(250.00)	(250.00)	(250.00)
DB027	Interest	CS048	(150.00)	(135.00)	(120.00)
DB028	Junior debt C retired		(400.00)	(385.00)	(370.00)
DB029	Minimum Cover	DB024/DB027	2.77x	2.21x	3.50x
DB030					
DB031	Cash for retirement of Junior debt D	DB024+DB028	706.17	464.53	923.55
DB032	Percentage repaid		10.0%	10.0%	10.0%
DB033	Junior debt D mandatory repayment	CS014	(200.00)	(200.00)	(200.00)
DB034	Interest	CS049	(125.00)	(112.50)	(100.00)
DB035	Junior debt D retired		(325.00)	(312.50)	(300.00)
DB036	Minimum Cover	DB031/DB034	2.17x	1.49x	3.08x
DB037					
DB038	Cash for retirement of Junior debt E	DB031+DB035	381.17	152.03	623.55
DB039	Percentage repaid		20.0%	20.0%	20.0%
DB040	Junior debt E mandatory repayment	CS015	(400.00)	(400.00)	(400.00)
DB041	Interest	CS050	(130.00)	(104.00)	(78.00)
DB042	Junior debt E retired		(530.00)	(504.00)	(478.00)
DB043	Minimum Cover	DB038/DB041	0.72x	0.30x	1.30x

Each section follows through to the next such that there is a reducing amount of cash to pay the junior debt. The final section in lines 54 to 56 in Figure 9.11 includes those items excluded from cash available for finance. These are items such as dividends, other interest and preference coupons, which need to be included to ensure that the total cash is the same as the balance change.

You need checks (see Figure 9.11) to be certain that there are no errors:

■ Cash is equal to the change in cash on the balance sheet.

■ That the check is equal to the last one. This is to ensure that you do not have a positive of, for example, 50 in one column and –50 in the next such that the total balance is zero.

Figure 9.11

Reconciliation to cash

Line No / Start / Finish	Label	Ref	6 / 01-Jan-17 / 31-Dec-17	7 / 01-Jan-18 / 31-Dec-18	8 / 01-Jan-19 / 31-Dec-19
DB042	Junior debt E retired		(530.00)	(504.00)	(478.00)
DB043	Minimum Cover	DB038/DB041	0.72x	0.30x	1.30x
DB044					
DB045	Cash for retirement of Other	DB038+DB042	(148.83)	(351.97)	145.55
DB046	Percentage repaid		20.0%	20.0%	20.0%
DB047	Other mandatory repayment	CS016	-	-	-
DB048	Interest	CS051	-	-	-
DB049	Other retired		-	-	-
DB050	Minimum Cover	DB045/DB048	na	na	na
DB051					
DB052	Net cash		(148.83)	(351.97)	145.55
DB053					
DB054	Finance income	FP030	298.8	328.7	361.5
DB055	Interest paid	FP031.FP032	-	(31.0)	(64.8)
DB056	Current portion long-term debt (CPLTD)	FB037			
DB057	Common stock (shares)	FB065	-	-	-
DB058	Preferred stock (shares)	FB066	(25.00)	(25.00)	(25.00)
DB059	Dividend payable	FB040	-	-	-
DB060	Dividends	FP052	(754.06)	(835.40)	(928.75)
DB061	Deferred taxes	FB047	-	-	-
DB062	Other deferred liability 1	FB048	(98.40)	59.76	65.74
DB063	Other deferred liability 2	FB049	153.79	179.28	197.21
DB064	Minority Interest	FB050	(47.00)	-	-
DB065	Retained earnings reconciliation		-	-	-
DB066	Total finance		(471.87)	(323.72)	(394.08)
DB067					
DB068	Additions to cash/overdraft		(620.70)	(675.69)	(248.54)
DB069					
DB070	Balance sheet comparison				
DB071	Balance sheet cash	FB011	-	-	-
DB072	Balance sheet overdraft	FB036	620.69	675.69	248.54
DB073	Total		620.69	675.69	248.54
DB074					
DB075	CheckSum: No Errors		-	-	-
DB076			-	-	-

CHART

Before starting further analysis, it is a good idea to plot the key lines to try to understand the loans servicing requirements against the cash available. Figure 9.12 is a combination of area, column and line charts. The first series is the cash available, which you format as an area chart. The next two are the total repayments and the capital payable. The chart type here is a column with the overlap set to 100 per cent, so that you can see the interest and principal clearly. The EBITDA and balance outstanding are line charts on the primary axis while the cash available divided by the total repayment is on the secondary right-hand scale. The data used in the chart is shown in Figure 9.13.

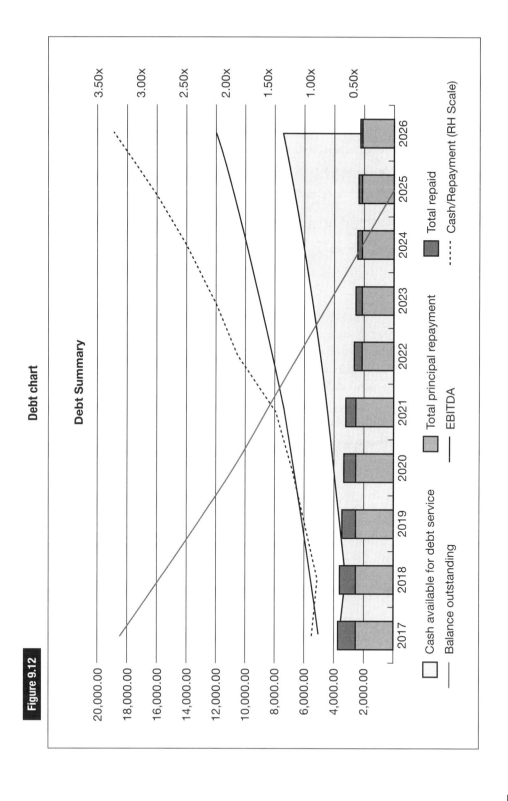

Debt chart

Figure 9.12

Figure 9.13

Chart data

Line No Start Finish	Label	Ref	6 01-Jan-17 31-Dec-17	7 01-Jan-18 31-Dec-18	8 01-Jan-19 31-Dec-19
DB076			–	–	–
DB077	Debt summary				
DB078	Cash available for debt service		3,596.17	3,260.53	3,625.55
DB079	Total principal repayment		2,550.00	2,550.00	2,550.00
DB080	Total interest payment		1,195.00	1,062.50	930.00
DB081	Total repaid		3,745.00	3,612.50	3,480.00
DB082	Cash//Repayment (RH Scale)		0.96x	0.90x	1.04x
DB083	EBITDA		5,021.02	5,528.98	6,087.74
DB084	Balance outstanding		18,400.00	15,850.00	13,300.00

You can now see clearly the lack of cash flow in the early stages to cover the total debt repayable and the increase in cash cover towards the end of the term.

SUMMARY

This chapter produces two cash flow statements: the first conforms to an international layout using the categories such as cash from operations, investing and finance. The second reworks the statement to show clearly the cash to service debt together with the waterfall of cash to individual debts and reconciles it to the variation in balance sheet cash. The next chapter calculates key financial ratios for further analysis and for checking the forecast.

Ratios

METHOD

This chapter sets out a workable ratios method for analysing and evaluating the accounting statements. With the accounts in a standardised format, you can then code templates to analyse the figures. The framework in Figure 10.1 shows the process of examining the strategy followed by the management and the results for both financial analysis and valuation purposes. You need to try to understand the factors that can influence the cash flow and assess the potential level of risk or downside. Whilst the absolute ratios will vary by industry and country, you need to assess whether the balance sheet or cash flow are becoming stronger or weaker with higher borrowings and less ability to service the debt. The grid in Figure 10.1 sets out the main factors for consideration: environment, industry, company, cash flow and management.

Framework

Figure 10.1

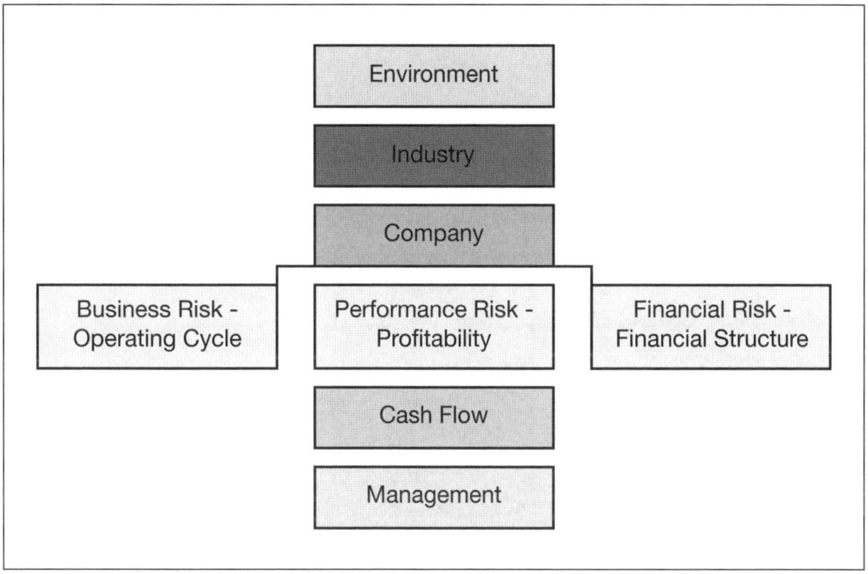

The environment contains all the outside factors beyond the control of management that affect the company's prospects for growth, stability and cash generation. This is a good starting point since an analysis of the company in isolation may not yield all the required information. Examples could include on-going economic cycles, political risk and changes such as the taxation system, social and demographic changes, technology shifts and environmental change. All companies are exposed to macro risk and it is necessary to consider the potential threats and consequences. This is sometimes categorised as a STEP or STEEP model (see Figure 10.2).

Figure 10.2

STEEP

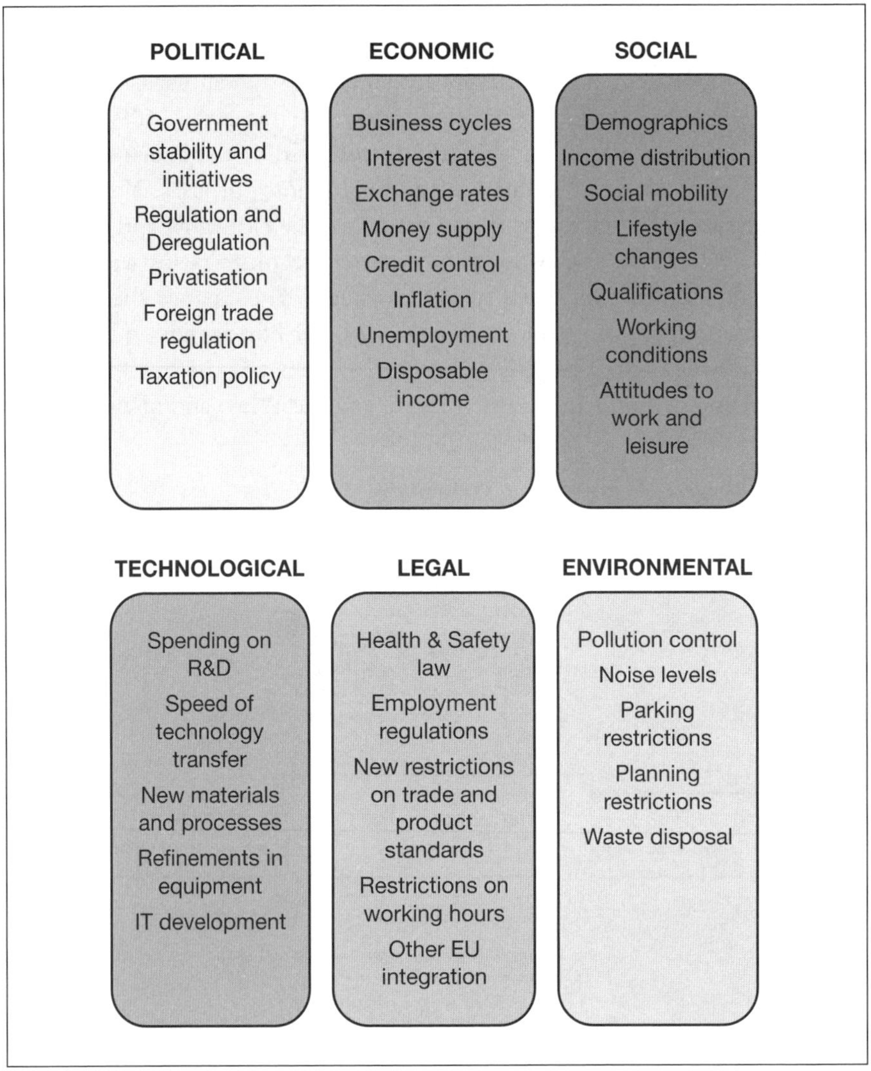

POLITICAL	ECONOMIC	SOCIAL
Government stability and initiatives	Business cycles	Demographics
Regulation and Deregulation	Interest rates	Income distribution
Privatisation	Exchange rates	Social mobility
Foreign trade regulation	Money supply	Lifestyle changes
Taxation policy	Credit control	Qualifications
	Inflation	Working conditions
	Unemployment	Attitudes to work and leisure
	Disposable income	

TECHNOLOGICAL	LEGAL	ENVIRONMENTAL
Spending on R&D	Health & Safety law	Pollution control
Speed of technology transfer	Employment regulations	Noise levels
New materials and processes	New restrictions on trade and product standards	Parking restrictions
Refinements in equipment	Restrictions on working hours	Planning restrictions
IT development	Other EU integration	Waste disposal

Second, the nature of the industry affects the company's ability to generate revenue and profit. Some industries with lower prices and oversupply are naturally more competitive than others. Alternatively, some industries face lower levels of competition and are able to set their prices accordingly. There are a number of business school models that seek to address the strategy issues. Probably the best known is the Porter model (see Figure 10.3), which looks at the forces on an industry and its ability to gain sustainable competitive advantage and attain an above average set of returns. Companies with unique products, facing little competition, can increase their margins and offer safer, more dependable cash flows than companies in industries with fierce competition and similar generic products.

Porter model

Figure 10.3

SUPPLIER POWER
See buyers

THREAT OF ENTRY
Economies of scale
Absolute cost advantages
Capital requirements
Product differentiation
Government and legal barriers
Retaliation by established producers

RIVALRY AMONG EXISTING FIRMS
Concentration
Diversity of competitors
Product differentiation
Excess capacity and exit barriers
Cost conditions

THREAT OF SUBSTITUTES
Buyer propensity to substitute
Relative price/performance of substitutes

BUYER POWER

PRICE SENSITIVITY
Cost of product relative to total costs
Product differentiation
Competition between buyers

BARGAINING POWER
Size and concentration of buyers relative to suppliers
Buyers' switching costs
Buyers' information
Buyers' ability to backwards integrate

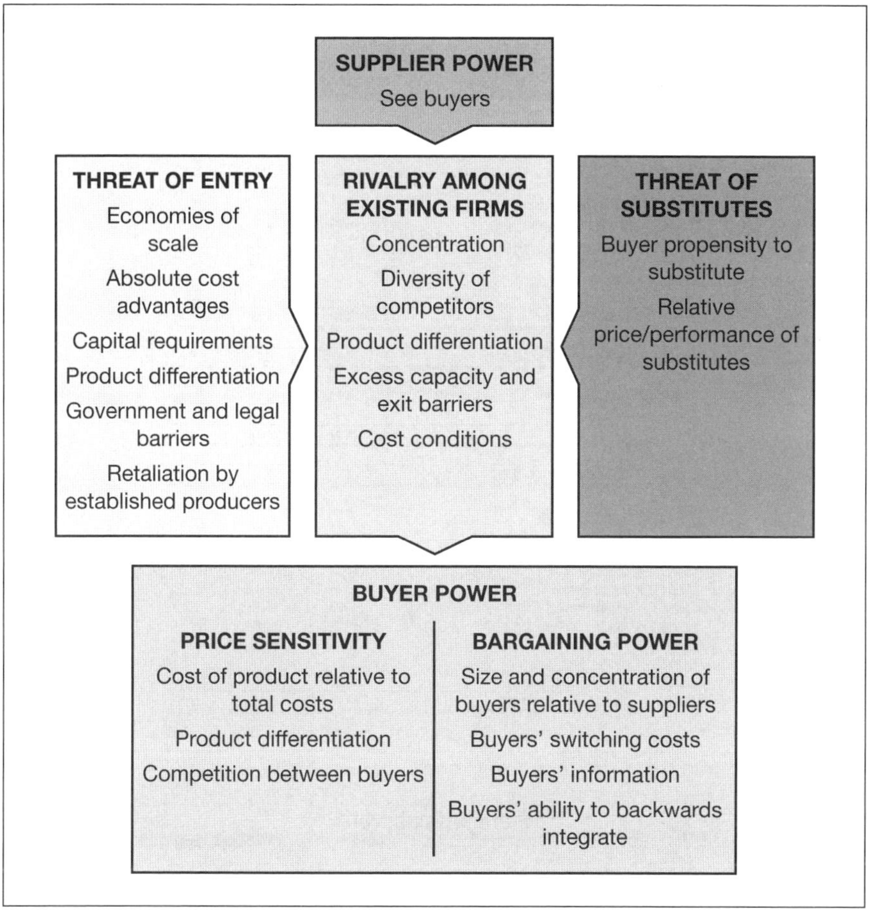

COMMON SIZE ANALYSIS

Before calculating ratios, it is a good idea to standardise the forecast statements as a percentage of the total sales, assets or liabilities. The alternative name is common size analysis. This is the same method as used in the historic accounts, but you now have the advantage of reviewing the historic and forecast figures on a single line. You can copy two more template sheets and then populate them with the same labels as the Income Statement and Balance sheet. The formulas follow this pattern:

```
Income J10: =Forecast_Income!J10/Forecast_
Income!J$10*cstHundred
```

You can generate all the formulas and then use Paste Special to copy the formats on the forecast Income Statement and Balance sheet to save formatting these schedules as new sheets. Figures 10.4–10.7 show the completed Income Statement and Balance sheet.

Figure 10.4

Standard Income Statement

Line No Start Finish	Label	Ref	6 01-Jan-17 31-Dec-17	7 01-Jan-18 31-Dec-18	8 01-Jan-19 31-Dec-19
SL010	Revenue		100.0	100.0	100.0
SL011	Cost of sales		(79.5)	(79.5)	(79.5)
SL012	**Gross profit**		**20.5**	**20.5**	**20.5**
SL013					
SL014	Operating expenses		-	-	-
SL015	Distribution costs		(10.0)	(10.0)	(10.0)
SL016	Administrative expenses		(2.0)	(2.0)	(2.0)
SL017	Depreciation		(1.8)	(1.9)	(2.0)
SL018	Amortisation		-	-	-
SL019	Other		-	-	-
SL020	**Subtotal costs**		**(13.8)**	**(13.9)**	**(14.0)**
SL021			-	-	-
SL022	**Operating profit (EBIT)**		**6.7**	**6.6**	**6.5**
SL023					
SL024	Fees write-off		(0.1)	(0.1)	(0.1)
SL025	New goodwill		-	-	-
SL026	**Subtotal**		**(0.1)**	**(0.1)**	**(0.1)**
SL027					
SL028	**Operating profit (EBIT post-transa**		**6.6**	**6.5**	**6.4**
SL029					
SL030	Finance income		0.5	0.5	0.5
SL031	Finance costs		-	(0.0)	(0.1)
SL032	Existing debt		-	-	-
SL033	Senior debt A		(0.9)	(0.7)	(0.6)
SL034	Senior debt B		(0.4)	(0.3)	(0.3)
SL035	Junior debt C		(0.3)	(0.2)	(0.2)
SL036	Junior debt D		(0.2)	(0.2)	(0.1)
SL037	Junior debt E		(0.2)	(0.2)	(0.1)
SL038	Other		-	-	-
SL039	Preference shares		(0.0)	(0.0)	(0.0)
SL040	**Total finance costs**		**(2.0)**	**(1.7)**	**(1.4)**

Figure 10.5

Standard net profit

Line No Start Finish	Label	Ref	6 01-Jan-17 31-Dec-17	7 01-Jan-18 31-Dec-18	8 01-Jan-19 31-Dec-19
SL040	**Total finance costs**		**(2.0)**	**(1.7)**	**(1.4)**
SL041					
SL042	Share of profit of associates		0.0	0.0	0.0
SL043	Gain (loss) on assets		0.0	0.0	0.0
SL044	**Profit before tax**		**5.1**	**5.3**	**5.5**
SL045					
SL046	Income tax expenses		(0.9)	(1.1)	(1.2)
SL047	**Profit for the year**		**4.2**	**4.2**	**4.3**
SL048					
SL049	Discontinued operations		-	-	-
SL050	**Profit for the year**		**4.2**	**4.2**	**4.3**
SL051					
SL052	Dividends		(1.3)	(1.3)	(1.3)
SL053	Minority interest		-	-	-
SL054					
SL055	**Net profit**		**2.9**	**3.0**	**3.0**

Assets

Figure 10.6

Line No Start Finish	Label	Ref	6 01-Jan-17 31-Dec-17	7 01-Jan-18 31-Dec-18	8 01-Jan-19 31-Dec-19
SA010	**Current assets**				
SA011	Cash & marketable securities		-	-	-
SA012	Accounts receivable		13.0	13.8	14.7
SA013	Inventories		5.9	6.3	6.7
SA014	Prepaid expenses		0.3	0.4	0.4
SA015	Prepaid income taxes		-	-	-
SA016	Other current assets 1		2.7	2.9	3.1
SA017	Other current assets 2		-	-	-
SA018	Other current assets 3		-	-	-
SA019	**Total current assets**		**22.0**	**23.3**	**24.8**
SA020					
SA021	**Non-current assets**				
SA022	Net land, property, plant & equipment		54.9	53.5	51.8
SA023	Investments		4.1	4.3	4.6
SA024	Intangibles		-	-	-
SA025	Other asssets		-	-	-
SA026	Transaction costs		0.5	0.4	0.2
SA027	New goodwill		11.7	11.3	10.9
SA028	Other non-current assets 1		2.7	2.9	3.1
SA029	Other non-current assets 2		4.1	4.3	4.6
SA030	Other non-current assets 3		-	-	-
SA031	**Total non-current assets**		**78.0**	**76.7**	**75.2**
SA032					
SA033	**Total assets**		**100.0**	**100.0**	**100.0**

Liabilities

Figure 10.7

Line No Start Finish	Label	Ref	6 01-Jan-17 31-Dec-17	7 01-Jan-18 31-Dec-18	8 01-Jan-19 31-Dec-19
SA035	**Current liabilities**				
SA036	Overdraft		1.4	2.8	3.3
SA037	Current portion long-term debt (CPLTD)		5.8	5.6	5.4
SA038	Accounts payable		8.9	9.4	10.0
SA039	Accrued expenses		2.7	2.9	3.1
SA040	Dividend payable		-	-	-
SA041	Income tax payable		0.7	0.7	0.8
SA042	Other current liabilities 1		5.4	5.8	6.1
SA043	Other current liabilities 2		1.4	1.4	1.5
SA044	Other current liabilities 3		10.9	11.5	12.3
SA045	**Total current liabilities**		**37.1**	**40.2**	**42.4**
SA046					
SA047	Deferred taxes				
SA048	Other deferred liability 1		1.4	1.4	1.5
SA049	Other deferred liability 2		4.1	4.3	4.6
SA050	Minority Interest		-	-	-
SA051			-	-	-
SA052	**Long term debt**		-	-	-
SA053	Existing debt		-	-	-
SA054	Senior debt A		21.8	18.4	15.2
SA055	Senior debt B		9.1	7.7	6.4
SA056	Junior debt C		4.5	3.8	3.2
SA057	Junior debt D		3.6	3.1	2.5
SA058	Junior debt E		2.7	1.8	0.8
SA059	Other		-	-	-
SA060	**Total long term debt**		**41.8**	**34.7**	**28.2**
SA061			-	-	-
SA062	**Short and long term liabilities**		**84.4**	**80.7**	**76.7**
SA063					
SA064	**Shareholders' equity**				
SA065	Common stock (shares)		10.5	10.1	9.8
SA066	Preferred stock (shares)		1.1	1.1	1.1
SA067	Retained earnings		4.0	8.1	12.4
SA068	**Shareholders equity**		**15.6**	**19.3**	**23.3**
SA069			-	-	-
SA070	**Total liabilities + shareholders equity**		**100.0**	**100.0**	**100.0**

CORE RATIOS

A tried and tested approach is to use core ratios to gain an overview of each of the key areas of profitability, liquidity and financial structure. An investigation here may show weaknesses in the component areas for further analysis. This section contains the three categories from Figure 10.7 above, which have a direct effect on cash flow:

- profitability – return on sales (ROS);
- liquidity – asset turnover (ATO);
- structure – asset leverage (ALEV).

You can summarise the overall performance as a single ratio from the ratios in each of these areas. The next blocks will then calculate further ratios in each of these sections, but the intention is to highlight areas of potential weakness.

Return on equity = Operating efficiency * Financial structure * Profitability

Alternatively:

Return on equity = Asset turnover * Asset leverage * Return on sales

On the other hand:

NPAT/Equity = Sales / Total assets * Total assets / Equity * NPAT / Sales

Core ratios		
Ratio	Definition	Description
Return on sales (%)	$\dfrac{Net\ profit\ after\ tax}{Sales} \times 100$	The portion of net revenue available to shareholders after costs have been deducted, expressed as a percentage of sales.
Asset turnover	$\dfrac{Sales}{Total\ assets}$	The sales, in units of currency, for each unit of currency that has been invested in assets. An overall measure of the efficiency in the use of assets.
Asset leverage	$\dfrac{Total\ assets}{Equity}$	The degree to which equity is funding the investment in assets. The higher the proportion of assets funded from internal sources (that is, equity and reserves) the lower the risk to external funds providers (i.e. trade creditors, banks, etc.).
Return on equity %	$\dfrac{Net\ profit\ after\ tax}{Equity} \times 100$	The net revenue attributable to shareholders for each unit of currency invested as equity or reserves, expressed as a percentage. A comprehensive measure of the financial performance of a company over a period of time.

Core ratios

Figure 10.8

Line No	Label	Ref	Units	6 01-Jan-17 31-Dec-17	7 01-Jan-18 31-Dec-18	8 01-Jan-19 31-Dec-19
Model Check: All balances OK						
RT010	**Core ratios**					
RT011	Return on sales (NPAT/sales %)	FP050/FP010	%	4.2%	4.2%	4.3%
RT012	Asset turnover (sales / total assets)	FP010/FB033	X	1.4x	1.4x	1.5x
RT013	Asset leverage (total assets/equity)	FB033/FB068	X	6.4x	5.2x	4.3x
RT014	Return on equity (NPAT/equity %)	FP050/FB068	%	36.5%	31.5%	28.2%

The line references in the 'Ref' column in Figure 10.8 show the sources of the formulas, e.g. FP050/FP010.

The return on sales will reflect factors in the particular sector as outlined in the sector or industry analysis. A high volume, low margin sector is very sensitive to changes in the margin. You also have the effect of cyclical industries and the point in the cycle. Nevertheless, you are seeking a consistent and growing return on sales ratio.

The asset turnover (sales/total assets) is a measure of operating efficiency and again will depend on the type of business. If the asset turnover is falling, this could indicate reduced liquidity, such as a build-up in inventory. Similarly, the asset leverage measures the total assets to equity or financial structure expressed as multiple. Where cash flows and revenues are volatile, you would expect to see low asset leverage with more of the company's assets funded through equity and not further debt. It is convenient to set out the other ratios in blocks to reflect each of the core ratios (see Figure 10.9 on page 144).

PROFITABILITY

The amount of cash produced depends first on the level of sales growth. Revenue drives total cost through the combination of fixed and variable cost, and future sales will depend on the investment in people and equipment. The standardised sales growth is in effect an X/Sales ratio for every line on the statement. This section picks out key lines such as the gross margin to show the trend from historic through to the forecast. The table on page 145 summarises the profitability ratios with their definitions and descriptions.

Core ratios chart

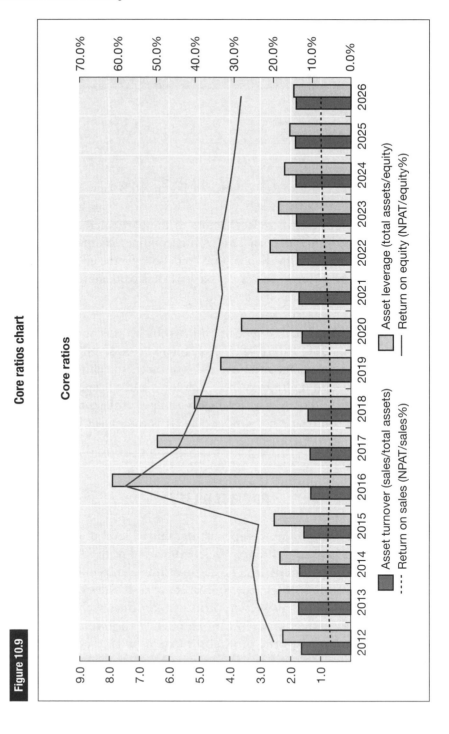

Figure 10.9

Profitability		
Ratio	Definition	Description
Sales	Sales	The level of sales for the year. It is included in the ratio sheet to help in the interpretation of the margins relative to sales calculated within this group of ratios.
Change in sales %	$\dfrac{Sales\ last\ year - Sales\ this\ year}{Sales\ this\ year} \times 100$	The change in sales relative to the level recorded in the previous year. This ratio may be compared with inflation rates to indicate volume growth.
$\dfrac{Gross\ profit\ \%}{Sales}$	$\dfrac{Gross\ profit}{Sales}$	The accrued revenues less cost of goods sold divided by sales.
Capital employed	Short-term debt + Long-term debt + Long-term taxes payable + Sundry long-term liabilities + Long-term provisions + Minority interests + Shareholders' equity	A measure of the total long-term funds used by the enterprise. Long-term debt, long-term liabilities, long-term provisions and equity provide obvious sources of long-term funding, but a further source is provided by the short-term debt.
Return on capital employed	$\dfrac{Operating\ profit}{Long\text{-}term\ debt + Shareholders'\ funds}$	Return on long-term capital.
Return on invested capital	$\dfrac{Net\ operating\ profit\ ^*(1-Tax)}{Short\text{-} + Long\text{-}term\ capital}$	Return to all providers of capital.
Return on assets	$\dfrac{Operating\ profit}{Total\ assets}$	Return for each currency unit of assets employed.

You also need to know the return against the amount of capital employed by the company. These are different definitions of capital and the intention is to match the correct profit line with the capital definition. The ratios in this section (see Figure 10.10) are:

■ gross profit/sales as the percentage gross margin;

■ net operating profit/sales as a percentage return on trading;

■ return on capital employed (ROCE) as net operating profit divided by long-term debt plus shareholders' funds;

■ return on invested capital (ROIC) as net operating profit multiplied by (1 – tax) divided by long- and short-term debt plus shareholders' funds;

■ return on assets as the net operating profit divided by total assets.

Figure 10.10

Profitability

Line No	Label	Ref		6	7	8
Start				01-Jan-17	01-Jan-18	01-Jan-19
Finish				31-Dec-17	31-Dec-18	31-Dec-19
RT016						
RT017	**Profitability**					
RT018	Sales growth	FP010	%	10.0%	10.0%	10.0%
RT019	Gross profit / sales (%)	FP012/FP010	%	20.5%	20.5%	20.5%
RT020	Operating profit / sales (%)	FP028/FP010	%	6.6%	6.5%	6.4%
RT021	Earnings before tax / sales (%)	FP044/FP010	%	5.1%	5.3%	5.5%
RT022	Return on capital employed (ROCE)	FP028/FB060+FB068		15.7%	17.3%	19.1%
RT023	Return on invested capital (ROIC)	FP028*(1-T)/FB060+FB068+FB036+FB0:		10.4%	11.2%	12.2%
RT024	Return on assets (ROA)	FP028/	%	9.0%	9.4%	9.8%

OPERATING EFFICIENCY

Operating efficiency looks at how the company manages short-term cash and materials. A company uses cash to purchase raw materials, which move through the production process into finished goods. The company delivers the goods, invoices its clients and has to wait for the customer to pay. It is a measure of management ability as to how fast it can 'turn' this cycle. If it cannot sell its finished goods, then they will remain in a warehouse and have to be funded from cash in the operating cycle, bank finance or new equity. More borrowings will increase the company's costs and reduce profits through an increased interest burden. In turn, the quantity of cash flow will fall and reduce the value of the business to shareholders. This is normally termed 'business risk'.

You need to understand how long it takes on average to get paid, how long the company holds raw materials and finished goods and how long they take to pay their suppliers. Important ratios are:

- Stock days – this is the number of stock days on hand. A rising number of stock days could demonstrate the company's inability to shift old or out-of-date stock. You could further subdivide this ratio into raw materials, work in progress and finished goods.

- Creditor days – this is the number of days taken to pay creditors. A high or rising ratio could indicate that the company was overtrading and using supplier cash to fund the business.

- Debtor days – indicates the accounts receivable days or collection period. The attitude towards credit policy and collection can illustrate the management's abilities or problems with sub-standard or returned products. A rising ratio could indicate a breakdown in credit control or a change of business.

- Funding gap or cash conversion cycle – this is the debtor days plus stock days minus creditor days. A longer cycle means more risk since the company has to wait longer to turn debtors and stock back into cash.

■ Working capital turnover – this is sales/(stocks + debtors – creditors) and represents the number of times in a year that the company turns the working capital. Again, different companies and industries require differing levels for efficient operation. The ratio may also indicate overtrading where the ratio is high and growing quickly. The level of growth may be too high for the financial resources of the company. In the short term, overtrading may be a source of low-cost financing, but in the longer term the risk of insolvency increases. Other symptoms are:

– decreasing liquidity;

– high stock turnover;

– increasing interest costs;

– high working capital turnover;

– reduced capital expenditure or increased investment in intangibles.

For a summary, see the following table and Figure 10.11.

Operating efficiency		
Ratio	Definition	Description
Inventory days Stock days	$\dfrac{Total\ inventory}{Cost\ of\ goods\ sold} \times Days\ in\ period$	The number of days, on average, that the enterprise holds raw material, work in progress and finished goods for sale in the normal course of business. It gives a rough guide to the length of the full cycle of production.
Raw material days	$\dfrac{Raw\ material}{Cost\ of\ good\ sold} \times Days\ in\ period$	The number of days, on average, during which the company holds raw materials to be used in the production process.
Work in progress days	$\dfrac{Work\ in\ progress}{Cost\ of\ goods\ sold} \times Days\ in\ period$	The number of days, on average, that the enterprise is taking to process raw materials into finished goods. It gives a rough guide to length of the physical production process.
Finished goods days	$\dfrac{Finished\ goods}{Cost\ of\ goods\ sold} \times Days\ in\ period$	The number of days, on average, that the enterprise is holding its finished goods for sale in the normal course of business.
Trade receivable days Debtor days	$\dfrac{Trade\ receivables}{Sales} \times Days\ in\ period$	The number of days, on average, of credit outstanding to the company's customers.

Ratio	Definition	Description
Trade creditor days	$$\frac{Trade\ creditors}{Cost\ of\ goods\ sold} \times Days\ in\ period$$	The number of days, on average, the enterprise is taking to pay its suppliers. Normal practice will vary from industry to industry, reflecting the purchasing company's bargaining power relative to suppliers.
Funding gap	$$Receivables + Inventory - Payables$$	The number of days in receivables and inventory less the payables to be funded by short-term debt.
Working capital turnover	$$\frac{Sales}{Re\,ceivables + Inventory - Payables}$$	Sales/Funding gap to provide a ratio against the sales turnover.

Figure 10.11

Operating efficiency

Line No	Label	Ref		6	7	8
Start				01-Jan-17	01-Jan-18	01-Jan-19
Finish				31-Dec-17	31-Dec-18	31-Dec-19
RT027	Operating efficiency					
RT028	Inventory	FB013/FP011	Days	20.0	20.0	20.0
RT029	Accounts receivable	FB012/FP010	Days	35.0	35.0	35.0
RT030	Accounts payable	FB038/FP011	Days	30.0	30.0	30.0
RT031	Funding gap receivables+inventory-pay RT028+RT029-RT030			25.0	25.0	25.0
RT032	Working capital turnover	FP010/FB012+FB013+FB038		13.5	13.5	13.5

FINANCIAL STRUCTURE

Financial risk is concerned with the structure of the balance sheet together with the sources of finance available to the company. Credit analysts are concerned with the liabilities taken on by companies and their ability to service debt. Prospects are often more volatile than originally anticipated and therefore the model needs to provide information about the financial strength. The company needs to manage debt and equity efficiently in order to reduce the cost of capital, but also not accept obligations, which it may not be able pay back from future cash flow. The ratios to be calculated by the model are:

■ Current ratio – basic measure of liquidity as the ratio of current assets to liabilities. The working capital requirement varies across industries so the absolute value is less important than the trend.

■ Quick ratio – this excludes stock from the current ratio. The rationale is that stock is often difficult to sell at book prices and may not be as realisable in the short-term.

■ Working capital – derived from the current assets minus current liabilities.

- Gross gearing (leverage) – short- plus long-term debt divided by share-holders' funds to show the level of borrowings.
- Net gearing (leverage) – gross gearing debt less cash and marketable securities divided by shareholders' funds showing the net borrowings.
- Solvency or time interest earned – measures the number of times the profit before interest and tax covers the interest payment.
- Total equity divided by total assets – a measure of financial strength or the amount of the company not funded with equity. Companies with a high ratio are financially more resilient since a company cannot waive interest in favour of dividends if there is insufficient cash.

For a summary, see the following table and Figure 10.12.

Financial structure		
Ratio	Definition	Description
Current ratio	$$\dfrac{Current\ assets}{Current\ liabilities}$$	A measure of 'liquidity'. The liabilities falling due for payment within a year relative to short-term assets. It seeks to indicate an organisation's ability to meet obligations falling due within the year through the liquidation proceeds of current assets.
Quick ratio Acid test	$$\dfrac{Current\ assets - Inventory}{Current\ liabilities}$$	A more stringent measure of liquidity than current ratio. The liabilities falling due for payment within one year relative to the enterprise's assets that are deemed to be closest to cash (i.e. cash, marketable securities, trade receivables).
Working capital	$$Current\ assets -\ \\ Current\ liabilities$$	An alternative measure of liquidity to the current ratio. Measures the extent to which current assets exceed (or fall short of) the liabilities falling due for payment within the next year. It considers all current assets and liabilities, not only receivables, stocks and payables.
Gross gearing %	$$\dfrac{Short\text{-}term\ debt}{+Long\text{-}term\ debt}{Shareholders'\ equity} \times 100$$	A measure of solvency or financial risk. Measures the use of debt (that is external funds with a fixed return and a fixed maturity) relative to the use of equity (that is internal funds with a flexible return and no obligation for repayment) in the financing chain.

149

Ratio	Definition	Description
Net gearing %	$$\dfrac{\begin{array}{c}\textit{Short-term debt} + \textit{Long-term debt}\\ - \textit{Cash} - \textit{Marketable securities}\end{array}}{\textit{Shareholders' equity}} \times 100$$	An alternative measure of solvency or financial risk, which also considers the holdings of the most liquid assets, cash and marketable securities.
Solvency (interest cover or times interest earned)	$$\dfrac{\textit{Net operating profit}}{\textit{Interest expense}}$$	This ratio compares the net revenue arising directly from the cycle of production to the interest expense for the period. Also called 'interest cover' and 'times interest earned' it is frequently used to indicate whether the organisation has a manageable debt.
Total equity/ Total assets	$$\dfrac{\textit{Shareholders' equity}}{\textit{Total assets}}$$	Measure of the financial strength of the balance sheet. A low figure implies a high gearing and an increase in the financial weakness.

The ratios together with the applicable references are shown in Figure 10.12.

Figure 10.12

Financial structure

Line No Start Finish	Label	Ref		6 01-Jan-17 31-Dec-17	7 01-Jan-18 31-Dec-18	8 01-Jan-19 31-Dec-19
RT035	Financial structure					
RT036	Current ratio	FB019/FB045	%	0.6	0.6	0.6
RT037	Quick ratio (acid test)	FB011+FB012/FB045		0.4	0.3	0.3
RT038	Working capital	FB019-FB045	USD Millions	(6,660.1)	(7,684.7)	(8,317.1)
RT039	Gross gearing (%)	FB036+FB037+FB060/FB068		313.6%	223.1%	158.2%
RT040	Net gearing (%)	FB036+FB037+FB060-FB011/FB068		313.6%	223.1%	158.2%
RT041	Solvency (times interest earned)	FP028/FP031:FP038	X	3.3	3.9	4.7
RT042	Total equity/total assets	FB068/FB033	%	15.6%	19.3%	23.3%
RT043						
RT044	Long term debt / book capitalization	FB060/FB060+FB068	%	72.8%	64.2%	54.7%
RT045	Long term debt / equity	FB060/FB068	%	267.5%	179.6%	121.0%
RT046	Long term debt / tangible equity	FB060/FB068-FB027	%	1063.4%	430.8%	227.5%
RT047	Total long term capital	FB060+FB068	USD Millions	25,278.2	24,677.5	24,294.6
RT048	EBIT / average capitalization	FP028/RT047	%	15.4%	17.1%	18.9%
RT049	Total senior debt	FB054:FB059	USD Millions	13,600.0	11,900.0	10,200.0
RT050	Senior debt / EBITDA	RT049/FP022-FP017-FP018	X	2.7x	2.1x	1.7x

Further possible ratios are:

- Long-term debt/book capitalisation (defined as shareholders' equity plus long-term debt).
- Long-term debt/shareholders' equity.
- Long-term debt/tangible equity (shareholders' equity less goodwill).
- Total long-term capital (long-term debt plus equity).

- EBIT/average capitalisation – this uses the average capital to check for distortions between different years.

- Total senior debt – debt is categorised as senior or junior on the Control sheet. The formula uses the function SUMPRODUCT since senior debt is equal to one and junior equal to zero. This construction is usually more efficient than using IF statements:

```
J49: =SUMPRODUCT(Control!$J$15:$J$20,Forecast_
Balance!J54:J59)
```

- Senior debt/EBITDA.

CASH FLOW

The sales ratio uses cash lines such as EBITDA or cash from operations and divides them into sales. Since profit is a function of accounting conventions and procedures, cash may be more dependable as a measure of performance (see the following table and Figure 10.13).

Cash flow ratios		
Ratio	Definition	Description
$\dfrac{EBITDA\ \%}{Sales}$	$\dfrac{Earnings\ before\ interest,\ Taxes,\ Depreciation\ and\ amortisation}{Sales} \times 100$	Earnings before the deduction of finance charges, taxes and depreciation or amortisation (EBITDA) relative to the level of sales.
NOPAT (net operating profit after tax)	$Net\ operating\ profit - tax\ paid$	NOPAT represents the earnings that are available to service all funds providers and contribute to long-term investment.
$\dfrac{NOPAT}{Interest\ paid}$	$\dfrac{NOPAT}{Interest\ paid}$	This is a ratio often used by lenders to measure how comfortably the earnings from operating activities after tax cover the interest expense relating to debt if operations continued at the current level.
$\dfrac{Cash\ from\ operations}{Sales}$	$\dfrac{Cash\ from\ operations}{Sales}$	Measure of cash from operations against sales to form a measure of the relative cash produced.

Figure 10.13

Cash flow

Line No Start Finish	Label	Ref		6 01-Jan-17 31-Dec-17	7 01-Jan-18 31-Dec-18	8 01-Jan-19 31-Dec-19
RT053	Cashflow ratios					
RT054	EBITDA / sales (%)	FP022-FP017-FP018/FP010	%	8.5%	8.5%	8.5%
RT055	Cash from operations/sales	CF038/FP010	%	4.0%	6.2%	6.3%

DEBT COVERAGE

This section provides more detail on the loans payments and the cash flow available to pay the debts. The formulas below extract the senior capital and interest from the Forecast_DebtCash sheet (see workings in Figure 10.14). The totals are already available so the junior entries are the difference between the total and the senior amount.

```
Senior capital O87: =O12*$J$12+O19*$J$19+O26*$J$2
6+O33*$J$33+O40*$J$40+O47*$J$47
Senior interest O88: =O13*$J$12+O20*$J$19+O27*$J$
26+O34*$J$33+O41*$J$40+O48*$J$47
```

Figure 10.14

Debt coverage

Line No Start Finish	Label	Ref		6 01-Jan-17 31-Dec-17	7 01-Jan-18 31-Dec-18	8 01-Jan-19 31-Dec-19
RT058	Interest coverage					
RT059	Senior interest expense	FP032.FP038	USD Millions	(790.0)	(711.0)	(632.0)
RT060	Junior interest expense	FP032.FP038	USD Millions	(280.0)	(351.5)	(298.0)
RT061	EBITDA / senior Interest	FP022-FP017-FP018/RT059	X	6.4x	7.9x	9.7x
RT062	EBITDA / total Interest	FP022-FP017-FP018/FP040	X	4.2x	5.0x	6.0x
RT063	EBIT / senior Interest	FP028/RT059	X	5.0x	6.0x	7.3x
RT064	EBIT / total interest	FP028/FP040	X	3.2x	3.8x	4.5x
RT067	Debt coverage					
RT068	Senior payment	FP043.FP049	USD Millions	(2,890.0)	(2,796.0)	(2,702.0)
RT069	Junior payment	FP043.FP049	USD Millions	(855.0)	(816.5)	(778.0)
RT070	Total payment	Sum	USD Millions	(3,745.0)	(3,643.5)	(3,544.8)
RT071	EBITDA / senior payment	FP022-FP017-FP018/RT068	X	1.8x	2.0x	2.3x
RT072	EBITDA / junior payment	FP022-FP017-FP018/RT069	X	5.9x	6.8x	7.9x
RT073	EBITDA / total payment	FP022-FP017-FP018/RT070	X	1.4x	1.5x	1.7x
RT074	EBIT / senior payment	FP028/RT068	X	1.4x	1.5x	1.7x
RT075	EBIT / junior payment	FP028/RT069	X	4.6x	5.2x	6.0x
RT076	EBIT / total payment	FP028/RT070	X	1.1x	1.2x	1.3x

The EBITDA and EBIT are available on the income and cash statements and you can divide them into the interest or the total payable at each level (see Figure 10.15). The cover number needed for the bank covenants will depend on the industry, prospects and forecast volatility, but the model can include a series of 'thresholds' as inputs. You can format the ratios as turns using this format style. With one character, Excel does not usually need to delineate the text with apostrophes.

```
Turns: _-* #,##0.0x_-;[Red](#,##0.0x);_-* "-"??_-
;_-@_-
```

Debt workings from Forecast_DebtCash

Figure 10.15

Line No Start Finish	Label	Ref	6 01-Jan-17 31-Dec-17	7 01-Jan-18 31-Dec-18	8 01-Jan-19 31-Dec-19
DB076			-	-	-
DB077	Debt summary				
DB078	Cash available for debt service		3,596.17	3,260.53	3,625.55
DB079	Total principal repayment		2,550.00	2,550.00	2,550.00
DB080	Total interest payment		1,195.00	1,062.50	930.00
DB081	Total repaid		3,745.00	3,612.50	3,480.00
DB082	Cash//Repayment (RH Scale)		0.96x	0.90x	1.04x
DB083	EBITDA		5,021.02	5,528.98	6,087.74
DB084	Balance outstanding		18,400.00	15,850.00	13,300.00
DB085					
DB086	Senior/junior split				
DB087	Senior capital		(1,950.00)	(1,950.00)	(1,950.00)
DB088	Senior Interest		(940.00)	(846.00)	(752.00)
DB089	Juntior Capital		(600.00)	(600.00)	(600.00)
DB090	Junior Interest		(255.00)	(216.50)	(178.00)

GROWTH

There are various models available to ascertain where the growth rate is sustainable. A company can grow quickly and use suppliers and short-term debt to fund the initial growth. This may work in the short-term but eventually the company may run out of cash if it is unable to raise more credit to fund the increasing requirement for raw materials, finished goods and debtors. This section uses one of the simpler formulas to compare the potential growth against the actual growth and decide whether it is above or below the threshold. The formulas are shown in Figure 10.16.

Growth

Figure 10.16

Line No Start Finish	Label	Ref		6 01-Jan-17 31-Dec-17	7 01-Jan-18 31-Dec-18	8 01-Jan-19 31-Dec-19
RT079	Growth formulas					
RT080	Retention rate (RR)	FP055/FP050	%	70.0%	70.0%	70.0%
RT081	Return on equity (ROE)	RT014	%	44.4%	39.6%	36.3%
RT082	Sustainable growth g=RR*ROE	RT080*RT081	%	31.1%	27.7%	25.4%
RT083	Actual growth	Change in FP010	%	10.0%	10.0%	10.0%
RT084	Variance actual-equilibrium	RT082-RT083	%	21.1%	17.7%	15.4%

The formula is: Sustainable growth g=RR*ROE
   Where:

RR = retention rate as the amount left after dividends divided by the profit after tax.

ROE = return on equity as calculated above.

MARKET RATIOS

Market ratios (see Figure 10.7) offer an alternative view of the prospects for the company. You entered the number of shares and the share prices on earlier sheets. You can code this information to generate the market capitalisation, earnings per share and dividends per share. The P/E ratio is an important and much-used market measure computed as:

> Formula: Price per share / [Earnings / Number of shares]

A high P/E confirms that the market has confidence in the stock and expects further growth and a low P/E reveals a lack of confidence. An alternative measure is the market price/EBITDA per share, which uses a profit line with the non-cash items excluded.

Market related data		
Ratio	Definition	Description
Number of shares issued and outstanding (in thousands)	$\dfrac{\textit{Number of shares issued and outstanding}}{1000}$	The number of shares issued and outstanding. You may choose to use the average number of shares when you are using this information to measure earnings or cash flow for a period relative to each share.
Date of share price	Date of share price	The date of the share price shown in the following line. Alternatively, the caption may indicate that the price reflects the high, low or mid-range share price for the period.
Share price	Share price	The share price that will be used to calculate market capitalisation and other price related ratios.
Market capitalisation	$\dfrac{\textit{Numbers of shares issued and outstanding}}{\textit{Share price}}$	The product of the number of ordinary shares issued and outstanding and the price of those shares, market capitalisation represents the market's valuation of the equity of a company. The share price, and hence the market capitalisation, can vary considerably.
Earnings per share	Earnings per share	The net operating profit for each share. This ratio changes with the number of shares issued; the annual report often provides adjusted earnings per share that allow comparisons to be made on a consistent basis when there have been share splits.

Ratio	Definition	Description
Dividends per share	Dividends per share	The declared dividends for each share. The annual report often provides adjusted dividends per share that allow comparisons to be made on a consistent basis when there have been changes such as share splits as outlined in the earnings per share definition.
Change in dividend per share (%)	$$\frac{\textit{Div. per share this year} - \textit{Div. per share last year}}{\textit{Div. per share last year}} \times 100$$	The percentage change in dividend per share.
$\dfrac{Price}{EBITDA\ per\ share}$	$EBITDA/Number\ of\ shares$	The market price of a share relative to earnings before the deduction of finance charges, taxes and depreciation or amortisation.
$\dfrac{Price}{Free\ cash\ flow\ per\ share}$	$\dfrac{Share\ price}{Free\ cash\ flow\ /\ Number\ of\ shares}$	The market price of a share relative to the cash flow after current operations less tax, interest and depreciation per share. This ratio relates the share price to the maximum cash flow that could go to shareholders in a 'no growth' situation.
$\dfrac{Price}{Book}$	$\dfrac{Share\ price}{(Shareholders'\ equity\ /\ Number\ of\ shares)}$	The market price of a share relative to the book value of net assets per share. A ratio above one may indicate that assets are undervalued in the balance sheet. As the share price is volatile and reflects many factors and sentiments.

Debt workings from Forecast_DebtCash

Figure 10.17

Line No Start Finish	Label	Ref		6 01-Jan-17 31-Dec-17	7 01-Jan-18 31-Dec-18	8 01-Jan-19 31-Dec-19
RT087	**Market ratios**					
RT088	Number of shares issued & outstanding	-	No	-	-	-
RT089	Current share price	-	USD	-	-	-
RT090	Market capitalisation	RT088*RT089	USD Millions	-	-	-
RT091	Earnings per share	FP050/RT088	USD	-	-	-
RT092	P / E ratio	RT089/RT091	X	-	-	-
RT093	Dividends per share	FP052/RT088	USD	-	-	-
RT094	Dividend cover	FP050/FP052	X	3.33	3.33	3.33
RT095	Market price / EBITDA per share	RT089/FP022-FP017-FP018/f	X			
RT096	Enterprise value	RT088*RT089+SUM(FB036.FB037)+SUI		22,070.69	20,196.37	17,894.91
RT097	Enterprise value / operating cash flow	RT096/CF038	X	9.27	4.96	3.90
RT098	Book price per share	FB068/RT088	USD	-	-	-
RT099	Market price / book	RT089/RT098	X	-	-	-
RT100	EV / EBITDA	RT096/FP022-FP018-FP017	X	4.34	3.61	2.91

The accounting net worth is simply share capital plus the retained earnings. This may bear no fixed relationship to the market value attributed by a stock market. The enterprise value tries to compute a market value for the whole enterprise as:

```
EV = Market value of share capital + market value
of preference share + market value of debt
```

Enterprise value/cash flow provides an alternative cover measure to show if cash flow is becoming a larger percentage of the overall market value.

The market price per share divided by the book price per share shows how the market views the share value against the accounting worth. This is correlated with failure, where the ratio is less than one, since you would expect the market value to be in excess of book value where assets such as human capital, knowledge or licences are taken into account. Similarly, EV/EBITDA provides a value measure that is often used as a multiple to compare companies from different countries or those using dissimilar accounting standards.

SUMMARY

Ratios offer a method for viewing the company over time and checking the forecast. It is important to view exterior macro and industry factors to see the company in context before calculating all the financial ratios. The core ratios approach shows how to dissect the return on equity to illustrate the changes in key areas of profitability, business risk and financial structure. The model also calculates the debt coverage, growth sustainability and market ratios. Together these provide a structured financial analysis of the example company.

Cost of capital

BACKGROUND

The model needs to value the cash flows generated by the forecast accounts and requires a risk-adjusted cost of capital to reflect the proportions and the cost of each source of capital. The cash flows produced by a distinct mix of capital can then be discounted at a suitable merged rate. It would be wrong to add a margin onto the debt rate and take an average as the discount rate since the resulting rate would over- or underestimate the real cost. The cash flow and the present value of these cash flows are the key sources of value. The selection of a reasonable rate will have a significant impact on the initial valuation of the entity.

The method for calculating the discount rate is:

- Find the different sources of capital and amounts.

- Calculate the cost of the individual sources of capital.

- Compute the weights or percentages based on market (not book) values. The book value of debt is difficult to determine unless publicly traded and therefore the book value as a proxy to market value is normally used.

- Factor the debt by (1 − marginal tax rate) if the company pays mainstream corporate tax.

- Multiply the relevant equity and after-tax debt cost by their percentage weighting.

- Add the constituents to derive the weighted average cost of capital.

The formula is:

$$WACC = \frac{D}{D+E} * R_d * (1 - Tax) + \frac{E}{D+E} * R_e$$

Corporate finance generally refers to this rate as the weighted average cost of capital (WACC), where the cost and proportions are multiplied out to form a composite rate. Given that different sources may have different values, the leverage will influence the cost of capital.

You can place the inputs for the cost of capital on the Forecast sheet and you will need the historic number of shares and share prices in addition to the debt entries from previous sheets (see Figures 11.1 and 11.2).

Figure 11.1

Historic data

Line No	Label	Ref		Total	1	2	3	4
Start					01-Jan-12	01-Jan-13	01-Jan-14	01-Jan-15
Finish					31-Dec-12	31-Dec-13	31-Dec-14	31-Dec-15
F110								
F111	(3) Cost of capital							
F112	Risk-free rate							
F113	Market risk premium							
F114	Levered beta							
F115								
F116	Number of shares				7,000.00	7,000.00	7,000.00	7,000.00
F117	Market share price				1.75	1.75	1.75	1.75
F118								
F119	Free cash flow							
F120	Terminal value method							
F121	Perpetuity	4.0%						
F122	Multiple EBITDA	4.0x						
F123								
F124	Multiple range	2.0x						
F125	Discount rate range	1.0%						
F126	Perpetuity range	1.0%						

Figure 11.2

Rates

Line No	Label	Ref	6	7	8	9	10
Start			01-Jan-17	01-Jan-18	01-Jan-19	01-Jan-20	01-Jan-21
Finish			31-Dec-17	31-Dec-18	31-Dec-19	31-Dec-20	31-Dec-21
F110							
F111	(3) Cost of capital						
F112	Risk-free rate		5.0%	5.0%	5.0%	5.0%	5.0%
F113	Market risk premium		6.0%	6.0%	6.0%	6.0%	6.0%
F114	Levered beta		0.8	0.8	0.8	0.8	0.8
F115							
F116	Number of shares		10,000.00	10,000.00	10,000.00	10,000.00	10,000.00
F117	Market share price		2.00	2.10	2.20	2.30	2.40

COST OF DEBT

Make a copy of the landscape template, call it WACC and use the labels shows in Figure 11.3.

The theory states that the debt should be expressed at market value. Without other information, the model assumes that the debt is at market value with no adjustments. The annual interest rates are available on the Forecast sheet while the amounts outstanding are on the Debt sheet. You need a weighted rate and the best function for this is SUMPRODUCT. You multiply out the two arrays of interest and capital and divide by the amount of capital present:

```
O28:=SUMPRODUCT(O11:O17,O19:O25)/SUM(O19:O25)
```

Figure 11.3

Line No Start Finish	Label	Ref	6 01-Jan-17 31-Dec-17	7 01-Jan-18 31-Dec-18	8 01-Jan-19 31-Dec-19
WA010	(A) Estimated cost of debt				
WA011	Existing debt	F100	5.00%	5.00%	5.00%
WA012	Senior debt A	F101	4.50%	4.50%	4.50%
WA013	Senior debt B	F102	5.00%	5.00%	5.00%
WA014	Junior debt C	F103	6.00%	6.00%	6.00%
WA015	Junior debt D	F104	6.25%	6.25%	6.25%
WA016	Junior debt E	F105	6.50%	6.50%	6.50%
WA017	Other	F106	6.75%	6.75%	6.75%
WA018					
WA019	Existing debt	CS010	–	–	–
WA020	Senior debt A	CS011	10,800.00	9,600.00	8,400.00
WA021	Senior debt B	CS012	4,500.00	4,000.00	3,500.00
WA022	Junior debt C	CS013	2,250.00	2,000.00	1,750.00
WA023	Junior debt D	CS014	1,800.00	1,600.00	1,400.00
WA024	Junior debt E	CS015	1,600.00	1,200.00	800.00
WA025	Other	CS016	–	–	–
WA026	Total debt		20,950.00	18,400.00	15,850.00
WA027					
WA028	Pre-tax of debt		5.07%	5.05%	5.03%
WA029					
WA030	Tax rate	F029	25.00%	25.00%	25.00%
WA031					
WA032	Net of tax rate		3.80%	3.79%	3.77%

Interest on debt is subject to tax relief and therefore you need a tax rate to calculate the net tax rate. In the case in Figure 11.3, the first year pre-tax cost is 5.07%, which is multiplied by $(1 - 25\%)$ to give a net figure of 3.80%.

PREFERENCE CAPITAL

The example case includes some preference share capital, which carries in this case a coupon of 5 per cent as listed on the Forecast sheet (see Figure 11.4). This is a distinct category of capital and its price and weighting have to be calculated separately.

Distribution of capital

Figure 11.4

Sources of funds			%
Existing debt	Senior	–	–
Senior debt A	Senior	12,000.00	41.93%
Senior debt B	Senior	5,000.00	17.47%
Junior debt C	Junior	2,500.00	8.74%
Junior debt D	Junior	2,000.00	6.99%
Junior debt E	Junior	2,000.00	6.99%
Other	Junior	–	–
Preferred stock		500.00	1.75%
Outside equity		1,118.77	3.91%
Management equity A		3,000.00	10.48%
Management equity B		500.00	1.75%
Total sources		28,618.77	100.00%

The table in Figure 11.5 shows the value as 100, or 100 per cent, which means that the cost is 5 per cent. If not, the calculation at a market value of 0.90 would be:

Market value/Coupon rate, e.g. 5%/Market price of 90 = 5.55% and not 5%

Figure 11.5   **Finance rates**

Line No	Label	Ref	-	6	7	8	9
	Start			01-Jan-17	01-Jan-18	01-Jan-19	01-Jan-20
	Finish			31-Dec-17	31-Dec-18	31-Dec-19	31-Dec-20
F097							
F098	Debt interest rates						
F099	Finance income	IP030		0.50%	0.50%	0.50%	0.50%
F100	Existing debt	IP032		5.00%	5.00%	5.00%	5.00%
F101	Senior debt A	IP033		4.50%	4.50%	4.50%	4.50%
F102	Senior debt B	IP034		5.00%	5.00%	5.00%	5.00%
F103	Junior debt C	IP035		6.00%	6.00%	6.00%	6.00%
F104	Junior debt D	IP036		6.25%	6.25%	6.25%	6.25%
F105	Junior debt E	IP037		6.50%	6.50%	6.50%	6.50%
F106	Other	IP038		6.75%	6.75%	6.75%	6.75%
F107	Preferred stock coupon			5.00%	5.00%	5.00%	5.00%
F108	Preferred stock par value			100.00	100.00	100.00	100.00

Figure 11.6   **Preference shares**

Line No	Label	Ref	6	7	8	9
	Start		01-Jan-17	01-Jan-18	01-Jan-19	01-Jan-20
	Finish		31-Dec-17	31-Dec-18	31-Dec-19	31-Dec-20
WA033						
WA034	(B) Preferred stock					
WA035	Amount	FB066	500.00	500.00	500.00	500.00
WA036	Coupon	F107	5.00%	5.00%	5.00%	5.00%
WA037	Par value	F108	100.00	100.00	100.00	100.00
WA038	Preferred Stock Rate	WA036/WA037	5.00%	5.00%	5.00%	5.00%
WA039						
WA040	(C) Equity					
WA041	Risk free rate	F112	5.00%	5.00%	5.00%	5.00%
WA042	Risk premium	F113	6.00%	6.00%	6.00%	6.00%
WA043	Levered beta	F114	0.80	0.80	0.80	0.80
WA044	Cost of equity		9.80%	9.80%	9.80%	9.80%

Figure 11.6 shows the amount and cost of funding.

HISTORIC COST OF EQUITY

The model uses the standard method of the Capital Asset Pricing Model (CAPM), which tries to derive the rate of return that investors expect before they decide to invest in a firm. Investors have a range of investment options and this calculation shows the expected rate of return of the highest-yielding alternative asset of equivalent risk. Whilst there is a wealth of academic criticism of this model, most practitioners still use it for its simplicity and wide adoption. The formula is:

```
Re = Rf + ße [Rm - Rf]
```

where:

Re = expected rate of return on equity
Rf = risk-free rate of return
ße = equity beta
Rm = expected rate of return on the market portfolio of risky assets
[Rm – Rf] = market risk premium

In the CAPM model (see Figure 11.7), the two components of the risk premium are the market risk premium and the firm's beta. The market risk premium is the excess expected return of the market portfolio over the return of the risk-free asset. The beta is really a measure of the variance of the share to the market. If the share is more risky than the market the beta will be greater than one and if less risky it will be below one.

CAPM

Figure 11.7

Line No	Label	Ref	6	7	8	9
Start			01-Jan-17	01-Jan-18	01-Jan-19	01-Jan-20
Finish			31-Dec-17	31-Dec-18	31-Dec-19	31-Dec-20
WA039						
WA040	(C) Equity					
WA041	Risk free rate	F112	5.00%	5.00%	5.00%	5.00%
WA042	Risk premium	F113	6.00%	6.00%	6.00%	6.00%
WA043	Levered beta	F114	0.80	0.80	0.80	0.80
WA044	Cost of equity		9.80%	9.80%	9.80%	9.80%

The CAPM inputs are from the Forecast sheet. Where a company is not publicly traded, another approach involves estimating the cost of equity based on variables such as:

■ discount rate for companies in the same industry;

■ discount rates for companies at similar points in their development;

■ estimated risk factor in future cash flows;

■ general market discount for stocks in the particular region.

Using this method you could estimate an appropriate cost without using the CAPM model.

FORECAST COST OF EQUITY

The historic cost of equity is a basic formula and it needs to be reworked to use the forecast debt and equity values since the beta will be affected by the forecast level of debt, its cost and the relative weightings of debt and equity. A company with higher debt is more risky and investors should demand a higher return to compensate for the increased risk. A higher rate will reduce the present value of the cash flows.

The leveraged or equity beta has to be first unleveraged and then releveraged using the forecast debt to equity ratio (see Figure 11.8). The model uses the average debt to equity for the historic years since there is a large difference between the two last years. The formula in N57 is:

```
N57 =SUM(M47:N47)/SUM(M53:N53)  = 109.69%
```

The leveraging formulas are:

```
Unlevered ß or asset ß = ß/(1+(1-Tax)*Debt/Equity)
Relevered or equity ß = ß* (1+(1-Tax)*Debt/Equity)
```

Figure 11.8

Leveraged cost of equity

Line No	Label	Ref	4	5	6	7	8
Start			01-Jan-15	01-Jan-16	01-Jan-17	01-Jan-18	01-Jan-19
Finish			31-Dec-15	31-Dec-16	31-Dec-17	31-Dec-18	31-Dec-19
WA045							
WA046	(D) Leverered cost of equity						
WA047	Total debt incl preferred	WA026+WA035	8,249.29	16,705.11	21,450.00	18,900.00	16,350.00
WA048	Total debt excl preferred	WA026	8,249.00	16,705.00	20,950.00	18,400.00	15,850.00
WA049							
WA050	Total book equity	FB065	393.00	395.00	4,618.77	4,618.77	4,618.77
WA051	No of shares	F116	7,000.00	7,000.00	10,000.00	10,000.00	10,000.00
WA052	Market price	F117	1.75	1.50	2.00	2.10	2.20
WA053	Total equity	WA051*WA052	12,250.00	10,500.00	20,000.00	21,000.00	22,000.00
WA054							
WA055	Total value		20,499.29	27,205.11	41,450.00	39,900.00	38,350.00
WA056							
WA057	Debt/equity	WA047/WA053		109.69%	107.25%	90.00%	74.32%
WA058							
WA059	Debt/value	WA048/WA055		61.40%	50.54%	46.12%	41.33%
WA060	Preferred/value	WA035/WA055		-	1.21%	1.25%	1.30%
WA061	Equity value	WA053/WA055		38.60%	48.25%	52.63%	57.37%
WA062				100.00%	100.00%	100.00%	100.00%
WA063							
WA064	Unleveraged beta	WA043/(1+(1-WA030)*WA057	0.44	0.44	0.48	0.51	
WA065	Check releveraged beta	WA064*(1+(1-WA030)*WA057		0.80	0.74	0.69	
WA066							
WA067	Releveraged beta	WA064*(1+(1-WA030)*WA057		0.80	0.74	0.69	
WA068	Cost of equity	WA041+WA042*WA067		9.80%	9.45%	9.14%	

The table in Figure 11.8 looks up the amount of debt and preferred shares and multiplies the share price by the number of shares to derive the market value of equity. The beta is unleveraged to 0.44:

```
Asset beta N64: 0.8 / [ 1 + ( 1 - Tax at 26.54% )
* D/E of 109.69% ]
```

You then need to calculate the forecast amounts where the initial debt to equity ratio is 107.25%:

```
Equity beta N64: 0.44 * [ 1 + ( 1 - Tax at 25.00% )
* D/E of 107.25% ]
```

The forecast cost of equity is:

```
Re = Rf + ße [Rm – Rf]
Re = 5% + 0.8 * 6% = 9.80%
```

COST OF CAPITAL

You now have the costs and proportions of debt and equity. The model needs to multiply out the proportions and costs in the form:

$$WACC = \frac{D}{D+E} * R_d * (1-Tax) + \frac{E}{D+E} * R_e$$

```
WACC = Debt% * Cost + Preference% * Cost +
Equity% * Cost
WACC = 50.54% * 3.8% + 1.21% * 5% + 48.25% *
9.80% = 6.71%
```

The WACC to be used in the valuation sheet is 6.71% (see Figure 11.9).

WACC

Figure 11.9

Line No	Label	Ref	4	5	6	7	8
Start			01-Jan-15	01-Jan-16	01-Jan-17	01-Jan-18	01-Jan-19
Finish			31-Dec-15	31-Dec-16	31-Dec-17	31-Dec-18	31-Dec-19
WA063							
WA064	Unleveraged beta	WA043/(1+(1-WA030)*WA057	0.44	0.44	0.48	0.51	
WA065	Check releveraged beta	WA064*(1+(1-WA030)*WA057		0.80	0.74	0.69	
WA066							
WA067	Releveraged beta	WA064*(1+(1-WA030)*WA057		0.80	0.74	0.69	
WA068	Cost of equity	WA041+WA042*WA067		9.80%	9.45%	9.14%	
WA069							
WA070	(E) Cost of capital						
WA071	Weighted average cost of capital (WA	WA032*WA059+WA038*WA060+WA068*W,		6.71%	6.79%	6.87%	
WA072	Cumulative WACC	WA072*(1+WA071)		1.07	1.14	1.22	
WA073							
WA074	Asset (unleveraged) beta	BetaU = BetaL / [1+(1-tax) * (D/E)]					
WA075	Unlevered beta = Adjusted (levered) Beta * [MVE / (Market Cap - (T * Book Value Of Debt))]						
WA076	Equity (leveraged) beta	BetaL = BetaU * [1+(1-tax) * (D/E)]					
WA077	Relevered beta = Unlevered Beta / [MVE / (Market Cap - (T * Book Value of Debt))]						

The WACC increases as the debt is paid down since the after-tax cost of debt is cheaper than equity. There is very little preference capital and this makes little difference to the overall cost.

You can also calculate a cumulative WACC by accumulating each year's rate. This could be an alternative rate to a single discount rate on the Valuation sheet in the next chapter.

```
Cumulative: Previous Year * (1 + Rate)
```

WACC

WACC = **6.71%**
Re(E/D+E) + Rd(1-Tax)(D/D+E)

Cost of Debt, Rd = **5.07%**
Rf + ßd(Rm - Rf)

Debt Beta, **ßd = 1.00**
Debt Premium / (Rm - Rf)

Debt Premium = **0.00%**

Preference
Rp = **5.00%**

Preference
Coupon 5.00%

Cost of Equity, Re = **9.80%**
Rf + ße(Rm - Rf)

Risk Free Rate
Rf = 5.00%

Market Premium
Rm - Rf = 6.00%

Equity Beta, **ße = 0.80**
ba * (1+(1-Tax)*D/E)

Asset Beta **0.44**
ße / (1+(1-Tax)*D/E)

Target Gearing
D/V = 109.69%

Effective Corp Tax Rate, Tc
Tc = 25.00%

Historic Equity Beta	0.80
Effective Corporate Tax Rate	25.00%
Historic D/E	1.10
Asset Beta ß	0.44
Forecast Debt/Equity	1.10
Equity Beta ß	0.80
Risk Free Rate	5.00%
Market Risk Premium	6.00%
Cost of Equity	9.80%
Preference shares	5.00%
Par value	100.00
Cost of preference shares	5.00%
Forecast P/D+E+P	1.21%
Cost of Debt	5.07%
Debt Premium	-
Debt Beta	1.00
Forecast D/D+E+P	50.54%
WACC	6.71%

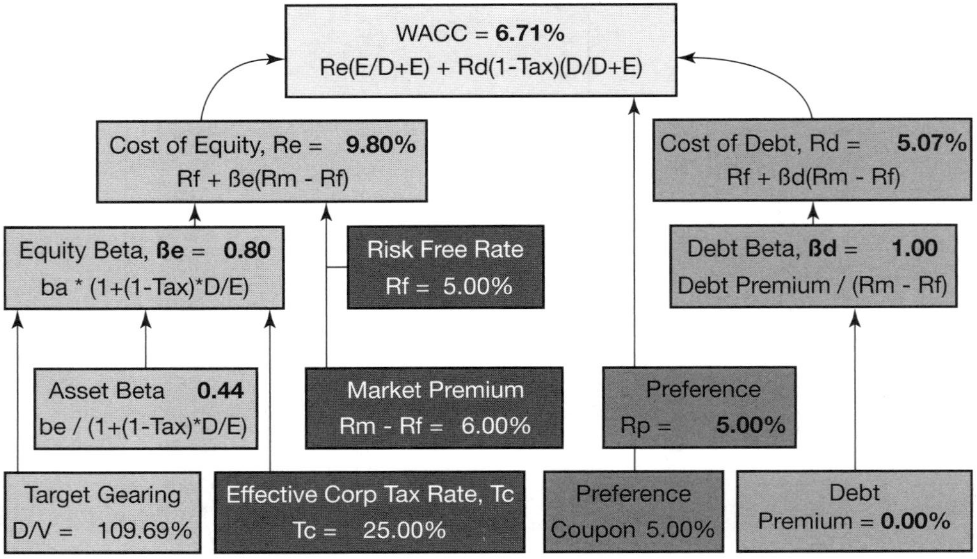

Figure 11.10

GRAPHICAL REPRESENTATION

You could also show the WACC in graphical form by starting with a copy of one of the templates and renaming it WACC_Calculation (see Figure 11.10). The sheet needs many narrow columns to display the data. The cells on the left bring forward the data from previous sheets. The basic shapes are on the Shapes menu as boxes and lines. In Figure 11.10 you can see more clearly the strands that make up the overall discount rate.

SUMMARY

The workings sheet for the cost of capital brings forward debt and equity data as a further building block in the cash valuation. This chapter lays out the key steps for calculating the cost of debt, preference capital and equity share capital and then puts the costs together in proportion to their percentage of total market value. The result is a discount rate that reflects the costs and risk of each source of capital. The next stage is to produce a single-point value for the firm.

Valuation

CASH FLOWS

This chapter brings together all the workings from the previous sheets, such as the cash flows and cost of capital. Since the model is valuing the company as the present value of future cash flows, this schedule needs to set out the cash flows to show the source and the stages of the valuation. The valuation conforms to Figure 12.1 with the forecast cash flows, discount rate and terminal value.

Copy a further template sheet and call it Valuation to uphold the consistent structure of the worksheets.

Framework

Figure 12.1

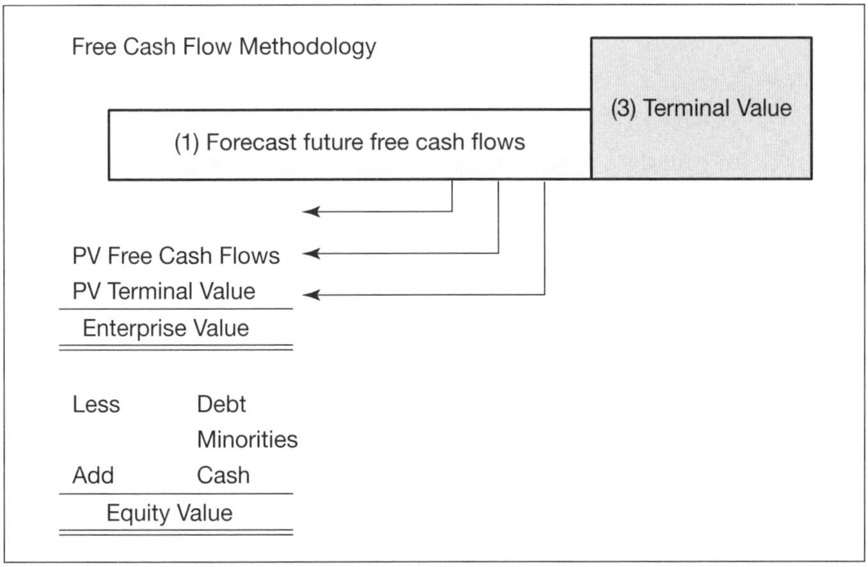

The valuation cash flow starts with the net operating profit before interest and tax and adds back non-cash items such as depreciation, amortisation and any transaction fees (see Figure 12.2). This is EBITDA, or the earnings before interest, tax, depreciation and amortisation. The EBITDA needs to be taxed at the marginal rate and you need to subtract capital expenditure and the changes in working capital. These items are all available on the Forecast Income and Cash sheets.

Figure 12.2

Cash flow

Line No Start Finish	Label	Ref	Total	1 01-Jan-12 31-Dec-12	6 01-Jan-17 31-Dec-17	7 01-Jan-18 31-Dec-18
VA010	Operating profit (EBIT post-transaction)	FP028	USD Millions		3,962.76	4,272.38
VA011						
VA012	Depreciation	FP017+FP018			1,058.27	1,256.60
VA013	Fees write-off	FP024			58.55	58.55
VA014	New goodwill	FP025			-	-
VA015	EBITDA				5,079.57	5,587.53
VA016						
VA017	Tax at 25.00% on EBIT	VA010*F029			(990.69)	(1,068.10)
VA018						
VA019	Net of tax EBITDA				4,088.88	4,519.44
VA020						
VA021	Changes in working capital	CF015.CF023			(5,592.17)	1,024.63
VA022	Capital expenditure	CF054			318.57	(1,575.85)
VA023						
VA024	Free cash flow				(1,184.71)	3,968.21

TERMINAL VALUE

You need to calculate a value for the company at the end of the forecast period since the forecast is only for a defined period. There are a number of methods, which will produce a range of values such as book value at one end and multiples of sales or profits at the other. Your model should incorporate two of the most common choices:

■ multiple of the final EBITDA;

■ value based on Gordon's growth model using the formula shown below.

The growth formula is a shortcut for the present value of a cash flow growing at a constant rate in perpetuity:

```
=(EBITDA * (1 + Growth rate))/(WACC - Growth rate)
```

If you were to start with a cash flow of 100 growing at a rate of 1 per cent per period with a discount rate of 10 per cent, the formula would be:

```
PV = [ 100 * (1 + 1%) ] / (10% - 1%) = 1,122.22
```

The chart in Figure 12.3 shows the effect of present valuing one, two and then three cash flows at the rate of 10 per cent. The line series shows this growing present value, which becomes close to the formula value after around 40 periods. Mathematically the two series will not meet but the distance between the figures grows smaller and smaller.

Figure 12.3

Growth model

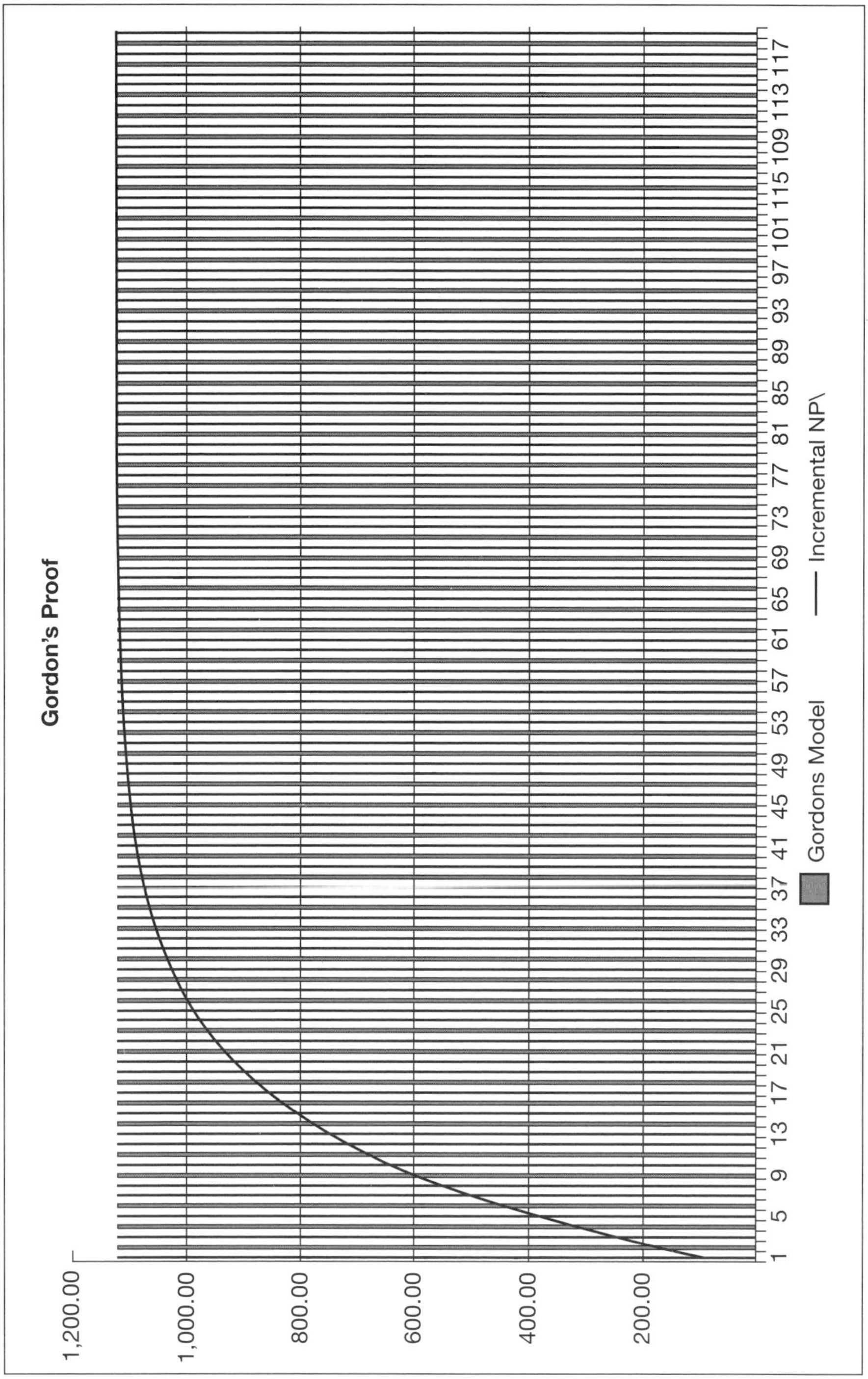

The final cash flow in the model is 2,261.45.

```
Perpetuity Formula :  =(X24*(cstOne+J44))/(X29-
J44)
```

The growth rate on the Forecast sheet is 4 per cent and the final WACC is 7.65%, which results in a final value of 64,490.65 at the final forecast period.

An alternative method uses a multiple of the final forecast year EBITDA. This is perhaps a simpler method as a multiple for a specific industry or sector is more readily available. The final EBITDA is 11,977.37 multiplied by four, which equals 47,909.48. The multiplier and perpetuity rates are inputs on the Forecast sheet in Figure 12.4.

Figure 12.4

Terminal value inputs

F119	Free cash flow	Perpetuity ▾
F120	Terminal value method	
F121	Perpetuity	4.0%
F122	Multiple EBITDA	4.0x
F123		
F124	Multiple range	2.0x
F125	Discount rate range	1.0%
F126	Perpetuity range	1.0%

CHOICE OF METHOD

You could also use a drop-down (combo) box from the Developer, Insert, Form Controls menu to generate a 1 or a 2 as a cell link and allow a selection between the two methods using CHOOSE, OFFSET or INDEX. Figure 12.4 displays the control against line 119. These controls are similar to a list validation, except that they also generate an index number to save you using MATCH to extract the index. Therefore, a user does not have to remember that they need to enter '1' for the terminal value method and '2' for the EBITDA multiplier.

Two further advantages of a combo box are:

■ two controls can access the same link cell, i.e. from the Forecast and Valuation sheets;

■ the link cell can be located on another sheet without having to name the cell as a range, as you would need to do with list validation.

INITIAL VALUATION

The terminal values are positioned at the end of the forecast period and these have to be discounted back at the WACC rate of 6.71 per cent. The formula is:

```
PV = Terminal value / (1+ WACC ) ^5
```

You could also use a PV function since this is a single cash flow problem.

Figure 12.5 displays the present value of the cash flows to the firm in line 24 at the WACC rate. Line 27 shows the total cash flows after the inclusion of the terminal value. The formula uses a standard NPV function and assumes 12 months to the first cash flow and equal periods.

The present value of the terminal value and the cash flows equates to the enterprise value as the market value of debt and equity. To obtain an equity value you have to subtract the debt and minorities values for the initial period. The debt is located on the Debt sheet and the minorities on the Balance sheet. This reduces the initial valuation to 32,221.21.

Cash flow to equity

Figure 12.5

Line No Start Finish	Label	Ref	Total	1 01-Jan-12 31-Dec-12	6 01-Jan-17 31-Dec-17	7 01-Jan-18 31-Dec-18
VA023						
VA024	Free cash flow				(1,184.71)	3,968.21
VA025						
VA026	Terminal value	VA044,VA045				
VA027	Cash flow to firm		16.20%		(1,184.71)	3,968.21
VA028						
VA029	WACC	WA071	%		6.71%	6.79%
VA030	Cumulative WACC	WA072	%		1.07	1.14
VA031	Net cash	VA024/VA030		22,289.99	(1,110.22)	3,482.40
VA032	Cumulative NPV				22,289.99	23,400.20
VA033						
VA034	Debt repayments	DB012.DB037	(23,500.00)		(2,550.00)	(2,550.00)
VA035	Debt interest	FP032.FP038	(6,247.50)		(1,195.00)	(1,062.50)
VA036	Preference shares	FP039			(25.00)	(25.00)
VA037	Cash flow to equity	-	395.53%	210,115.65	16,226.19	27,214.52
VA038						
VA039	Terminal value					
VA040						
VA041	Select method	Perpetuity ▼				
VA042	WACC	6.71%				
VA043						
VA044	Perpetuity		64,490.95	Perpetuity	4.00%	
VA045	Multiple EBITDA		47,909.48	Multiple	4.00	
VA046						
VA047	Enterprise and equity value		Single	Cumulative		
VA048	NPV of free cash flows at 6.71%		22,581.13	22,289.99		
VA049						
VA050	Terminal value		64,490.95	64,490.95		
VA051	NPV of terminal value		33,687.09	32,377.60		
VA052	Enterprise value		56,268.21	54,667.59		
VA053						
VA054	Debt		(24,000.00)	(24,000.00)		
VA055	Minorities		(47.00)	(47.00)		
VA056	Equity value		32,221.21	30,620.59		

The model also uses the cumulative WACC from the previous sheet and divides each cash flow by its cumulative factor. Since the capital structure changes as the debt is paid down, this means that the cost of capital rises. This change results in a slightly lower valuation of 30,620.59.

CHART

You could also generate a chart to show the value creation over the period. For convenience, the model places the workings at the bottom of the Valuation sheet (see Figure 12.6). Press F11 or use the chart wizard to enter this data as several y axes and the forecast dates at the top of the sheet as the x axis (see Figure 12.7). The present value of the cash flows is an area chart while the cumulative NPV and free cash flow are columns. The percentage WACC and return on invested capital are line charts on the right-hand secondary axis. You could save this chart as a template for future use by selecting Chart Tools and this would save reformatting the chart types and colours if you wanted to use it again.

Figure 12.6

Chart workings

Line No	Label	Ref	Units	6 01-Jan-17 31-Dec-17	7 01-Jan-18 31-Dec-18	8 01-Jan-19 31-Dec-19
	Valuation Chart Workings					
VA061	NPV of free cash flows at 6.71%	NPV		22,581.13	25,280.94	23,008.98
VA062	Cumulative NPV	VA037/WA072		15,205.93	23,882.73	19,505.22
VA063	Free cash flow	VA024		(1,184.71)	3,968.21	4,029.66
VA064	EBITDA	VA015		5,079.57	5,587.53	6,146.29
VA065	WACC	VA042		6.71%	6.71%	6.71%
VA066	ROIC	RT023		10.45%	11.23%	12.24%

Figure 12.7

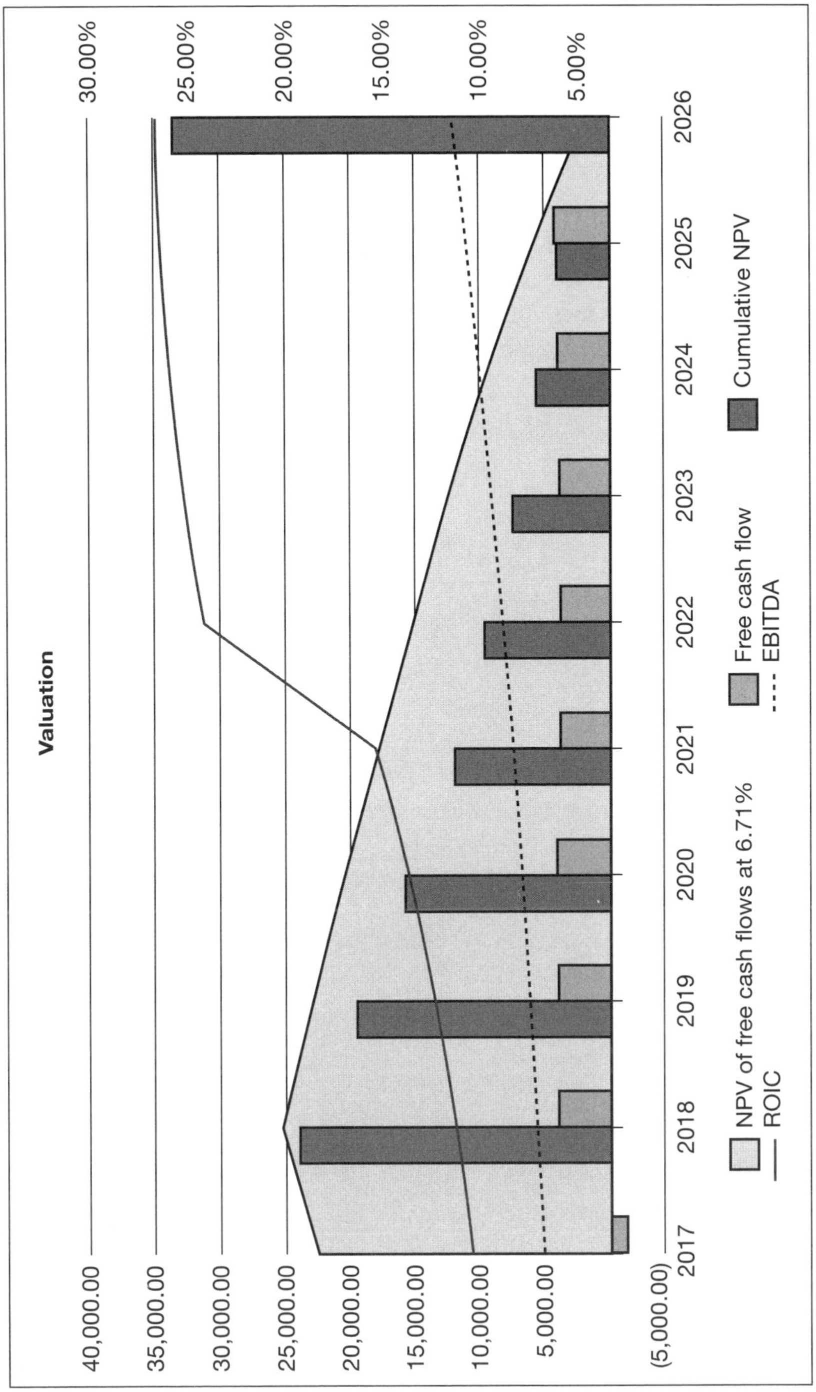

Valuation chart

Valuation

SUMMARY

The Forecast drivers feed through into the accounting statements and cash flows. Using the calculated cost of capital, this sheet discounts the free cash available to pay debt and equity and calculates a discounted terminal value. The addition of the cash flows and terminal values produces an enterprise value and when debt and minorities are deducted, the model generates an initial equity value. The next stages add more detail and sensitivity to these figures in order to assess risk and the value of the forecast percentages together with checking the model for accuracy.

Other approaches

	Method
	Book value
	Adjusted book value
	Market value
	Multiples
	Peer data
	Summary

METHOD

The discounted cash flow sheet computes a valuation from the forecasted cash flows as 32,221; however, it is useful as a comparison to consider other valuation methods or other companies in the same sector. An optimistic forecast can produce a high valuation relative to book or market values. Alternatively, a takeover can result in a high market value because of scarcity or takeover premiums. This chapter looks at accounting, market and peer groups to add a set of comparison figures.

BOOK VALUE

Copy a template sheet and rename it Market. Most of the share and market information is available on earlier sheets and you can bring it forward and multiply out the figures. For example, shareholders' funds are the addition of share capital and retained earnings on the Forecast Balance Sheet (Figure 13.1). Alternatively, you can view it as the total assets less the short- and long-term liabilities.

Forecast Balance sheet

Figure 13.1

Line No Start Finish	Label	Ref	Total	1 01-Jan-12 31-Dec-12	2 01-Jan-13 31-Dec-13
FB064	Shareholders' equity				
FD005	Common stock (shares)	IN022+IN023+IN024		389.0	395.0
FB066	Preferred stock (shares)	IN021		3,744.0	4,028.0
FB067	Retained earnings	FB067+FP055		4,873.0	4,957.0
FB068	Shareholders equity			9,006.0	9,380.0
FB070	Total liabilities + shareholders equity			20,410.0	22,563.0

Figure 13.2

Book value

Line No Start Finish	Label	Ref	Total	1 01-Jan-12 31-Dec-12	2 01-Jan-13 31-Dec-13	3 01-Jan-14 31-Dec-14
MA010	Book Value					
MA011	Shareholders' Funds GBP '000	FB068		9,006.00	9,380.00	10,506.00
MA012	Number of Shares Issued & Outstandi	F116		7,000.00	7,000.00	7,000.00
MA013	Book Value per Share	MA011/MA012		1.29	1.34	1.50
MA014						
MA015						
MA016	Adjusted Book Value					
MA017	Book Value of Total Assets	FB033		20,410.00	22,563.00	24,807.00
MA018	Adjustments to Book Value					
MA019	Tangible Assets			-	-	-
MA020	Intangibles			-	-	-
MA021	Pension Fund			-	-	-
MA022	Other			-	-	-
MA023	Other			-	-	-
MA024	**Adjusted Book Value**			**20,410.00**	**22,563.00**	**24,807.00**
MA025	Other Adjustments					
MA026	Less Current Liabilities	FB045		(6,072.00)	(7,547.00)	(8,152.00)
MA027	Less Long-term Liabilities	FB060		(4,531.00)	(5,248.00)	(4,574.00)
MA028	Less Contingent (Legal) Liabilities			-	-	-
MA029	Operating Leases			-	-	-
MA030	Other			-	-	-
MA031	**Adjusted Book Value of Equity**			**9,807.00**	**9,768.00**	**12,081.00**
MA032						
MA033	Adjusted Book Value per Share	MA031/MA012		1.40	1.40	1.73

The number of shares is an input on the Forecast sheet so the book value per share is the shareholders' funds divided by the number of shares (see Figure 13.2). This is useful as a low value against the calculated discounted cash flow equity value.

ADJUSTED BOOK VALUE

The book value is simply the accounting value of the company and has no direct link to market or investor values. Accounting figures may need upward or downward adjustment due to some of the factors below:

- Lack of uniformity in preparation of statements, where companies choose different accounting rules such as depreciation periods or recognition of contingent liabilities.

- Historical information that is backward looking given that companies publish their annual reports some months after a year-end.

- Off-balance sheet items such as operating leasing that tend to understate borrowings and therefore gearing ratios.

- Contingent liabilities such as litigation, pension liabilities or environmental damage that does not appear as liabilities on the balance sheet can affect value.

- Understatement of value where, for example, land is valued at historic cost leading to a reduced accounting value.

- Intangible assets such as goodwill or research and development are subject to an impairment test rather than an amortisation period.

- Changes in the external environment after the balance sheet date, which may affect asset values.

- A single estimate of balance sheet, for example where borrowings at the year-end are lower than average during the year.

- Comparisons with other companies can be difficult due to individual and market factors.

- In diversified and acquisitive organisations that regularly buy and sell other companies it is difficult to compare year-by-year performance.

- Window dressing or creative accounting which usually leads to an overstatement of revenue or understatement of cost with some form of capitalisation in the balance sheet in order to enhance short-term profits.

- International differences in presentation, where countries and companies interpret generally accepted practice differently.

The schedule in Figure 13.2 starts with the book value of the assets and inserts some input cells for manual entry of the adjustments leading to an alternative book value.

MARKET VALUE

Market value is simply the number of shares multiplied by the current share price with the figures on the Forecast sheet (see Figure 13.3). Shares in publicly listed companies are readily tradable by stock exchanges and the price represents the views of buyers and sellers. If the share is in a closely held company, or on an emerging market exchange, it may be more volatile and the price may not be realistic.

Market value

Figure 13.3

Line No	Label	Ref	Total	1	2	3
Start				01-Jan-12	01-Jan-13	01-Jan-14
Finish				31-Dec-12	31-Dec-13	31-Dec-14
MA035						
MA036	Market Value					
MA037	Number of Shares Issued & Outstanding	F116		7,000.00	7,000.00	7,000.00
MA038	Current Share Price GBP	F117		1.75	1.75	1.75
MA039	Market Capitalisation (Thousands)	MA037*MA038		12,250.00	12,250.00	12,250.00
MA040	Market Price to Book	MA038/MA013		1.36	1.31	1.17

Several factors can affect the market value:

- 'Short termism' of the stock market where values can be under- or over-stated.
- Shareholder loyalty, for example football clubs, which results in higher valuations.
- Fashion such as social networking or IT companies leading to a 'herd' instinct.
- Control premium, since the price is higher due to speculator interest.
- Employee loyalty or available benefits such as discounts available solely to shareholders.

Nevertheless, a market value offers a benchmark for comparison with the discounted cash flow value. A useful measure is the ratio of the market to the book value. This provides a measure of the sentiment of the stock market – a value less than one would signify that the market has little confidence in the management or the company, whereas a high multiple indicates a higher level of confidence or the prospect of future growth.

MULTIPLES

Values such as EBITDA do not allow you to compare companies directly but it is useful to add more elements to the market schedule. The price to earnings per share ratio is a popular measure and is often referred to as the P/E ratio. A high P/E suggests that investors are expecting a higher future earnings growth compared to companies with a lower P/E. However, the P/E ratio does not tell us the whole story by itself since it is usually more useful to compare the P/E ratios of one company to the sector in general or against the company's own historical P/E. The formula is:

```
PE ratio = Share price / Earnings per share
PE ratio = Market capitalisation / Sustainable
earnings available to shareholders
```

The earnings may need adjustment for one-offs as you need the available sustainable earnings. This may be partly subjective, but you need to make sure that the model does not overvalue the company due to unusual factors.

You can calculate P/E ratios for companies and sectors, and these can easily be adjusted for forward prospects (see Figure 13.4). The more confident an investor is in a company's future prospects, the more he will be prepared to pay, and therefore the higher the P/E ratio will be. If the investor considers the company to be risky or volatile, he will not be prepared to pay so much, and so you would expect to see a lower P/E ratio.

Multiples

Figure 13.4

Line No Start Finish	Label	Ref	Total	1 01-Jan-12 31-Dec-12	2 01-Jan-13 31-Dec-13	3 01-Jan-14 31-Dec-14
MA042						
MA043	PE Multiple					
MA044	NPAT	FP050		1,407.00	1,712.00	1,981.00
MA045	Earnings per Share	MA044/MA012		0.20	0.24	0.28
MA046	P / E Ratio	MA038/MA045		8.71	7.16	6.18
MA047	Net Profit after Tax (NPAT) * P/E Ratio	MA044*MA046		12,250.00	12,250.00	12,250.00
MA048						
MA049						
MA050	Price to Cash Flow					
MA051	Valuation Free Cash Flow GBP '000	VA037				
MA052	Valuation Free Cashflow per Share	MA051/MA012				
MA053	Share Price / Cashflow per Share	MA038/MA052				
MA054	Enterprise Value	MA039+FB036.FB037+FB053.FB059		17,258.00	19,412.00	18,465.00
MA055	Enterprise Value / Valuation Free Cashflc	MA054/MA051				
MA056						
MA057						
MA058	Enterprise Value to EBITDA					
MA059	Enterprise Value (EV)	MA039+FB036.FB037+FB053.FB059		17,258.00	19,412.00	18,465.00
MA060	EBITDA	FP022-FP017-FP018		2,682.00	3,089.00	3,502.00
MA061	EV / EBITDA	MA059/MA060		6.43	6.28	5.27
MA062	EV/Sales	MA059/FP010		0.51	0.49	0.43
MA063						
MA064						
MA065	Summary					
MA066	Book Value	MA011		9,006.00	9,380.00	10,506.00
MA067	Adjusted Book Value	MA031		9,807.00	9,768.00	12,081.00
MA068	Market Value	MA039		12,250.00	12,250.00	12,250.00

The net profit after tax (NPAT) is available on the Forecast Income statement and this allows you to easily calculate the earnings per share. As a check, the NPAT multiplied by the PE ratio should return the market value.

Price to cash flow is also a useful measure of the value of cash as opposed to accounting profit, and uses the formula:

```
Price to cash flow = Share price / Cash flow per
share
Price to cash flow = Market capitalisation / Cash
flow
```

There are a number of definitions of free cash flow and this model uses the valuation free cash flow from the previous schedule. You could also adjust the ratio for net interest paid and taxation.

Enterprise value also has several definitions, but in simple form, it is the market value of all debt plus the market value of equity. You could also add excess cash to the value or subtract any off-balance sheet debt and make adjustments due to contingent liabilities or other factors. An alternative cash flow measure would be to divide the enterprise value by the cash flow per share.

The final section compares the enterprise value (EV) to EBITDA and to sales. EV/EBITDA has become a popular comparison measure as it uses the market value of the whole enterprise together with a profit line before interest, tax and financing choices, or accounting differences such as the depreciation method. This may be useful for comparing the company.

PEER DATA

The above data provides trends but it does not tell you how the company stands against other companies in its sector. The file Peer_Group.xls on the CD-ROM contains some specimen sector data and you can copy the figures to a new template schedule. Call it Peer_Group and format the data (see Figure 13.5).

The data in the table below is a simple average of the companies. You can bring forward the data from previous sheets and calculate a variance.

Ratio	Source
Market cap/EV	Market
Market/book	Market
Current PE	Market
EV/EBITDA	Market
Debt to equity	WACC
Beta	WACC, forecast or valuation
EV/Sales	Market
Return on equity	Ratios
Return on capital	Ratios
Net profit margin	Ratios
Pre-tax operating margin	Ratios
EBITDA	Cash flow or valuation

The company shows a higher market to book and return on equity and a lower P/E than the peer group. It is broadly similar to the peer group ratios; however, you could perform more analysis by weighting the figures based on company size or market capitalisation.

The 'thermometer' charts in Figure 13.6 on page 188 are an alternative method of showing the variance and are useful for budgets and charts. The company is the wide column while the average is the middle column. This is not a standard Excel chart, however, and so you have to 'fool' the chart wizard to produce it.

Figure 13.5

Peer group data

Line No	Name	Market Cap	Enterprise Value	Stock price	Market Cap / EV	Market / Book	Current PE	EV/EBITDA	Debt to Equity	Beta	EV/Sales	Return on Equity	Return on Capital	Net Profit Margin	Pre-tax Operating Margin	EBITDA
Model Check: All balances OK																
PE008	AA	5,374.67	5,253.20	34.01	102.3%	4.66	18.09	9.67	1.0%	0.08	0.86	30.0%	58.0%	5.0%	7.0%	543.13
PE009	BB	4,964.67	6,839.53	49.41	72.6%	1.14	10.11	4.82	51.0%	0.47	0.36	11.0%	22.0%	3.0%	5.0%	1,419.80
PE010	CC	3,041.00	3,392.47	30.89	89.6%	1.61	25.43	13.21	14.0%	0.71	0.42	10.0%	10.0%	3.0%	3.0%	256.80
PE011	DD	7,200.47	11,775.07	65.21	61.2%	1.30	12.75	7.57	83.0%	0.68	0.46	8.0%	16.0%	2.0%	4.0%	1,554.53
PE012	EE	234.07	236.88	26.08	98.8%	3.08	18.68	9.30	3.0%	0.39	0.73	23.0%	25.0%	5.0%	7.0%	25.47
PE013	FF	10,091.20	11,051.73	8.83	91.3%	2.01	11.82	5.64	31.0%	0.42	0.41	19.0%	22.0%	3.0%	5.0%	1,957.87
PE014	GG	6,404.40	7,140.73	10.19	89.7%	7.95	33.46	14.18	11.0%	0.99	1.02	33.0%	27.0%	3.0%	5.0%	503.53
PE015	HH	35,506.80	46,059.60	4.43	77.1%	2.33	15.02	10.51	35.0%	0.57	0.80	18.0%	12.0%	4.0%	5.0%	4,380.80
PE016	II	7,400.93	8,289.13	2.79	89.3%	1.40	11.59	6.98	15.0%	0.42	0.50	11.0%	14.0%	4.0%	5.0%	1,187.53
PE017	JJ	7,278.53	9,283.67	3.92	78.4%	1.37	12.43	8.04	37.0%	0.65	0.46	16.0%	13.0%	3.0%	4.0%	1,154.73
PE018	**Mean**	**8,749.67**	**10,932.20**	**23.58**	**85.0%**	**2.69**	**16.94**	**8.99**	**28.1%**	**0.54**	**0.60**	**17.9%**	**21.9%**	**3.5%**	**5.0%**	**1,298.42**
PE019																
PE020	Case	20,000.00	41,570.69	2.00	205.1%	2.91	7.96	8.18	107.3%	0.80	0.70	44.4%	15.7%	5.1%	6.6%	4,370.00
PE021	Variance	11,250.33	30,638.49	(21.58)	120.1%	0.22	(8.98)	(0.81)	79.2%	0.26	0.09	26.5%	(6.2%)	1.6%	1.6%	3,071.58

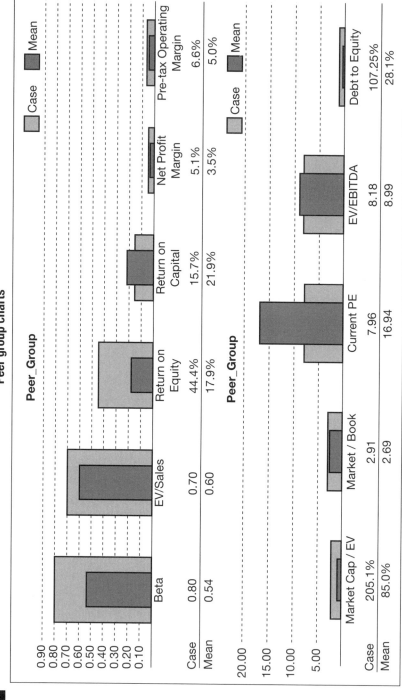

Figure 13.6

The narrow column is on the secondary axis with a large gap width (see Figure 13.7). The wide column is plotted on the primary axis with a gap width of 60 per cent. Since the two series are on separate axes, they will overlap without difficulty. You can also remove the lines on the secondary axis and you do not need to repeat the labels. Since you may need the chart again, save it as a template using Chart Tools, Save as Template.

Narrow column options

Figure 13.7

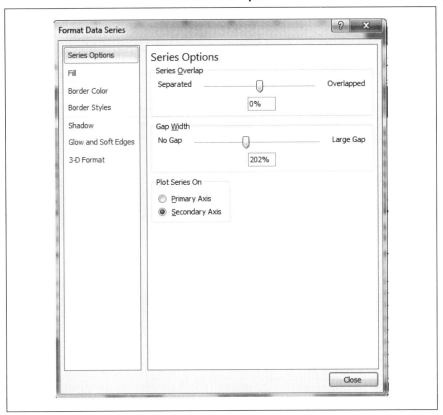

You can also vary the options to the chart by adding a data table below the chart to show the data more clearly (see Figures 13.8 and 13.9).

Chart data table

Figure 13.8

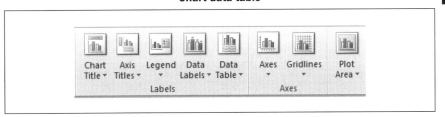

Figure 13.9

Narrow column options

Line No	Label	Ref	5	6	7
			01-Jan-16	01-Jan-17	01-Jan-18
			31-Dec-16	31-Dec-17	31-Dec-18
MA065	Summary				
MA066	Book Value	MA011	5,118.77	6,878.24	8,827.51
MA067	Adjusted Book Value	MA031	7,500.75	9,268.63	11,456.93
MA068	Market Value	MA039	10,500.00	20,000.00	21,000.00

SUMMARY

The discounted cash flow valuation values the forecast cash flows and this chapter compares the value against the accounting and book values and calculates some useful ratios for comparison against similar companies. The company in the model is broadly similar to the other companies on the sector list.

Alternative methods

METHOD

Traditional analysis using discounted cash flows finds a single value but does not provide detailed information on the constituents of value or the breakdown of constituents. Figure 14.1 shows the sources of potential value in terms of:

■ current market value;

■ internal improvements such as cost cutting and savings;

■ external improvements such as liquidations, acquisitions, disposals and strategic improvements;

■ financial engineering, which includes borrowing costs, changing leverage and lowering the cost of capital.

Value gap

Figure 14.1

Share Price

| 1.60 | Optimal Restructuring Value | Value Gap: 0.60 |

| 1.40 | Potential Value after External Improvements |

| 1.20 | Potential Value after Internal Improvements |

| 1.00 |

Activity

Internal Improvements	**External Improvements**	**Financial Engineering**

* Increasing revenues
* Decreasing unit costs
* Reducing corporate overheads
* Efficiency savings
	* Liquidation
	* Disposals
	  - Sale
	  - MBO
	  - Demerger
	* Acquisitions
		* Share repurchase
		* Financing mix (D/E)
		* Borrowing costs

Since you have all the information on previous schedules, you can use it to find out more about the sources of value by breaking down the calculations. The two approaches covered in this chapter are adjusted present value and economic profit.

Adjusted present value (APV) tries to show the constituents by first valuing the company with discounted cash flows as if it had no debt by using a non-leveraged cost of capital. Models then generate further cash flows for the interest shield and structural or strategic changes as layers that can be discounted at an appropriate rate for that specific cash flow. The adjusted present value is the sum of the individual components and should approximate to the single cash flow value.

Economic profit or residual profit generates an adjusted profit after tax and makes a charge for the capital employed at the beginning of each period. The starting point is that the capital employed has a real cost and the company should earn more than its cost of capital if it is indeed adding shareholder value. This is closely aligned with the EVA methodology outlined by Stern Stewart as a remuneration approach to make managers more conscious of their contribution to total value. These two methods are modelled below.

ADJUSTED PRESENT VALUE

Adjusted present value (APV) concentrates on value enhancement by concentrating on value drivers. To create value you have to increase revenue, reduce costs to increase free cash flow or reduce the cost of capital. Any method that does not change the cash volume, such as increasing depreciation periods or changing inventory valuation, will not contribute to value. Examples of adding value are:

- generating higher cash flows from existing assets without affecting growth prospects or risk profile;
- reinvesting more with excess returns without affecting risk;
- reducing the cost of financing without lowering returns.

The basic procedure is as follows:

- Develop the free cash flow forecast as in the traditional discounted cash flow method. These figures are available on the Valuation sheet.
- Discount the free cash flow using the cost of equity based on unlevered beta.
- Calculate the actual interest tax shield and discount at the cost of debt (or another appropriate cost of capital).
- Develop free cash flows for all other synergies and benefits of the transaction. These figures should be adjusted for tax if the company is paying mainstream tax.
- Discount each free cash flow using its own cost of capital. Where appropriate the discount rate should be adjusted for tax.
- Add together all elements to obtain the adjusted present value (which is equivalent to the target company's enterprise value) (see Figure 14.2).

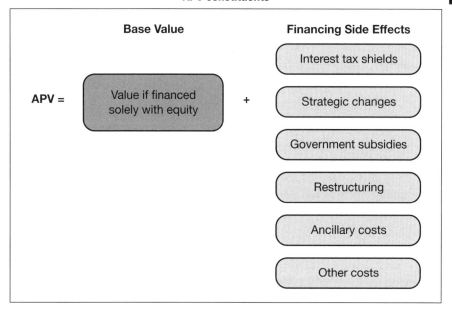

APV constituents

Figure 14.2

Copy two more template sheets and call them APV and Economic_Profit. On the APV sheet, bring forward the valuation cash flow and terminal value using the line references below. You need to site the terminal value in the final year:

```
O12:  =IF(YEAR(O8)=YEAR(Exit_
Year),Valuation!$E$50,cstZero)
```

The unleveraged beta on the WACC sheet (Figure 14.3) is 0.44 and the cost of equity given by:

$$Ka = Rf + (\beta * MRP)$$

FCF at unleveraged cost of equity

Figure 14.3

Line No	Label	Ref		Total	6	7	8
Start					01-Jan-17	01-Jan-18	01-Jan-19
Finish					31-Dec-17	31-Dec-18	31-Dec-19
AP-10	(1) Free cash flow						
AP-11	Valuation free cash flow	VA024	USD Millions		(1,184.71)	3,968.21	4,029.66
AP-12	Terminal value	VA050			-	-	-
AP-13	Total cash flow				(1,184.71)	3,968.21	4,029.66
AP-14							
AP-15	Unleveraged cost of equity	WA041+WA042*WA064	=		7.66%	7.66%	8.08%
AP-16	Cumulative	Cum AP-15			1.08	1.16	1.25
AP-17	Discounted cash	AP-13/AP-16			(1,100.41)	3,423.61	3,216.66
AP-18							
AP-19	Cumulative discounted cash				49,007.75	50,108.17	46,684.55
AP-20							
AP-21	Equity net present value at 7.66%	NPV AP-11		21,485.16			
AP-22	PV of terminal value	NPV AP-12		30,828.11			
AP-23	Total			52,313.27			

where:

Ka	=	*cost of the asset*
Rf	=	*local risk-free yield such as long-term government debt*
MRP	=	*market risk premium*
Beta (β)	=	*unleveraged or asset beta for target*

```
Unleveraged cost of equity = 5% + 6% * 0.44 = 7.66%
```

You can discount the cash flows at this single rate or calculate a cumulative cost of equity by multiplying it out:

```
P16: = O16 * (cstOne + P15)
```

The starting value is the present value of the cash flows and terminal value as if the company is debt-free.

Figure 14.4

APV

Line No	Label	Ref	Total	1	2	3
Start				01-Jan-12	01-Jan-13	01-Jan-14
Finish				31-Dec-12	31-Dec-13	31-Dec-14
AP-24						
AP-25	(2) Interest shield					
AP-26	Interest	VA035				
AP-27	Terminal value	VA035*(1+F121))/(AP-33-F121)				
AP-28	Total		-			
AP-29						
AP-30	Tax	IP046				
AP-31	Net of tax amount					
AP-32						
AP-33	Cost of debt	F100.F106				
AP-34	Cum WACC	Cum AP-33				
AP-35	Discounted interest	AP-31/AP-34				
AP-36						
AP-37	Cumulative discounted interest					
AP-38						
AP-39	(3) Adjusted present value					
AP-40	Net of tax cost of debt	AP-33*(1-T)	3.81%			
AP-41	Debt NPV at 5.09%	AP-31	3,352.77			3,366.40
AP-42						
AP-43	Enterprise value	AP-23+AP-4 Single	55,666.04	Cumulative	52,360.52	
AP-44	Debt	VA054	(24,000.00)		(24,000.00)	
AP-45	Minorities	VA055	(47.00)		(47.00)	
AP-46	Equity value		31,619.04		31,679.93	

The second stage (Figure 14.4) is to generate other layers: you can find the interest payable on the Valuation sheet. Interest payable is subject to tax relief and the leverage effect constitutes the interest multiplied by the tax rate. The cost of debt changes each year as the company pays off the debt. A SUMPRODUCT function allows you to multiply out the interest rate and the amount outstanding and find the net of tax rate:

```
O33: =SUMPRODUCT(Forecast!O100:O106,Debt_
Schedule!N10:N16) / SUM(Debt_Schedule!N10:N16)
O34: =(cstOne+O33*(1-Forecast!O29))
```

You can derive the adjusted present value by adding these two elements and you could add further layers for different sources, such as:

- margin improvement;
- plant closures or cost reductions;
- financial or operational synergies;
- working capital improvements;
- asset sales.

This is close to the original discounted cash flow valuation. The result provides an indication of the effect of the financing option together with other strategic changes.

ECONOMIC PROFIT

Economic profit calculations and discounted cash flow values should result in the same answer. The intention here is to make a charge for the capital employed by the company. The basic formulas for economic profit (see Figure 14.5) are:

```
Economic profit = (Return on capital employed -
Cost of capital) * Capital employed
Economic profit = After-tax operating income -
(Cost of capital * Capital invested) = NOPAT -
(WACC * EV)
```

Economic profit

Figure 14.5

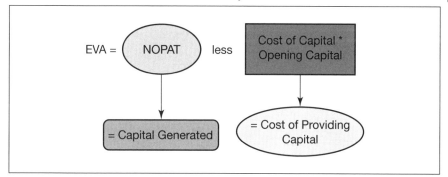

The first section generates the same figures as the Valuation schedule and discounts the cash flows at the cumulative weighted average cost of capital. The method is:

Operating profit (EBIT post-transaction)
+ Depreciation
+ Fees write-off
+ New goodwill
= EBITDA
Less tax on EBIT
= Net of tax EBITDA
− Changes in working capital
− Capital expenditure
= Free cash flow
+ Terminal value
= Cash flow to firm

The depreciation, amortisation, changes in working capital and capital expenditure together with the terminal value and cost of capital can be sourced on the Valuation sheet. The example in Figure 14.6 uses the cumulative cost of capital and derives the answer of 30,620.59, which is the same as the cumulative figure on the Valuation sheet (Figure 14.7).

The first task is to find the starting and finishing capital for each period:

Initial capital
− Depreciation
+/− Change in WC
− Capital expenditure
= Ending capital

You can also calculate the return on capital employed as the after-tax EBT divided by the opening capital. In the terminal value year, you need a different formula:

```
Y41: =Forecast!D121/((X36+X37+X38)/X44)
Y41 = Terminal value growth rate / (Previous year
depreciation + Change in WC + Capital expenditure)
/ EBIT * (1-T) for last year
```

The economic profit is computed as the after-tax profit less the capital charge:

EBIT (1−t)	*2,972.07*
WACC	*6.71%*
*WACC * capital*	*(2,781.13)*
Economic profit	*190.94*

Figure 14.6

FCF cash flow

Line No	Label	Ref	Units	Total	6 01-Jan-17 31-Dec-17	7 01-Jan-18 31-Dec-18	8 01-Jan-19 31-Dec-19	9 01-Jan-20 31-Dec-20	10 01-Jan-21 31-Dec-21	11 01-Jan-22 31-Dec-22	12 01-Jan-23 31-Dec-23	13 01-Jan-24 31-Dec-24	14 01-Jan-25 31-Dec-25	15 01-Jan-26 31-Dec-26	16 01-Jan-27 31-Dec-27
EP10	Earning before interest and tax (EBIT)	FP028	USD Millions		3,962.76	4,272.38	4,632.80	5,132.43	5,693.52	6,909.05	7,712.12	8,597.00	9,571.87	10,645.72	
EP11		F029			25.00%	25.00%	25.00%	25.00%	25.00%	25.00%	25.00%	25.00%	25.00%	25.00%	
EP12	EBIT * (1-tax)				2,972.07	3,204.29	3,474.60	3,849.32	4,270.14	5,181.79	5,784.09	6,447.75	7,178.90	7,984.29	
EP13	Tax reconcilation to FCFF														
EP14	EBIT (1-t)	EP12			2,972.07	3,204.29	3,474.60	3,849.32	4,270.14	5,181.79	5,784.09	6,447.75	7,178.90	7,984.29	
EP15	Depreciation	VA012+VA013+FP025			1,116.82	1,315.15	1,513.48	1,628.48	1,743.48	1,271.65	1,286.65	1,301.65	1,316.65	1,331.65	
EP16	Change in WC	VA021			(5,592.17)	1,024.63	632.37	224.30	(627.72)	(941.65)	(1,430.81)	(1,940.26)	(2,495.21)	(5,249.24)	
EP17	Capital expenditure	VA022			318.57	(1,575.85)	(1,590.79)	(1,607.22)	(1,625.30)	(1,703.74)	(1,725.61)	(1,749.67)	(1,776.14)	(1,805.25)	
EP18	Free cash flow (FCFF)	EP14:EP17		–	(1,184.71)	3,968.21	4,029.66	4,094.88	3,760.60	3,808.06	3,914.32	4,059.48	4,224.21	2,261.45	
EP19															
EP20	Terminal value	VA050													64,490.95
EP21	Total free cash			–	(1,184.71)	3,968.21	4,029.66	4,094.88	3,760.60	3,808.06	3,914.32	4,059.48	4,224.21	66,752.40	
EP22															
EP23	(1) Equity and WACC														
EP24	Cumulative WACC	VA030			1.07	1.14	1.22	1.30	1.39	1.49	1.60	1.72	1.85	1.99	
EP25	Present value				(1,110.22)	3,482.40	3,309.06	3,143.89	2,696.99	2,548.62	2,442.28	2,368.68	2,282.93	33,512.96	
EP26															
EP27	(2) Free cash valuation														
EP28	Value of firm	EP25		54,667.59											
EP29	Investments														
EP30	Debt	IN014:IN021		(24,000.00)											
EP31	Minorities	FB050		(47.00)											
EP32	Value of equity			30,620.59											

Figure 14.7

Economic profit

Line No	Label	Ref	0	Total	6 01-Jan-17 31-Dec-17	7 01-Jan-18 31-Dec-18	8 01-Jan-19 31-Dec-19	9 01-Jan-20 31-Dec-20	10 01-Jan-21 31-Dec-21	11 01-Jan-22 31-Dec-22	12 01-Jan-23 31-Dec-23	13 01-Jan-24 31-Dec-24	14 01-Jan-25 31-Dec-25	15 01-Jan-26 31-Dec-26	16 01-Jan-27 31-Dec-27
EP42	Capital Invested				41,450.00	45,606.78	44,842.85	44,287.70	44,042.23	44,551.77	45,925.50	47,796.28	50,183.55	53,138.24	148,793.80
EP43															
EP44	EBIT (1-t)	EP12			2,972.07	3,204.29	3,474.60	3,849.32	4,270.14	5,181.79	5,784.09	6,447.75	7,178.90	7,984.29	8,303.66
EP45	WACC	WA071			6.71%	6.79%	6.87%	6.96%	7.05%	7.16%	7.27%	7.38%	7.51%	7.65%	
EP46	WACC * capital	EP35:EP45			(2,781.13)	(3,094.75)	(3,079.80)	(3,081.18)	(3,106.63)	(3,188.46)	(3,337.16)	(3,529.25)	(3,769.07)	(4,063.42)	(11,378.09)
EP47	Economic profit				190.94	109.54	394.80	768.14	1,163.31	1,993.33	2,446.93	2,918.50	3,409.84	3,920.87	(3,074.43)
EP48															
EP49	PV of terminal EVA	EP47/(EP45-F121)													
EP50	Total economic profit				190.94	109.54	394.80	768.14	1,163.31	1,993.33	2,446.93	2,918.50	3,409.84	(84,302.85)	
EP51															
EP52	PV				178.93	96.13	324.20	589.75	834.29	1,334.08	1,526.72	1,695.74	1,842.81	(80,381.98)	(40,355.67)
EP53															
EP54	PV of total economic profit	EP52:EP52		(31,933.02)											
EP55	Capital invested	EP35		41,450.00											
EP56															
EP57	PV of change terminal capital	(EP42-EP35)/EP24		45,150.61											
EP58	Enterprise value			54,667.59											
EP59															
EP60	Debt	VA054		(24,000.00)											
EP61	Minorities	VA055		(47.00)											
EP62	Equity value			30,620.59											

The final after-tax profit is made up of the previous year multiplied by 1 + growth rate. The final capital is:

```
Y42: Final after-tax profit / terminal return on
capital
Y42: 8,303.60 / 5.58% = 148,793.80
```

You can calculate the final capital charge as the capital multiplied by the last cost of capital of 7.65 per cent. This results in an economic profit of minus 3,074.43. If you divide this by the cost of capital less the terminal growth rate, the capital decrease is minus 84,302.85.

If you calculate the present value of the economic profit line using the cumulative cost of capital you produce the enterprise value. Rather than using a function, you divide the cash flow by the cumulative discount factor and then add the sum of the yearly figures to derive the valuation. If you subtract debt and minorities, you gain the equity value:

PV of total economic profit	(31,933.02)
Capital invested	41,450.00
PV terminal EP	
PV of change terminal capital	45,150.61
Enterprise value	54,667.59
Debt	(24,000.00)
Minorities	(47.00)
Equity value	30,620.59

SUMMARY

Adjusted present value tries to show the sources of value as separate streams while economic profit charges a cost for the use of capital to demonstrate the company's ability to earn more than its cost of capital. These are alternative valuation methods that fit in with the overall cash flow framework and add to the analysis on the basic discounted cash flow template.

Sensitivity

OUTLINE

The model now produces a single valuation that you can compare to the accounting value, market value or alternative methods such as adjusted present value or economic profit. On the other hand, the model considers the lenders' position since it computes the debt service coverage ratios and gearing. If covenants or thresholds were introduced you would find that you could increase the value by increasing the gearing but possibly breach the specimen banking covenants. Alternatively, you could improve the lenders' security by increasing the proportion of equity capital, although this would worsen returns to equity investors. The available cash flow to different classes of capital provider drives the model and the key factors that influence this are:

- equity valuation;
- debt proportion and gearing;
- required debt service coverage;
- cost of capital.

The model now allows you to change the capital, income statement and balance sheet variables to see their overall effect; however this process is slow and there is no facility to save the outcomes. A model should answer a management need for analysis and information. In particular, there are two key questions:

- What happens to the outcomes if variable A or B changes?
- Is variable A more important that B, C or D?

Framework

Figure 15.1

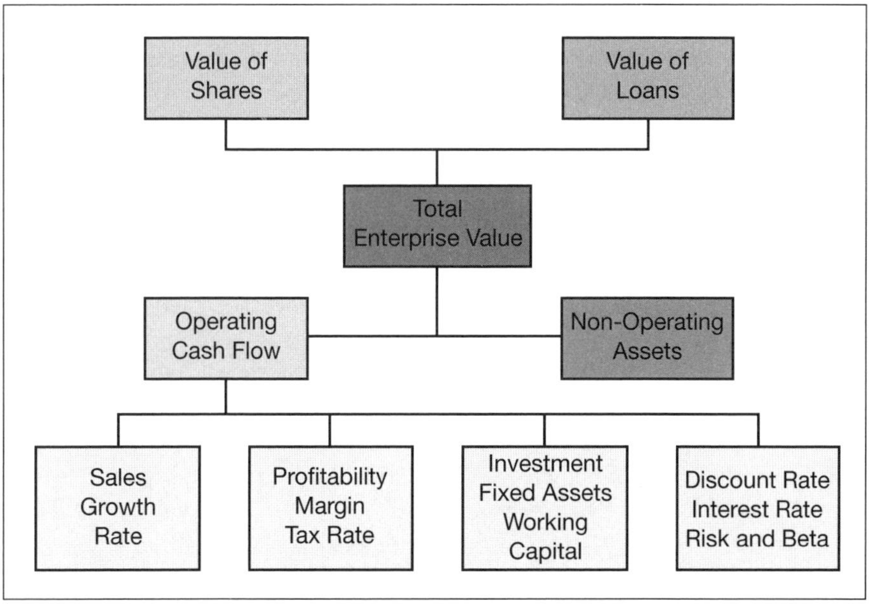

The framework shown in Figure 15.1 shows the elements that generate the enterprise value together with non-operating assets and adjustments. A company's accounting statements should be read with care, taking into consideration such issues as:

- lack of uniformity in the preparation of statements between countries;
- historical information/backward looking instead of forecast values;
- changes in external environment leading to future radical change in company prospects;
- a single estimate of balance sheet – in particular, where borrowing can be suppressed at the year and does not show the same pattern during the year;
- comparisons may be difficult due to geographical or sector differences;
- diversified organisations which buy and sell companies every year can be difficult to assess using trends;
- window dressing or creative accounting leading to enhanced revenue and profit and increased balance sheet capitalisation of cost;
- international accounting practice (GAAP) where presentation, method and interpretation can materially differ.

Nevertheless, the various factors in the forecast form a jigsaw (see Figure 15.2), where each factor exerts an influence on other elements.

The model in its current form does not tell us about risk or how likely the company is to meet the forecast cash flows. Risk is often used interchangeably with uncertainty; however, it usually means some of the following:

- chance of loss or gain since risk is symmetrical with up- and downsides;
- possibility of the occurrence of an undesirable contingency;
- uncertainty of the level of losses;
- possibility of loss due to uncontrollable circumstances;
- unknown hazards such as environmental changes;
- divergence of the actual outcome from expected results;
- condition with a high possibility of a loss.

In corporate finance, risk usually means the possibility of an occurrence of an undesirable contingency, or alternatively downside risk. You could also split risk into risk and uncertainty defined as follows:

- Risk that is measurable or probabilistic with expected outcomes.
- Uncertainty, defined as variability or the effect of chance and a function of the system, e.g. earthquakes or model risk, since models simplify the system, or generally a lack of knowledge about the complexity of the system.

Credit jigsaw

Figure 15.2

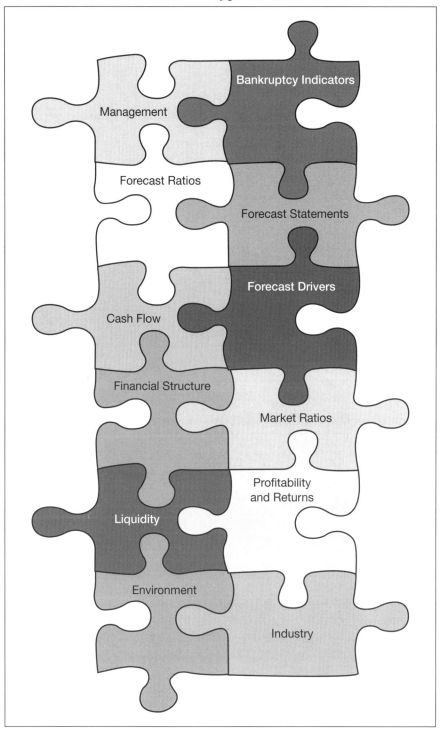

In addition, there are elements that are not easily modelled. For example, you input sales growth to a model, but in reality you are entering the management's ability to deliver future sales growth. Other examples include:

■ Commercial and legal relationships where reality may be different to the legal framework.

■ Economic circumstances and economic cycles.

■ Human behaviour where you assume that people are rational.

■ Natural events such as earthquakes.

■ Political circumstances such as a change in government.

■ Technological and technical issues leading to market-changing shifts in demand.

■ Management activities and controls.

■ Individual activities where managers may work more for themselves than for the company. This is the problem addressed by Agency Theory and moral hazard, where managers may sub-optimise in pursuit of their own agenda.

Figure 15.3   **Inter-linkages**

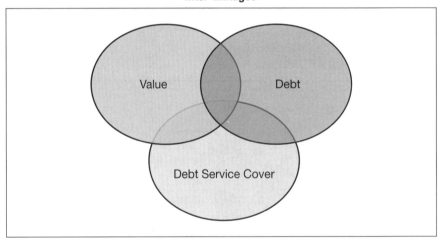

Therefore the model needs to produce more information since the answer is similar to the Venn diagram in Figure 15.3. As noted above, increasing value may lead to unacceptable levels of debt or breached coverage covenants so the model needs to find an acceptable position where all factors and covenants are satisfied. With more information and analysis, you could:

■ increase growth as the initial plan may be too cautious;

■ do nothing since the extra costs outweigh the potential benefits;

■ collect more data or run more tests to better understand the risk;

■ add a contingency and allow for potential downside risk;

■ reduce the forecast or increase the equity capital to adopt a less risky approach.

RETURNS

A further answer constitutes the internal rate that shareholders could yield on their investment if the company sells to a third party at the end of the forecast period. The investors accept the risks and uncertainty as in the financial analysis grid in Figure 15.4. You need to generate the initial investment, cash flows and terminal exit value for each of the investors and all investors.

Business risks

Figure 15.4

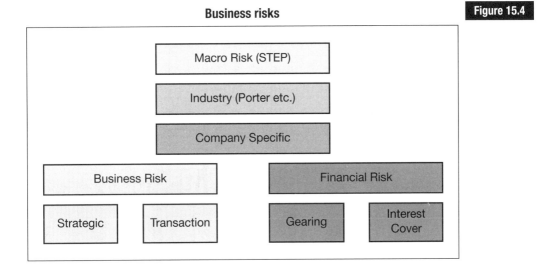

Copy another template landscape sheet and call it Returns. The dividends flow is available on the Forecast sheet to bring forward (see Figure 15.5).

Dividends flow

Figure 15.5

Line No	Label	Ref	6	7	8
Start			01-Jan-17	01-Jan-18	01-Jan-19
Finish			31-Dec-17	31-Dec-18	31-Dec-19
FP047	Profit from continuing	IP047	2,513.54	2,784.66	3,095.84
FP048					
FP049	Discontinued operations	IP049	–	–	–
FP050	Profit for the year	IP050	2,513.54	2,784.66	3,095.84
FP051					
FP052	Dividends	IP052	(754.06)	(835.40)	(928.75)
FP053	Minority interest	IP053	–	–	–
FP054					
FP055	Net profit	IP055	1,759.48	1,949.26	2,167.09

Returns

Figure 15.6

Equity allocation

Line No	Label	Ref	Investment	Percent
RE010	Exit Year:	31-Dec-26		
RE011	Start			
RE012	Finish			
RE013	Equity allocation		Investment	Percent
RE014	Senior debt A	IN015	12,000.0	41.9%
RE015	Senior debt B	IN016	5,000.0	17.5%
RE016	Junior debt C	IN017	2,500.0	8.7%
RE017	Junior debt D	IN018	2,000.0	7.0%
RE018	Junior debt E	IN019	2,000.0	7.0%
RE019	Other	IN020		
RE020	Preferred stock	IN021	500.0	1.7%
RE021	Outside equity	IN022	1,118.8	3.9%
RE022	Management equity A	IN023	3,000.0	10.5%
RE023	Management equity B	IN024	500.0	1.7%
RE024	Total initial equity		4,618.8	
RE025	Total overall investment		28,618.8	100.0%
RE026				
RE027	Final net proceeds to allocate	VA056	32,221.2	
RE028				
RE029	Allocation		%	Allocation
RE030				
RE031	Outside equity		24.2%	7,804.7
RE032	Management equity A		65.0%	20,928.5
RE033	Management equity B		10.8%	3,488.1
RE034	Totals		100.0%	32,221.2

Returns

	4	5	6	7	8	9	10	11	12	13	14	15
Start	01-Jan-15	01-Jan-16	01-Jan-17	01-Jan-18	01-Jan-19	01-Jan-20	01-Jan-21	01-Jan-22	01-Jan-23	01-Jan-24	01-Jan-25	01-Jan-26
Finish	31-Dec-15	31-Dec-16	31-Dec-17	31-Dec-18	31-Dec-19	31-Dec-20	31-Dec-21	31-Dec-22	31-Dec-23	31-Dec-24	31-Dec-25	31-Dec-26
Outside equity returns												
Investment	(1,118.8)											
Dividends			182.65	202.35	224.96	258.12	296.11	380.98	433.83	489.16	549.61	615.59
Participation												7,804.7
Cash	(1,118.8)		182.7	202.4	225.0	258.1	296.1	381.0	433.8	489.2	549.6	8,420.3
IRR	34.59%											
Management equity A returns												
Investment	(3,000.0)											
Dividends			489.78	542.61	603.25	692.15	794.02	1,021.60	1,163.34	1,311.69	1,473.78	1,650.72
Participation												20,928.5
Cash	(3,000.0)		489.8	542.6	603.2	692.1	794.0	1,021.6	1,163.3	1,311.7	1,473.8	22,579.2
IRR	34.59%											
Management equity B returns												
Investment	(500.0)											
Dividends			81.63	90.44	100.54	115.36	132.34	170.27	193.89	218.61	245.63	275.12
Participation												3,488.1
Cash	(500.0)		81.6	90.4	100.5	115.4	132.3	170.3	193.9	218.6	245.6	3,763.2
IRR	34.59%											
Equity returns												
Investment	(4,618.8)											
Dividends			754.1	835.4	928.8	1,065.6	1,222.5	1,572.8	1,791.1	2,019.5	2,269.0	2,541.4
Participation												32,221.2
Cash	(4,618.8)		754.1	835.4	928.8	1,065.6	1,222.5	1,572.8	1,791.1	2,019.5	2,269.0	34,762.6
IRR	34.59%											

You can work out the proportions as in the left-hand table in Figure 15.6 since the data inputs are on the Control sheet. You need to compute the proportions of all capital including debt and the percentages of equity capital.

The cash flow on the right-hand side of Figure 15.6 uses the equity capital for the outside equity, management equity and equity returns. You can then split the dividends in proportion to the total and similarly use the same method for the terminal value. The simplest function is an IRR function, but you could also use the XIRR function if you want to include dates as well as cash flows:

```
N35: =IF(N34<0,IRR(N34:X34,Workings!$K$27),0)
```

Workings!K27 is an input guess. Since the internal rate uses iterative mathematics to find the rate at which the net present value is zero, you often have to give the function a starting point to prevent it generating an error.

DATA MATRIX

Some people try to add sensitivity to their models as an afterthought by duplicating sheet and models or writing macros to enter data and print reports. The author prefers to use data tables or matrices as the basic sensitivity tool. These enable you to generate multiple answers dynamically without the need for macros.

As an example, you want to plot changes in the cost of capital against the terminal growth rate. As the cost of capital increases, value declines, whereas the opposite is true with the terminal growth rate. Set out a matrix on the Valuation sheet as in Figure 15.7 with a link in the left-hand corner to the equity value in line 56. You need specimen values for the WACC across and value for the terminal value growth down. The inputs for a table have to be on the same sheet so the table must reside on the sheet with the variables 'driving' the answer.

Data table

Figure 15.7

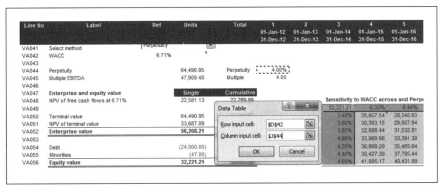

Figure 15.8

Two-way table

Line No	Label	Ref		Total	1	2	3	4	5	6	7	8	9	10
Start					01-Jan-12	01-Jan-13	01-Jan-14	01-Jan-15	01-Jan-16	01-Jan-17	01-Jan-18	01-Jan-19	01-Jan-20	01-Jan-21
Finish					31-Dec-12	31-Dec-13	31-Dec-14	31-Dec-15	31-Dec-16	31-Dec-17	31-Dec-18	31-Dec-19	31-Dec-20	31-Dec-21
VA039	Terminal value													
VA040														
VA041	Select method	Perpetuity												
VA042	WACC		6.71%											
VA043														
VA044	Perpetuity			64,490.95	Perpetuity	4.00%									
VA045	Multiple EBITDA			47,909.48	Multiple	4.00									
VA046														
VA047	Enterprise and equity value			Single	Cumulative									
VA048	NPV of free cash flows at 6.71%			22,581.13	22,289.99									
VA049														
VA050	Terminal value			64,490.95	64,490.95									
VA051	NPV of terminal value			33,687.09	32,377.60									
VA052	Enterprise value			56,268.21	54,667.59									
VA053														
VA054	Debt			(24,000.00)	(24,000.00)									
VA055	Minorities			(47.00)	(47.00)									
VA056	Equity value			32,221.21	30,620.59									

Formula:
= TABLE(D42,J44)

Sensitivity to WACC across and Perpetuity down

32,221.21	6.32%	6.44%	6.58%	6.71%	6.84%	6.98%	7.11%
3.40%	28,857.54	28,340.83	27,819.95	27,295.01	26,776.59	26,264.62	25,758.99
3.60%	30,393.15	29,857.94	29,318.45	28,774.77	28,237.88	27,707.68	27,184.07
3.80%	32,088.44	31,532.81	30,972.77	30,408.40	29,851.11	29,300.78	28,757.33
4.00%	33,969.66	33,391.39	32,808.54	32,221.21	31,641.28	31,068.63	30,503.15
4.20%	36,069.20	35,465.64	34,857.34	34,244.40	33,639.19	33,041.62	32,451.57
4.40%	38,427.39	37,795.44	37,158.54	36,516.83	35,883.24	35,257.68	34,640.02
4.60%	41,095.17	40,431.09	39,761.86	39,087.58	38,421.89	37,764.66	37,115.77

Highlight the whole grid and go to `Data, What-if Analysis, Data Table` to insert the function. The inputs are the WACC in the row and the terminal value growth rate in the column.

The completed table is shown in Figure 15.8. You can use conditional formatting to highlight the answer. The model now generates 49 outcomes showing you how the equity value changes with amendments to two key variables.

You cannot place the table on a sheet where the input variables are not present but you can look up the values from the table sheet on a separate report. You could copy a portrait template, call it Sensitivity and simply look up the values with simple formulas. The first grid repeats the table on the Valuation sheet but your next question is: by how much does that combination change? The first table calculates the monetary variance and the second table the percentage change (see Figure 15.9).

Sensitivity report

Figure 15.9

Select:	Perpetuity				Client: AAAAA : Rev 1-Jan-2012		
Tolerance	5.00%		Low	30,610.15	High		33,832.27

Units: USD Millions

Sensitivity to WACC across and Perpetuity down

32,221.21	6.32%	6.44%	6.58%	6.71%	6.84%	6.98%	7.11%
3.40%	28,857.54	28,340.83	27,819.95	27,295.01	26,776.59	26,264.62	25,758.99
3.60%	30,393.15	29,857.94	29,318.45	28,774.77	28,237.88	27,707.68	27,184.07
3.80%	32,088.44	31,532.81	30,972.77	30,408.40	29,851.11	29,300.78	28,757.33
4.00%	33,969.66	33,391.39	32,808.54	32,221.21	31,641.28	31,068.63	30,503.15
4.20%	36,069.20	35,465.64	34,857.34	34,244.40	33,639.19	33,041.62	32,451.57
4.40%	38,427.39	37,795.44	37,158.54	36,516.83	35,883.24	35,257.68	34,640.02
4.60%	41,095.17	40,431.09	39,761.86	39,087.58	38,421.89	37,764.66	37,115.77

Variance

	6.32%	6.44%	6.58%	6.71%	6.84%	6.98%	7.11%
3.40%	(3,363.67)	(3,880.39)	(4,401.26)	(4,926.21)	(5,444.62)	(5,956.59)	(6,462.22)
3.60%	(1,828.06)	(2,363.27)	(2,902.76)	(3,446.44)	(3,983.34)	(4,513.54)	(5,037.14)
3.80%	(132.78)	(688.40)	(1,248.44)	(1,812.81)	(2,370.11)	(2,920.43)	(3,463.88)
4.00%	1,748.45	1,170.17	587.32	-	(579.94)	(1,152.59)	(1,718.06)
4.20%	3,847.99	3,244.43	2,636.13	2,023.18	1,417.98	820.41	230.35
4.40%	6,206.18	5,574.22	4,937.33	4,295.61	3,662.03	3,036.46	2,418.80
4.60%	8,873.96	8,209.88	7,540.64	6,866.37	6,200.68	5,543.45	4,894.56

Percentage variance

	6.32%	6.44%	6.58%	6.71%	6.84%	6.98%	7.11%
3.40%	(10.4%)	(12.0%)	(13.7%)	(15.3%)	(16.9%)	(18.5%)	(20.1%)
3.60%	(5.7%)	(7.3%)	(9.0%)	(10.7%)	(12.4%)	(14.0%)	(15.6%)
3.80%	(0.4%)	(2.1%)	(3.9%)	(5.6%)	(7.4%)	(9.1%)	(10.8%)
4.00%	5.4%	3.6%	1.8%	-	(1.8%)	(3.6%)	(5.3%)
4.20%	11.9%	10.1%	8.2%	6.3%	4.4%	2.5%	0.7%
4.40%	19.3%	17.3%	15.3%	13.3%	11.4%	9.4%	7.5%
4.60%	27.5%	25.5%	23.4%	21.3%	19.2%	17.2%	15.2%

A chart of one of the options is also useful since it shows graphically the sensitivity to change. The chart in Figure 15.10 plots the 4 per cent line from the first grid and uses a chart template as discussed earlier.

Figure 15.10

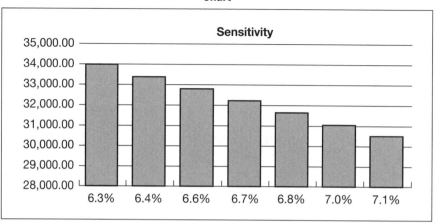

Chart

SCENARIO MANAGER

It is perhaps artificial to change up to two variables in isolation and Excel contains a scenario manager to allow you to 'remember' up to 32 input values so that you can reload them at a later stage. This removes the need to duplicate sheets and models. Each variable has a certain impact on the model outcome and a probability of occurrence. From a management point of view, you need to consider the items in the top right-hand corner of the matrix in Figure 15.11.

Figure 15.11 **Impact probability matrix**

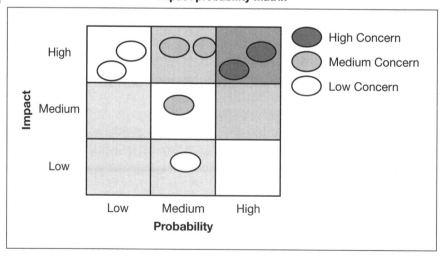

Scenarios belong to sheets so you need to access the Forecast sheet and save a scenario using Data, What-If Analysis, Scenario Manager. The example in Figure 15.12 uses sales growth, cost of goods sold and distribution costs together with the terminal growth rate and EBITDA multiple. You enter a range followed by a comma and then a new range with no comma at the end.

Inserting scenarios

Figure 15.12

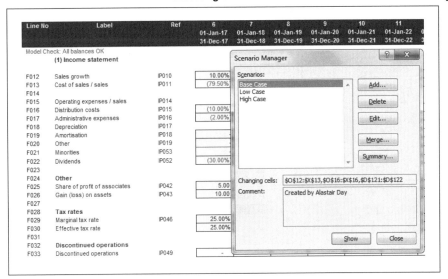

You can enter a number of scenarios and use it as an audit data trail. The values are saved in the model so you can always load them back in again using the dialog box. The scenario answers are control numbers since the model should continue to generate the same results. A change could indicate a model error or an unauthorised amendment to the code.

You might also want a report for presentation purposes and you can produce this with the Summary button in Figure 15.12. The dialog box for this option (see Figure 15.13) requests some answer cells which must be on the same sheet. The solution is to create a set of answers to the right of the schedule and bring forward the answers as below. The enterprise and equity values are on the Valuation sheet and the IRR on the Returns sheet.

Figure 15.13

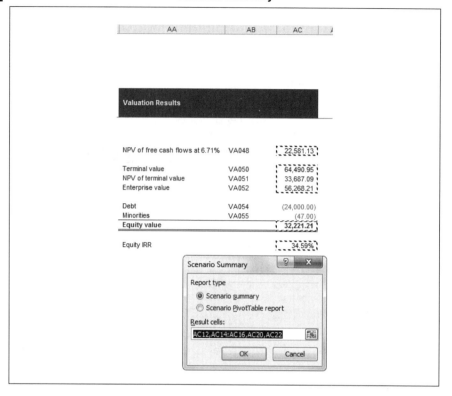

The Excel scenario report presents the inputs at the top in columnar format and the answers at the bottom (see Figure 15.14). If you name ranges, then the names are used rather than cell references, but you can always update the labels manually as shown.

MANUAL SCENARIOS

Excel scenarios are limited to 32 cells, and whilst this is satisfactory for small models, you may need to change more cells at a time. The solution involves setting up individual sheets to hold scenarios and then use a table method to gain a table of answers for all the scenarios. This is the procedure:

- Copy the Forecast sheet three times and rename them Base, Case_1 and Case_2.

- Type in a label and an input cell to hold the scenario name: Base, Low, High.

- Amend the values on the Low and High sheets using the same values as in the Scenario Manager example above, which changed the sales growth, cost of goods sold and distribution costs (see Figures 15.15 and 15.16).

Scenario report

Figure 15.14

Scenario Summary		Current Values:	Base Case	Low Case	High Case
Changing Cells:					
Sales	$O$12	10.00%	10.00%	9.00%	11.00%
	$P$12	10.00%	10.00%	9.00%	11.00%
	$Q$12	10.00%	10.00%	9.00%	11.00%
	$R$12	10.00%	10.00%	9.00%	11.00%
	$S$12	10.00%	10.00%	9.00%	11.00%
	$T$12	10.00%	10.00%	9.00%	11.00%
	$U$12	10.00%	10.00%	9.00%	11.00%
	$V$12	10.00%	10.00%	9.00%	11.00%
	$W$12	10.00%	10.00%	9.00%	11.00%
	$X$12	10.00%	10.00%	9.00%	11.00%
COGS	$O$13	(79.50%)	(79.50%)	(80.00%)	(79.00%)
	$P$13	(79.50%)	(79.50%)	(80.00%)	(79.00%)
	$Q$13	(79.50%)	(79.50%)	(80.00%)	(79.00%)
	$R$13	(79.50%)	(79.50%)	(80.00%)	(79.00%)
	$S$13	(79.50%)	(79.50%)	(80.00%)	(79.00%)
	$T$13	(79.50%)	(79.50%)	(80.00%)	(79.00%)
	$U$13	(79.50%)	(79.50%)	(80.00%)	(79.00%)
	$V$13	(79.50%)	(79.50%)	(80.00%)	(79.00%)
	$W$13	(79.50%)	(79.50%)	(80.00%)	(79.00%)
	$X$13	(79.50%)	(79.50%)	(80.00%)	(79.00%)
Distribution	$O$16	(10.00%)	(10.00%)	(10.00%)	(9.50%)
	$P$16	(10.00%)	(10.00%)	(10.00%)	(9.50%)
	$Q$16	(10.00%)	(10.00%)	(10.00%)	(9.50%)
	$R$16	(10.00%)	(10.00%)	(10.00%)	(9.50%)
	$S$16	(10.00%)	(10.00%)	(10.00%)	(9.50%)
	$T$16	(10.00%)	(10.00%)	(10.00%)	(9.50%)
	$U$16	(10.00%)	(10.00%)	(10.00%)	(9.50%)
	$V$16	(10.00%)	(10.00%)	(10.00%)	(9.50%)
	$W$16	(10.00%)	(10.00%)	(10.00%)	(9.50%)
	$X$16	(10.00%)	(10.00%)	(10.00%)	(9.50%)
	$D$121	4.0%	4.0%	4.0%	4.0%
	$D$122	4.0x	4.0x	4.0x	4.0x
Result Cells:					
	NPV of free cash flows at 6.71%	22,581.13	22,581.13	21,507.03	24,671.42
	Terminal value	64,490.95	64,490.95	55,323.21	79,746.95
	NPV of terminal value	33,687.09	33,687.09	28,898.28	41,656.11
	Enterprise value	56,268.21	56,268.21	50,405.31	66,327.53
	Equity value	32,221.21	32,221.21	26,358.31	42,280.53
	Equity IRR	34.59%	34.59%	31.20%	39.61%

Scenario sheet – low

Figure 15.15

| Line No | Label | Ref | | | 6 | 7 | 8 |
| Start | | | | | 01-Jan-17 | 01-Jan-18 | 01-Jan-19 |
Finish					31-Dec-17	31-Dec-18	31-Dec-19
	(1) Income statement		Name	Low			
F012	Sales growth	IP010	USD Millions		9.00%	9.00%	9.00%
F013	Cost of sales / sales	IP011			(80.00%)	(80.00%)	(80.00%)
F014							
F015	Operating expenses / sal	IP014					
F016	Distribution costs	IP015			(10.00%)	(10.00%)	(10.00%)
F017	Administrative expenses	IP016			(2.00%)	(2.00%)	(2.00%)

Figure 15.16

Scenario sheet – high

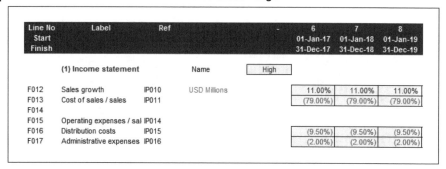

Enter a label on the original forecast sheet and validate it with `Data,`
`Validation` so that it can only accept integer values between 1 and 3 (see
Figure 15.17). You cannot use 4 since there are only three scenario sheets.

■ Name the cell ScenarioNo by overwriting the cell reference in the Name
box in the top-left corner of the screen.

■ Amend all the input cells on the Forecast sheet to ensure that they lookup
a value based on the scenario number. A CHOOSE function is simplest:

```
O12:  =CHOOSE(ScenarioNo,Base!O12,Case_1!O12,Case_
2!O12)
```

Figure 15.17

Data validation

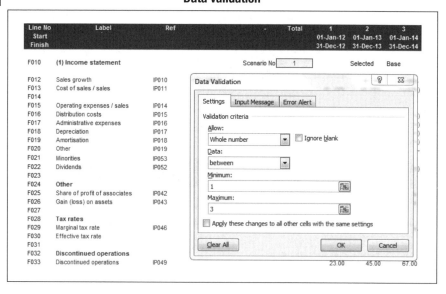

This now means that you can redirect the model at each of the three scenarios simply by changing the value of the ScenarioNo cell. Since this is a pivotal cell, you can generate a data table based on changing this value. Add another section to the Forecast sheet and type 1, 2 and 3 across the top. Down the left-hand side bring forward the label from the Valuation, Returns and Ratio sheets. In this table, you want to know about each of the answers as the model varies the ScenarioNo cell automatically. Again, highlight the whole table and go to `Data, What-if Analysis, Data Table` and generate the table with only a row input as the ScenarioNo cell. You should see a result similar to the table in Figure 15.18 providing the information on how the model flexes with each set of entries. The values are the same as the Excel Scenario Manager.

The completed table brings together information about value, gearing, returns and debt service cover. Whereas the Excel Scenario Manager is static and values only, this method is dynamic since any changes you make to the individual scenario sheets are immediately reflected in the output table.

Scenario report

Figure 15.18

			Current	1	2	3
F129	(4) Scenario Summary					
F130	The results of the Base, High and Low Sheets					
F131			Current	1	2	3
F132	Case Name	F010	High	Base	High	Low
F133	NPV of free cash flows at 6.71%	VA047	24,671.4	22,581.1	24,671.4	21,507.0
F134	Terminal value	VA049	79,746.9	64,490.9	79,746.9	55,323.2
F135	NPV of terminal value	VA050	41,656.1	33,687.1	41,656.1	28,898.3
F136	Enterprise value	VA051	66,327.5	56,268.2	66,327.5	50,405.3
F137	Debt	VA053	(24,000.0)	(24,000.0)	(24,000.0)	(24,000.0)
F138	Minorities	VA054	(47.0)	(47.0)	(47.0)	(47.0)
F139	Equity value	VA055	42,280.5	32,221.2	42,280.5	26,358.3
F140	IRR	RE034	39.61%	34.59%	39.61%	31.20%
F141	Gross gearing (%)	Max RT039	293.98%	313.61%	293.98%	324.82%
F142	Net gearing (%)	Max RT040	293.98%	313.61%	293.98%	324.82%
F143	EBITDA / senior Interest	Min RT060	7.25x	6.43x	7.25x	6.00x
F144	EBITDA / total Interest	Min RT072	1.53x	1.36x	1.53x	1.26x

A chart is also useful and the example in Figure 15.19 plots the enterprise and equity value on the primary axis and the debt service covers on the secondary axis.

Figure 15.19

Chart report

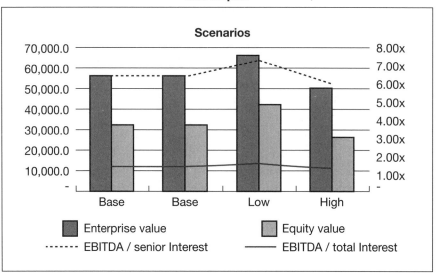

SUMMARY

The chapter introduces three methods for generating multiple results since a model with a single-point answer is not sufficient for management purposes. You need to understand how a model 'flexes' and the combination of scenarios, tables and manual scenarios provides a framework for further analysis.

Optimisation

OUTLINE

The case model provides information about valuation and debt servicing using the sensitivity methods but does not illustrate how (or whether) the amounts are 'enough' to satisfy the competing demands of returns and debt covers. The model needs to have some targets and to include some degree of optimisation as a means of checking the outcomes. You should always be looking at the flexibility of the model and seeing if it is possible to gain more management information. The model currently uses:

■ inputs–calculations–outputs information flow as a basic model design;

■ data tables or matrices;

■ a built-in Scenario Manager.

Since the model has been developed using best practice principles, it should be straightforward to add more techniques. The two optimisation techniques that we will look at here are Goal Seek and Solver, which allow you to change one cell and multiple cells respectively and target specific outcomes.

You have an answer in the model but you now want to test the result to check if it is the 'best' result in satisfying the competing demands of the shareholders and lenders. This is 'what-if' in reverse since you want to work backwards through the model from the answer to the inputs. This will answer questions such as:

■ What share price is required for the equity value to increase to XX?

■ Will changing the debt mix within certain bounds enhance the shareholder value?

■ What is the optimum debt to equity mix?

You could enter combinations yourself but this will quickly become tedious and difficult, especially if you have multiple inputs and several scenarios. Goal Seek and Solver take your model and work backwards through it from output to input (see Figure 16.1). The methods that they use are listed below.

Goal Seek (Data, What-if Analysis, Goal Seek):

■ Make X, Y by changing Z (i.e. target an answer by changing an input cell).

■ For single-cell problems only.

■ No constraints or rules are allowed.

Solver uses multiple variables (Data, Analysis, Solver):

■ X – target minimum, maximum or a value in a specific output cell.

■ Allows you to change multiple cells or ranges of cells.

■ Allows you to add constraints, e.g. sales growth < 10%.

Figure 16.1   **Information flow**

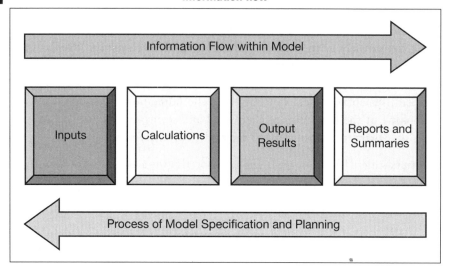

GOAL SEEK

Goal Seek allows you to undertake a quick 'what-if' analysis by allowing Excel to change one input cell only. You cannot enter any rules or provide any constraints in this simple targeting. Goal Seek will simply try to find a mathematical solution that works within a number of iterations.

The changing cells and answers have to be on the same sheet so you should amend the Control sheet by entering some required targets and answers below the main inputs, as in Figure 16.2.

Figure 16.2   **Answer box**

A	B	C	D	E	F	G	H
33							
34	IN034	Results					
35	IN035	Initial equity valuation	IN019			11,550.00	
36	IN036	FCFF valuation	VA056			32,221.21	
37	IN037	Sponsor X mgt equity	IN022/IN023			37.29%	
38	IN038	Ratio entry exit multiplier	IN036/IN035			2.79	
39	IN039	Equity IRR	RE035		40.00%	34.59%	-
40	IN040	Firm IRR	VA027		16.50%	16.20%	-
41	IN041	Purchase EV/EBITDA	IN026/IP022–IP017–IP018		7.00	6.50x	1
42	IN042	Max senior debt/EBITDA	Max RT050		2.60	2.70x	-
43	IN043	Exit EV/EBITDA	VA049/IP022–IP017–IP018		5.00	7.37x	1
44	IN044	Max total debt/EBITDA	Max RT050		4.00	3.50x	1
45	IN045						
46	IN046	Number of tests satisfied					3 Tests
47	IN047						
48	IN048	Number of tests		6 Tests			
49	IN049						
50	IN050	Result: Model fails minimum conditions					

Figure 16.2 shows the sources of the answers on the Control, Valuation and Ratios sheets. The input cells in row F are target outputs and the code in row H decides whether the output meets the target by means of a binary one and zero:

```
H39:  =IF(G39>=F39,cstOne,cstZero)
```

With gearing you are seeking a lower borrowing percentage and you would reverse the sign in the formula above. You can use the function COUNTIF to check how many of the available tests are satisfied:

```
E48:  =COUNTIF(F39:F44,"<>0")
```

You may want to find out the share price needed to reach a specific output equity valuation. Whilst you could enter values randomly in the share price input cell, it is more efficient to use Goal Seek. The problem needs to be expressed in Goal Seek vocabulary (see Figure 16.3) as:

```
X: G36
Y: 32,500
Changing Z: E14
```

Goal Seek inputs

Figure 16.3

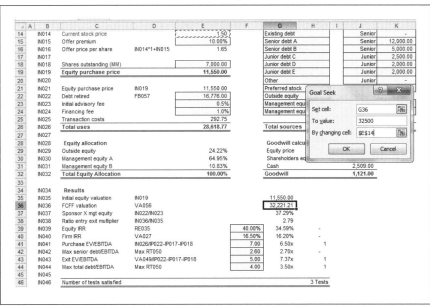

Notice that you cannot enter any rules and that the target must be a hard-coded cell. If you want to make the process easier, record a macro using `Developer`, `Code`, `Record Macro` and link it to a button. Goal Seek will record a single line of code, such as:

```
Range("G36").GoalSeek Goal:=32500,
ChangingCell:=Range("E14")
```

If you format and name a target cell as a range, you can amend the code as follows and assign it to an object or button:

```
Range("G36").GoalSeek Goal:=Range("GSTarget"),
ChangingCell:=Range("E14")
```

Goal Seek sometimes does not produce a solution and you should then examine your model for breaks in the line of calculations, such as mixed formulas (e.g. C6/12) or hard-coded cells. Alternatively, you can access `Options`, `Formulas` and check the iteration settings as these also control Goal Seek calculations (see Figure 16.4).

Figure 16.4   **Iteration settings**

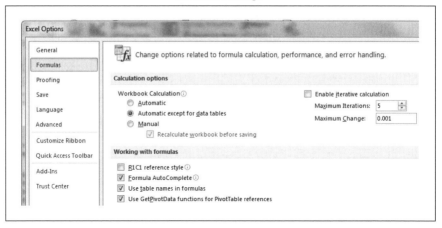

Using Goal Seek you can review individual answers and find the input value that generates the desired output value. You can overcome the need to enter all the values every time you use it by recording a macro or copying the code above. While useful, there are limitations with this approach since it does not allow you to optimise the ouput cell by changing multiple input cells. If the problem requires changes to multiple cells, therefore, you will need to use Solver.

SOLVER

Solver is an add-in to Excel which should be visible under `Data, Analysis, Solver` on the right-hand side of the ribbon (Figure 16.5). If it is not visible, go to `File, Options, Add-Ins` and tick the box to force it to open. If it is still not visible you may need to check your Office installation and install it with your Office disk.

Add-ins

Figure 16.5

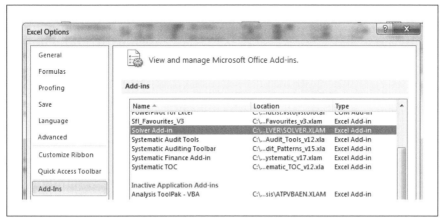

As the problem needs to be expressed in Solver language, before opening Solver it is usually a good idea to think about what you are trying to find out or write down the problem. It is easy to solve the wrong problem or not be clear about the rules. The elements are:

■ Inputs – the model follows best practice and all are clearly marked in blue.

■ Decision variables – the variables which Solver will change in order to produce the desired result in the target cell.

■ Objective function or target cell – the quantity you want to maximise, minimise or set at a particular value.

■ Constraints – the rules that you want the model to follow. For example, senior debt is between 12,000 and 20,000.

A blank Solver dialog box is shown in Figure 16.6.

Figure 16.6
Solver dialog box

In this example, you want to know the debt and equity mix that would produce an equity valuation of 33,000 and if it is possible within the constraints. As there may be many solutions to this problem it is up to you to define the exact model rules. Excel will not continue to optimise unless you tell it to keep trying by refining the rules. It will simply find a set of inputs that create the desired output within the rules and then stop.

Rather than typing the rules into the Solver dialog box, it is a good idea to create a workings area on the sheet so that you can see the inputs and modify them quickly (see Figure 16.7).

Figure 16.7
Solver inputs

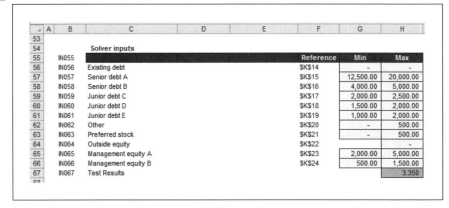

					Reference	Min	Max
54		Solver inputs					
55	IN055				Reference	Min	Max
56	IN056	Existing debt			$K$14	-	-
57	IN057	Senior debt A			$K$15	12,500.00	20,000.00
58	IN058	Senior debt B			$K$16	4,000.00	5,000.00
59	IN059	Junior debt C			$K$17	2,000.00	2,500.00
60	IN060	Junior debt D			$K$18	1,500.00	2,000.00
61	IN061	Junior debt E			$K$19	1,000.00	2,000.00
62	IN062	Other			$K$20	-	500.00
63	IN063	Preferred stock			$K$21	-	500.00
64	IN064	Outside equity			$K$22		-
65	IN065	Management equity A			$K$23	2,000.00	5,000.00
66	IN066	Management equity B			$K$24	500.00	1,500.00
67	IN067	Test Results					3.350

You want to target an equity value of 32,500 and check the mix using the limits shown in Figure 16.7. You can enter this data into the Solver dialog box (see Figure 16.8). Click the `Solve` button to run the routine. The routine sets up the problem and will generate a series of iterations until it reaches a feasible solution (see Figure 16.9). If the routine continues running beyond about 90 seconds, an interim box will open asking you if you want to continue. If you have constrained the problem too much or have made an error in the assumptions, such as mixing up maximums and minimums, Solver will generate a 'no feasible solution' error and give you the option to roll back to the original figures.

Solver inputs

Figure 16.8

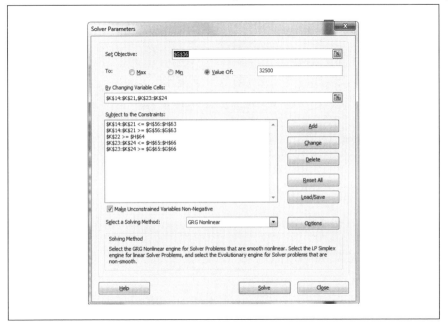

Solver results

Figure 16.9

Figure 16.10

Solver answer report

	A	B	C	D	E	F	G
1		Microsoft Excel 14.0 Answer Report					
2		Worksheet: [MCFM_16a.xls]Control					
3		Result: Solver found a solution. All Constraints and optimality conditions are satisfied.					
4		Solver Engine					
5		Engine: GRG Nonlinear					
6		Solution Time: 66.222 Seconds.					
7		Iterations: 2 Subproblems: 0					
8		Solver Options					
9		Max Time Unlimited, Iterations Unlimited, Precision 0.000001, Use Automatic Scaling					
10		Convergence 0.0001, Population Size 100, Random Seed 0, Derivatives Forward, Require Bounds					
11		Max Subproblems Unlimited, Max Integer Sols Unlimited, Integer Tolerance 1%, Assume NonNegative					
12							
13		Objective Cell (Value Of)					
14		Cell	Name	Original Value	Final Value		
15		$G$36	VA056 Goodwill	32,221.21	32,500.00		
16							
17							
18		Variable Cells					
19		Cell	Name	Original Value	Final Value	Integer	
20		$K$14	Existing debt	-	-	Contin	
21		$K$15	Senior debt A	12,000.00	12,500.00	Contin	
22		$K$16	Senior debt B	5,000.00	4,184.72	Contin	
23		$K$17	Junior debt C	2,500.00	2,244.77	Contin	
24		$K$18	Junior debt D	2,000.00	1,828.43	Contin	
25		$K$19	Junior debt E	2,000.00	1,706.86	Contin	
26		$K$20	Other	-	-	Contin	
27		$K$21	Preferred stock	500.00	487.40	Contin	
28		$K$23	Management equity A	3,000.00	3,000.00	Contin	
29		$K$24	Management equity B	500.00	500.13	Contin	
30							

Figure 16.11

Constraints

	A	B	C	D	E	F	G
31							
32		Constraints					
33		Cell	Name	Cell Value	Formula	Status	Slack
34		$K$22	Outside equity	2,156.10	$K$22>=$H$64	Not Binding	2,156.10
35		$G$36	VA056 Goodwill	32,500.00	$G$36=32500	Binding	0
36		$K$14	Existing debt	-	$K$14<=$H$56	Binding	0
37		$K$15	Senior debt A	12,500.00	$K$15<=$H$57	Not Binding	7500
38		$K$16	Senior debt B	4,184.72	$K$16<=$H$58	Not Binding	815.2770168
39		$K$17	Junior debt C	2,244.77	$K$17<=$H$59	Not Binding	255.2314768
40		$K$18	Junior debt D	1,828.43	$K$18<=$H$60	Not Binding	171.5741438
41		$K$19	Junior debt E	1,706.86	$K$19<=$H$61	Not Binding	293.1385246
42		$K$20	Other	-	$K$20<=$H$62	Not Binding	500
43		$K$21	Preferred stock	487.40	$K$21<=$H$63	Not Binding	12.60142795
44		$K$14	Existing debt	-	$K$14>=$G$56	Binding	-
45		$K$15	Senior debt A	12,500.00	$K$15>=$G$57	Binding	-
46		$K$16	Senior debt B	4,184.72	$K$16>=$G$58	Not Binding	184.72
47		$K$17	Junior debt C	2,244.77	$K$17>=$G$59	Not Binding	244.77
48		$K$18	Junior debt D	1,828.43	$K$18>=$G$60	Not Binding	328.43
49		$K$19	Junior debt E	1,706.86	$K$19>=$G$61	Not Binding	706.86
50		$K$20	Other	-	$K$20>=$G$62	Binding	-
51		$K$21	Preferred stock	487.40	$K$21>=$G$63	Not Binding	487.40
52		$K$23	Management equity A	3,000.00	$K$23<=$H$65	Not Binding	2000
53		$K$24	Management equity B	500.13	$K$24<=$H$66	Not Binding	999.8677274
54		$K$23	Management equity A	3,000.00	$K$23>=$G$65	Not Binding	1,000.00
55		$K$24	Management equity B	500.13	$K$24>=$G$66	Not Binding	0.13

The Solver report details the starting and finishing positions (see Figure 16.10). Binding means that all the constraints have been used and not binding means that some is left and Solver will display the balance (see Figure 16.11).

Once you have managed to find a feasible solution, you can then add more rules or change the constraints. With the maximum and minimum values on the sheet it is straightforward to change the values, open the dialog box, and click `Solve` again.

CODING SOLVER

You can use the code Solver in the same way as Goal Seek. You would need to record the macro as you enter each of the stages:

- First reset Solver using the button on the dialog box.
- Enter the target, changing cells and each of the rules.
- Click `Solve`.
- Stop the macro recording.
- Assign the macro to a button or object using `Developer, Insert, Button`.

You need to add two stages to make the macro work successfully:

- Name the target cell as in the code specimen below, e.g. Target = Range("GSTarget"), and replace the hard-coded target values with the Visual Basic name 'Target'.
- Set Solver as a reference in `Tools, References` in Visual Basic (see Figure 16.12).

Solver reference

Figure 16.12

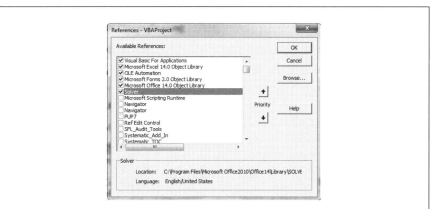

The completed code follows the same sequence as the manual Solver input:

```
Sub Solver_Inputs()
'
' Solver_Inputs Macro
    Target = Range("GSTarget")
    Sheets("Control").Select
    SolverReset
    SolverOk SetCell:="$G$36", MaxMinVal:=3,
ValueOf:=Target, ByChange:="$K$14:$K$21,$K$23:
$K$24"
    SolverAdd CellRef:="$K$14:$K$21", Relation:=1,
FormulaText:="$H$56:$H$63"
    SolverAdd CellRef:="$K$14:$K$21", Relation:=3,
FormulaText:="$G$56:$G$63"
    SolverAdd CellRef:="$K$23:$K$24", Relation:=1,
FormulaText:="$H$65:$H$66"
    SolverAdd CellRef:="$K$23:$K$24", Relation:=3,
FormulaText:="$G$65:$G$66"
    SolverAdd CellRef:="$K$22", Relation:=3,
FormulaText:="$H$64"
    SolverOk SetCell:="$G$36", MaxMinVal:=3,
ValueOf:=Target, ByChange:="$K$14:$K$21,$K$23:
$K$24"
    SolverSolve
End Sub
```

Test the macro by entering an amended NPV and pressing the button. Provided that you have not constrained the model too much, the model should reach a solution. You can of course save all of the runs as scenarios to allow you to reload them at a later stage without running Solver or Goal Seek.

SUMMARY

Goal Seek and Solver allow you to structure the model to target and optimise specific outputs by changing input cells. This is only possible if you are certain that you have a direct link from inputs through calculations to outputs. Solver is usually more useful since most problems entail the flexing of multiple cells with real-world rules and constraints. The method depends on having a well-written model and it acts as a further layer on the basic model for gaining more management information.

Reporting

REPORTING

Each chapter has increased the number of sheets in the model starting with the initial accounts and adding the forecast, debt servicing, valuation and sensitivity. You now need to communicate the answers to different types of audiences. One common error is to print the entire contents of the workbook like a 1980s computer report. Somebody is unlikely to want to read a 50 page workbook and so they need concise reports which summarise the key findings. You need to extract the main conclusions in summaries, dashboards, charts and reports. Different users need varying levels of detail and the model should report to each category of user. Exposure to peer group review could reveal further ideas for restructuring or redefinition of the required outcomes and analysis and provide useful model checking.

EXECUTIVE SUMMARY

Executive summaries should bring together information from the different sheets rather than performing new tasks and calculations. This is easier when you are auditing a model since you can disregard these sheets from the information process. A 'one sheet' summary approach is useful to try to place all the information you need on one sheet. The suggested categories are:

- initial shares and debt;
- input and exit multiples;
- goodwill calculation;
- results;
- sensitivity tables of three scenarios.

This means that users will be able to see at a glance how the initial debt is structured together with the debt equity mix leading to the results box. Using the manual scenarios approach detailed in Chapter 15, the tables are also advantageous for viewing three scenarios simultaneously.

Copy a template sheet and size it accordingly in landscape mode. You can then start to bring forward all the information using the sheet references below. Use the systematic built-in styles to format the cells quickly.

You can also produce quick in-cell charts using the REPT function (see Figures 17.1–17.3). This repeats a character a number of times, as in the sources table below which uses a capital 'I'. You could also use conditional formatting to emphasise differences of value. The result is a simple chart in the worksheet cells (see Figure 17.4).

```
Cell M8: =REPT("I",L8*50)
```

Figure 17.1

Source and uses of funds

	Uses of Funds	Ref		Sources of Funds	Ref	Rate	%	Chart
SM-05								
SM-06								
SM-07	Current Stock Price	IN014	1.50	Existing debt	F100.IN014	5.00%	-	-
SM-08	Offer Premium	IN015	10.00%	Senior debt A	F101.IN015	4.50%	12,000.00	41.93%
SM-09	Offer Price Per Share	IN016	1.65	Senior debt B	F102.IN016	5.00%	5,000.00	17.47%
SM-10				Junior debt C	F103.IN017	6.00%	2,500.00	8.74%
SM-11	Shares Outstanding (MM)	IN018	7,000.00	Junior debt D	F104.IN018	6.25%	2,000.00	6.99%
SM-12	Equity Purchase Price		11,550.00	Junior debt E	F105.IN019	6.50%	2,000.00	6.99%
SM-13				Other	F106.IN020	6.75%	-	-
SM-14	Debt Retired	IN022	16,776.00	Preferred stock	F107.IN021	5.00%	500.00	1.75%
SM-15	Transaction Costs	IN025	292.75	Outside equity	IN022		1,118.77	3.91%
SM-16				Management equity A	IN023		3,000.00	10.48%
SM-17				Management equity B	IN024		500.00	1.75%
SM-18								
SM-19	Total Uses	Sum	28,618.75	Total Sources	Sum		28,618.77	100.00%
SM-20								
SM-21	Acquisition and Exit Multiples			Equity Allocation			%	Chart
SM-22								
SM-23	EBITDA	IP022-IP017-IP018	4,370.00	Preferred stock	SM-14/SM-14.SM-17		9.77%	
SM-24	Multiple	SM-19/SM-23	6.5x	Outside equity	SM-15/SM-14.SM-17		21.86%	
SM-25	Exit Year	IN007+IN011	31-Dec-26	Management equity A	SM-16/SM-14.SM-17		58.61%	
SM-26	Exit EBITDA Multiple	F122	4.0x	Management equity B	SM-17/SM-14.SM-17		9.77%	
SM-27	Exit Book Multiple	VA056/FB068	0.9x					
SM-28				Total Equity Allocation			100.00%	

Figure 17.2

Results

Results	Ref	Result	Target	Pass/Fail
Initial equity valuation	IN019	11,550.00		
FCFF valuation	IN036	42,280.53		
Sponsor X mgt equity	IN037	37.29%		
Ratio entry exit multiplier	IN038	3.7x		
Equity IRR	IN039	39.61%	40.00%	No
Firm IRR	IN040	18.54%	16.50%	Yes
Purchase EV/EBITDA	IN041	6.5x	7.0x	Yes
Max senior debt/EBITDA	IN042	2.4x	2.6x	Yes
Exit EV/EBITDA	IN043	9.7x	5.0x	Yes
Max total debt/EBITDA	IN044	3.5x	4.0x	Yes

Result: Model fails minimum conditions

Goodwill Calculation				
Equity price	IN029	11,550.00		
Shareholders equity	IN030	(12,938.00)		
Cash	IN031	2,509.00		
Goodwill	IN032	1,121.00		

Figure 17.3

Data table results

	Results		Current	1	2	3
SM-30						
SM-31						
SM-32	Case Name	F132	High	Base	High	Low
SM-33	NPV of free cash flows at 6.71%	F133	24,671.4	22,581.1	24,671.4	21,507.0
SM-34	Terminal value	F134	79,746.9	64,490.9	79,746.9	55,323.2
SM-35	NPV of terminal value	F135	41,656.1	33,687.1	41,656.1	28,898.3
SM-36	Enterprise value	F136	66,327.5	56,268.2	66,327.5	50,405.3
SM-37	Debt	F137	(24,000.0)	(24,000.0)	(24,000.0)	(24,000.0)
SM-38	Minorities	F138	(47.0)	(47.0)	(47.0)	(47.0)
SM-39	Equity value	F139	42,280.5	32,221.2	42,280.5	26,358.3
SM-40	IRR	F140	39.61%	34.59%	39.61%	31.20%
SM-41	Gross gearing (%)	F141	293.98%	313.61%	293.98%	324.82%
SM-42	Net gearing (%)	F142	293.98%	313.61%	293.98%	324.82%
SM-43	EBITDA / senior Interest	F143	7.25x	6.43x	7.25x	6.00x
SM-44	EBITDA / total Interest	F144	1.53x	1.36x	1.53x	1.26x

Chart

Figure 17.4

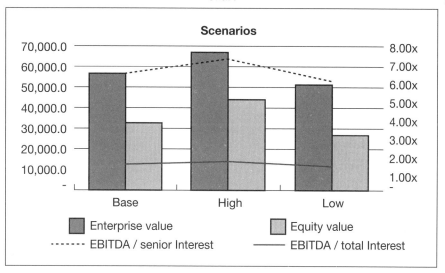

DASHBOARD

Models often include pages of individual charts; however, it can be better to produce a page of small charts or format them as a dashboard. You do not need large charts to understand the trends or relationships between variables and a single page of reports represents a quick way of understanding the key indicators. When you have produced a sheet of charts this can act as a template for use in future models. It is usually possible to place around 12 small charts on an A4 sheet of paper.

Copy a portrait sheet to bring forward the data and call it Chart_Nos (see Figure 17.5).

Chart data

Figure 17.5

		Jan-12 12	Jan-13 13	Jan-14 14	Jan-15 15	Jan-16 16	Ref
1	Total Sales	33,974.0	39,454.0	42,641.0	47,298.0	54,327.0	FP010
2	NOP / Sales (%)	5.7	5.8	6.2	5.9	5.9	RT020
3	Return on Equity	15.6	18.3	18.9	18.9	44.5	RT014
4	Return on Sales	4.1	4.3	4.6	4.7	4.2	RT011
5	Asset Turnover	1.7	1.7	1.7	1.6	1.3	RT012
6	Asset Leverage	2.3	2.4	2.4	2.6	7.9	RT013
7	Current Ratio	56.9	49.7	51.1	58.4	42.0	RT036
8	Gearing (%)	55.6	76.4	59.2	75.1	459.1	RT039
9	EBITDA / Sales	7.9	7.8	8.2	7.9	8.0	RT054
10	EBITDA/ Total Interest	-	0.1	0.1	0.1	0.1	RT055
11	Market to book	1.4	1.3	1.2	1.0	2.1	RT099
12	EV/EBITDA	7.8	7.6	6.5	6.8	7.9	RT100
13	Cash from Operations	-	2,340.0	2,771.0	3,401.0	3,725.0	RT038
14	Cash before Financing	-	(154.0)	262.0	(804.0)	(8,428.8)	CF038+CF054

This is the chosen data for the charts and the list on the right of Figure 17.5 shows the source of the data. The dashboard attempts to show key indicators of returns, gearing and debt cover on a single sheet:

(1) Total Sales

(2) NOP (net operating profit)/Sales (%)

(3) Return on Equity

(4) Return on Sales

(5) Asset Turnover

(6) Asset Leverage

(7) Current Ratio

(8) Gearing (%)

(9) EBITDA/Sales

(10) EBITDA/Total Interest

(11) Operating Cash/Interest Paid

(12) EV/EBITDA

(13) Cash from Operations

(14) Cash before Financing

You could introduce a choice into the model by selecting historic or forecast data. Name a cell ReportOption and validate it as an integer to accept either one or two:

```
Cell D8: =CHOOSE(ReportOption,Forecast_
Income!J10,Forecast_Income!O10)
```

If you want to be able to use the table on another sheet without having to format the cells, the only solution is to use the Camera tool. This is not available on the usual Excel ribbon and you have to find it in Excel, Options. Go to `File, Excel Options, Quick Access Toolbar` and choose `All Commands`. The commands are in alphabetical order. Find `Camera` and drag it across to the Quick Access Toolbar.

Copy another portrait template and call it Charts_Dashboard. Size the columns so that E, H and K are narrow. The other columns will have charts. You can select the table area on the Chart_Nos sheet and then paste the object onto this sheet using the Camera tools. This pastes an updating text box which can be sized and not interfere with the underlying cell structure. This is also useful for placing tables directly on charts.

Insert the first chart with the chart wizard using the top numbers as the x series and the data as the y series. In the example in Figure 17.6, the title is formatted cells rather than part of the chart. Size the chart to the cells using the gridlines on the sheet (see Figures 17.7 and 17.8 on pages 238 and 239).

Sheet column widths

Figure 17.6

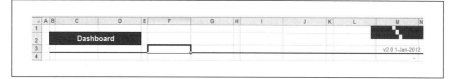

You can save the chart template in `Chart Tools, Type, Save as Template`. This creates a 'ctrx' file in a sub-directory to your nominated templates directory. You can then copy the chart several times and change the data to make up a sheet of charts. This is useful for this model but will also serve as a template.

DYNAMIC CHARTS

Dashboard charts provide much information on one sheet but there are times when you want to review individual lines. Dynamic charts can be useful here for three reasons:

- checking the forecast and trends to make sure they are 'sensible and achievable';
- auditing since unusual chart lines could indicate errors;
- data analysis.

You need to copy a landscape template with a timeline and insert around a hundred lines to accept the data down to row 130. Call the sheet Analysis. The sheet needs to have plenty of rows to accept any sheet data. As you want to be able to plot any line on any sheet, two lookups are needed: the sheet and the line number on the sheet.

Go to `Developer, Insert Form Controls, Combo Box` and insert two combo boxes on the sheet (see Figure 17.9 on page 240). The first will select the sheet and the second a line number in the data. You need a listing of sheets and the simplest location for this is on the Workings sheet (see Figure 17.10 on page 240).

Figure 17.7

Charts 1

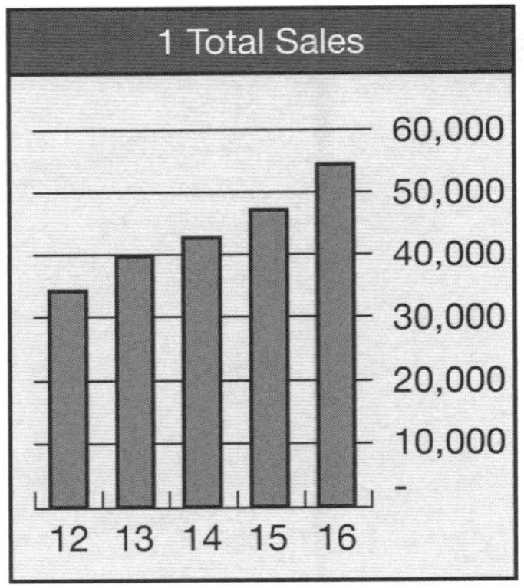

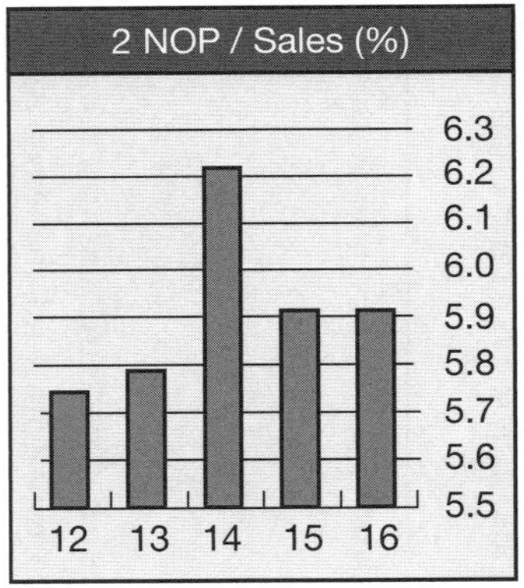

	12	13	14	15	16
Total Sales	33,974.0	39,454.0	42,641.0	47,298.0	54,327.0
NOP/Sales (%)	5.7	5.8	6.2	5.9	5.9
Return on Equity	15.6	18.3	18.9	18.9	44.5
Return on Sales	4.1	4.3	4.6	4.7	4.2
Asset Turnover	1.7	1.7	1.7	1.6	1.3
Asset Leverage	2.3	2.4	2.4	2.6	7.9
Current Ratio	56.9	49.7	51.1	58.4	42.0
Gearing (%)	55.6	76.4	59.2	75.1	459.1
EBITDA / Sales	7.9	7.8	8.2	7.9	8.0
EBITDA / Total Interest	–	0.1	0.1	0.1	0.1
Market to book	1.4	1.3	1.2	1.0	2.1
EV/EBITDA	7.8	7.6	6.5	6.8	7.9

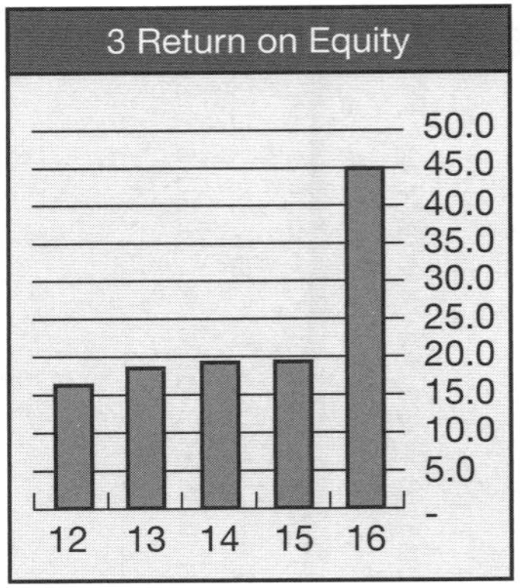

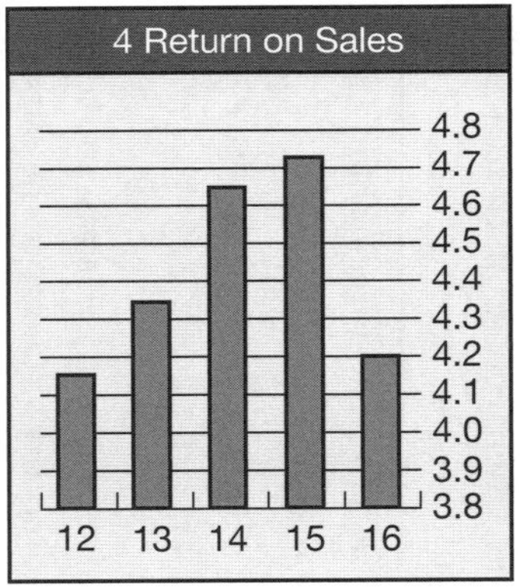

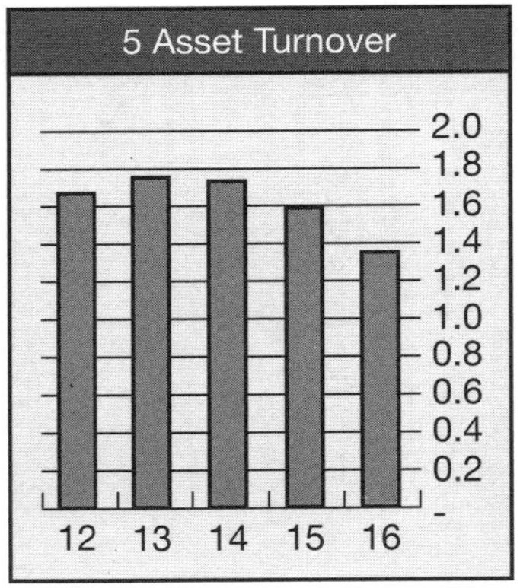

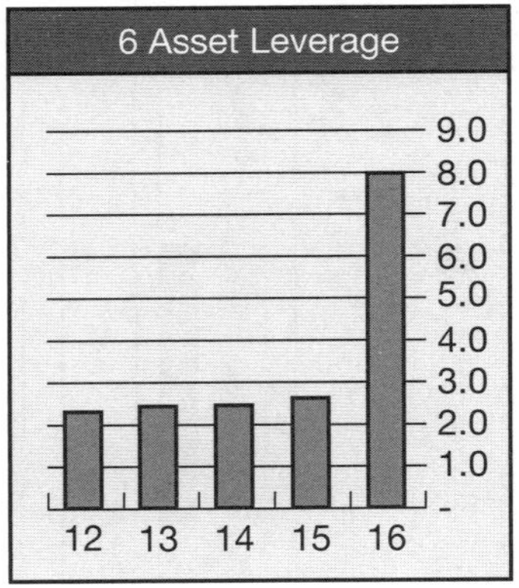

1 Total Sales

2 NOP / Sales (%)

3 Return on Equity

4 Return on Sales

5 Asset Turnover

6 Asset Leverage

Figure 17.8

Charts 2

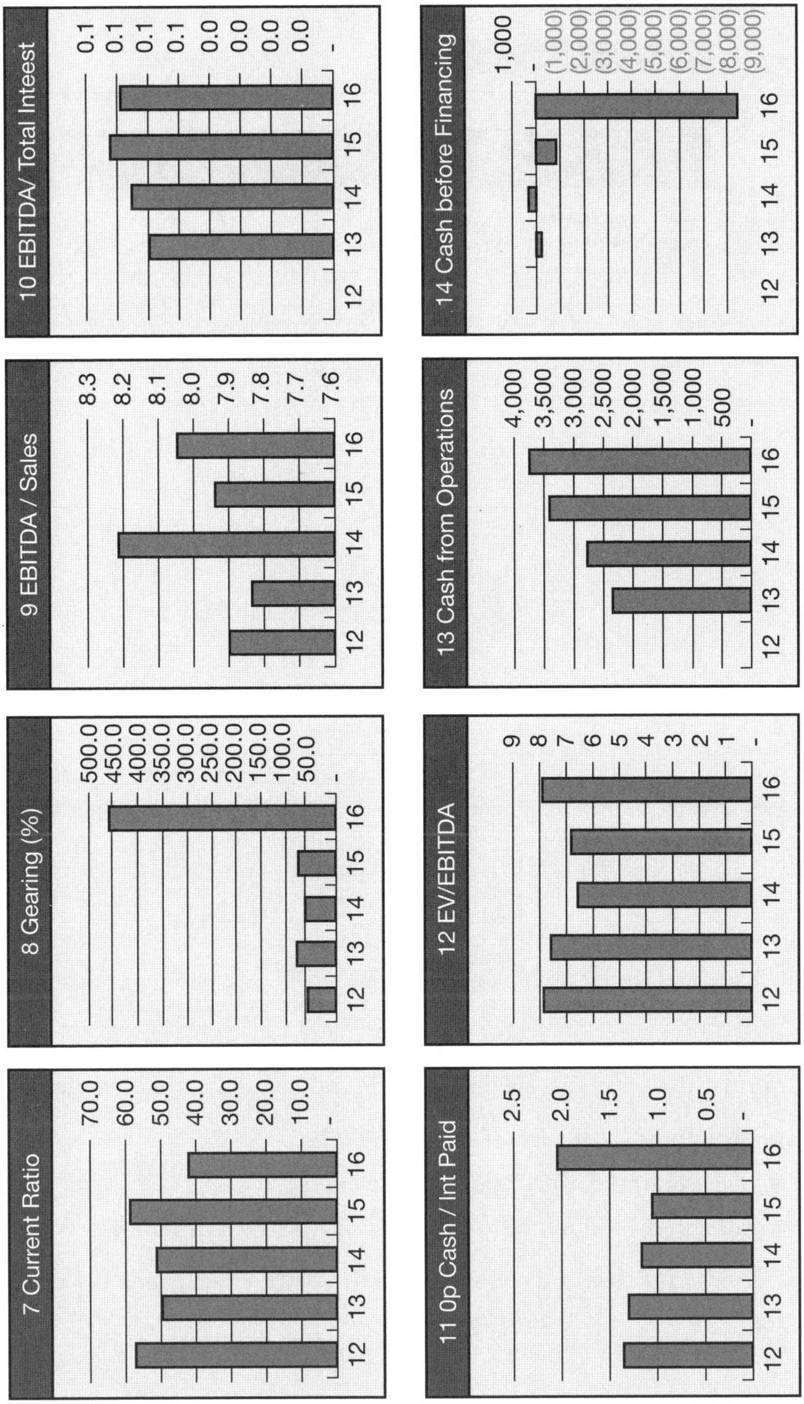
7 Current Ratio
70.0
60.0
50.0
40.0
30.0
20.0
10.0
-
12 13 14 15 16
8 Gearing (%)
500.0
450.0
400.0
350.0
300.0
250.0
200.0
150.0
100.0
50.0
-
12 13 14 15 16
9 EBITDA / Sales
8.3
8.2
8.1
8.0
7.9
7.8
7.7
7.6
12 13 14 15 16
10 EBITDA/ Total Inteest
0.1
0.1
0.1
0.1
0.0
0.0
0.0
0.0
-
12 13 14 15 16
11 0p Cash / Int Paid
2.5
2.0
1.5
1.0
0.5
-
12 13 14 15 16
12 EV/EBITDA
9
8
7
6
5
4
3
2
1
-
12 13 14 15 16
13 Cash from Operations
4,000
3,500
3,000
2,500
2,000
1,500
1,000
500
-
12 13 14 15 16
14 Cash before Financing
1,000
-
(1,000)
(2,000)
(3,000)
(4,000)
(5,000)
(6,000)
(7,000)
(8,000)
(9,000)
12 13 14 15 16

Figure 17.9

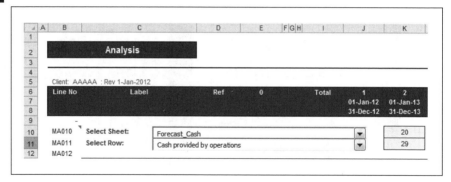

Combo boxes

Figure 17.10

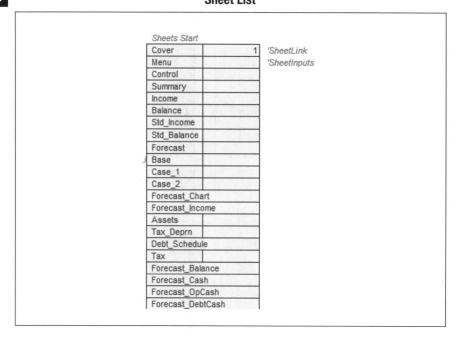

Sheet List

Format the cells with the inputs style and name the cells as follows:

- SheetInputs – the list of around 50 cells.
- SheetsStart – the cell above the sheets list.
- SheetsLink – a link cell to be used in a future chapter for navigation.

The macro below will populate the list with the current list of sheet and charts. If you insert or delete sheets and run the macro, it will loop around to generate a list of names and then paste the list into the named range.

```
Sub GetAllSheetNames()
'Macro by Alastair Day

Dim Number, Number1, Counter, SheetName(50)
Dim IndexNumber

On Error Resume Next
Application.Calculation = xlCalculationManual
Application.ScreenUpdating = False

Worksheets(1).Select
Range("sheetinputs") = ""

Range("A1").Select
Number = ActiveWorkbook.Sheets.Count
Number1 = ActiveWorkbook.Charts.Count

For Counter = 1 To Number

SheetName(Counter) = ActiveSheet.Name
   ActiveSheet.Next.Select
   Next Counter

On Error GoTo Error:
Worksheets("Workings").Select
Range("sheetsstart").Select
For Counter = 1 To Number

'SheetName(Counter) = Worksheets(Counter).Name

ActiveCell.Offset(1, 0).Range("A1").Select
'ActiveCell.FormulaR1C1 = Worksheets(Counter).Name
ActiveCell.FormulaR1C1 = SheetName(Counter)
Next Counter

Error:
Range("A2").Select
On Error Resume Next
IndexNumber = Range("sheetslink")
Sheets(IndexNumber).Select
Range("A2").Select
Application.ScreenUpdating = True
Application.Calculation = xlCalculationSemiautomatic

End Sub
```

Figure 17.11

First combo box

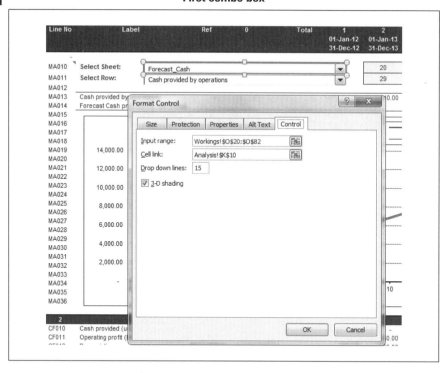

Figure 17.12

Second combo box

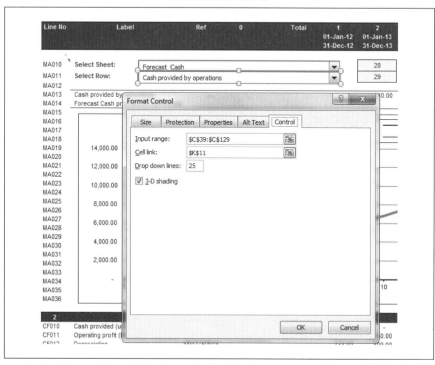

Each of the sheets has an index number from the first combo box (Figure 17.11). You can use the function OFFSET to gain the sheet name:

```
Cell L10: =OFFSET(SheetsStart,Analysis!K10,cstZero)
```

All of the schedules use the same template and all data starts on line 10. Place a list of row numbers on the right-hand side of the schedule starting at 10. If you have the sheet name you can use the functions INDIRECT (see Figure 17.13) and ADDRESS to generate a text reference to find the data. This is a two-dimensional lookup (see Figure 17.14).

INDIRECT **function**

Figure 17.13

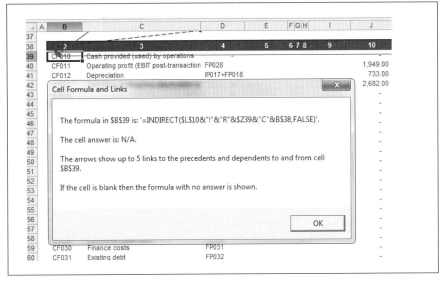

Row numbers

Figure 17.14

	T	U	V	W	X	Y	Z
37							
38	20	21	22	23	24		
39	-	-	-	-	-	-	10.00
40	8,381.68	9,428.55	10,592.22	11,885.54	13,322.78	-	11.00
41	1,271.65	1,286.65	1,301.65	1,316.65	1,331.65	-	12.00
42	9,653.33	10,715.20	11,893.87	13,202.19	14,654.44	-	13.00
43	-	-	-	-	-	-	14.00
44	(965.60)	(1,071.82)	(1,189.72)	(1,320.59)	(1,465.85)	-	15.00
45	(435.90)	(483.85)	(537.07)	(596.15)	(661.73)	-	16.00

Copy the formula across and down and populate the schedule with the data from a specific sheet. The second combo box (Figure 17.12) will generate a line or index number. Use OFFSET or INDEX to lookup a line in the data on this sheet at the top (see Figure 17.15):

```
Cell K13: =OFFSET(K38,$K$11,cstZero)
```

Figure 17.15

Data lookup

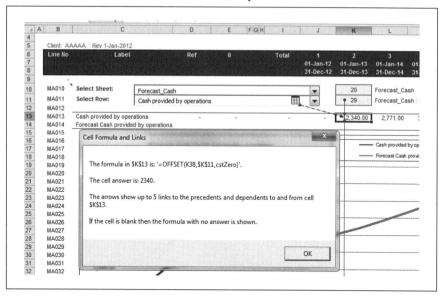

You can then insert a chart as one or two series. It can be helpful to use an xy scatter (Figure 17.16) and plot the historic data as the first series and the forecast data as the second series starting from the last historic data point rather than the first forecast element. You can concatenate the text with an '&' to add 'Forecast' to the name of the selected row.

Figure 17.16

xy scatter chart

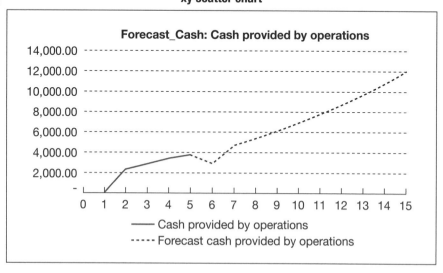

Column chart

Figure 17.17

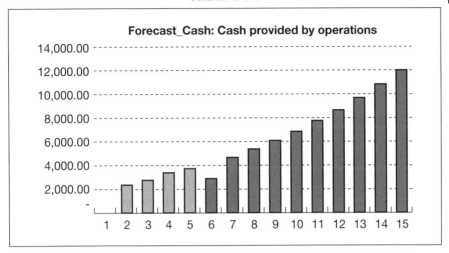

The second chart example (Figure 17.17) is a column chart with the historic block format with a different colour. If you right-click to select the series, left-click to select a particular data point and then right-click to format, you can change the colour of specific data points. Format the chart using themes and colours and again save the charts as templates for future use.

The result of the exercise is a graphic analysis tool whereby you can plot almost any line on all the different schedules. You now have a number of layers of flexibility built into the model to allow graphical analysis:

- Change the values on each of the three scenario forecast sheets.
- Load different scenarios into the model.
- View the Summary and Dashboard sheets.
- Select different sheets on the Analysis sheet.

SUMMARY

This chapter explores some ideas for presenting the information. You need succinct methods for demonstrating the findings in a model and exposure to peer group review. You can now use various methods to display the forecast, sensitivity and findings. The next chapter demonstrates some auditing methods to generate confidence in the model solution.

Auditing and review

MODEL REVIEW

The model now needs to be reviewed and checked to eradicate errors in the code. Most companies do not appear to have a formal auditing process in place and allow spreadsheet models to be used without formal testing or any kind of review. It is normally certain that errors exist in the model even if it is a simple case of a misspelt label. Models have to be checked and you should always assume that there are errors until you are satisfied otherwise.

The level and amount of testing required depend on the size of the spreadsheet, the amount of funds processed and its importance in a document chain. If a spreadsheet model is for your own use, the level of testing may be limited, but once a model is to be used by a team or third parties then the model should be subject to formal verification. It is better to test a model than allow it to be used with mistakes as the former must be more cost effective in the long run.

You could classify spreadsheet errors as:

- high-level errors solving the wrong problem or producing answers not in the specification;
- method errors by using the wrong formulas and techniques;
- cell errors;
- legacy errors where a number of people have worked on a model and compounded existing errors.

Most people appear to concentrate on cell errors but a model can fail or sub-optimise due to incorrect high-level or methodology errors. First, you should examine the model to decide if it generally produces the right kind of answers. This is a basic visual check. If there is an output block, you can ascertain if the model answers the basic questions contained in the specification. Where the author has not followed a predefined plan or has allowed the specification to wander, this is often a source of modelling errors.

The author emphasises the use of a modelling standard, such as:

- repeatable sheet layout using templates;
- physical separation of inputs, calculations, answers and reports;
- styles with specific colours to define cell types and delineate areas;
- number formats for dates, numbers, percentages, etc.;
- validation rules to prevent incorrect data input;
- polarity rules with cash out always a negative number;
- simple formulas to allow tracking of formula precedents and dependents.

While some modelling houses produce exacting methodologies, the design method in this book has used a few rules to build the model quickly and accurately. If there are no rules you have nothing to check since any form of code could be right or wrong. This is particularly true where modellers hard code variables into cell blocks or change the flow of code execution frequently. This chapter sets out a number of tests that you should perform on your models after first visually checking the model yourself and asking a third party to review it. A third party review is often useful for finding simple errors that the modeller misses. Similarly, you could enter another example in the model where a different pattern of inputs could highlight usability problems or coding errors.

SELF-CHECKS

Models should check themselves as much as possible. There are a number of sheets in the model where a self-check would be useful:

- historic balance sheet;
- forecast balance sheet;
- cash flow;
- debt cash flow;
- debt amortisation;
- cash reconciliation;
- economic profit reconciled to free cash flow;
- sources and uses of funds.

There should be checks at the bottom of the individual sheets, for example the historic balance sheet in Figure 18.1.

Figure 18.1 **Balance sheet check**

Line No	Label	1	2	3	4	5
Start		01-Jan-12	01-Jan-13	01-Jan-14	01-Jan-15	01-Jan-16
Finish		31-Dec-12	31-Dec-13	31-Dec-14	31-Dec-15	31-Dec-16
IB067						
IB068	Shareholders' equity					
IB069	Common stock (shares)	389.00	395.00	397.00	393.00	395.00
IB070	Preferred stock (shares)	3,744.00	4,028.00	4,416.00	4,551.00	4,678.00
IB071	Retained earnings	4,873.00	4,957.00	5,693.00	6,871.00	7,865.00
IB072	Shareholders equity	9,006.00	9,380.00	10,506.00	11,815.00	12,938.00
IB073						
IB074	Total liabilities + sharehc	20,410.00	22,563.00	24,807.00	30,164.00	41,515.00
	CheckSum: Balance Sheet	-	-	-	-	-

This line simply subtracts the assets from the liabilities to make sure there is a zero balance. A cash flow statement would make sure that the change in cash reconciles to the cash movement in the balance sheet. You want to know immediately if the model does not balance and where the error lies. The solution is to bring together all the error checks in one place and add them up (see Figure 18.2). If there are no errors, the sum of the error checks should be zero. If there is an error it will immediately show as a balance and warn any potential user. The simplest place to use is the Workings sheet as this will normally not be printed out.

Error check

Figure 18.2

Error checks		
Balance sheet	-	IB076
Forecast balance sheet	-	FB072.FB073
Balance sheet reconciliation	-	FB093+FB097+FB100
Cash flow	-	CF083
Cash reconciliation	-	DB061
Economic profit	-	EP62-VA056
Sources and users	-	IN026-IN026
Initial answer	-	
Check	-	

Scenario: Base : Model Check: All balances OK
N/A

You can then create a text string to note the selected scenario and the model check. You could name the cell ErrorCheck.

```
Cell S30: ="Scenario: "&Summary!G32&" : "&"Model
Check: "&IF(U28<>0, "ERRORS","All balances OK")&I
F(ROUND(U28,cstOne)=cstZero,""," : Source: "&S31)
```

If there are no errors it will say 'Model Check: All Balances OK' and if there are errors, the code will generate 'ERROR' and mark the element above with a non-zero balance. You need a second cell to find the balance using a MATCH function:

```
=IF(ROUND(U28,cstOne)=cstZero,"N/A",IF(ISERROR(IN
DEX(S19:S25,MATCH(U28,U19:U25,cstZero),cstZero)),
"N/K",INDEX(S19:S25,MATCH(U28,U19:U25,cstZero),cs
tZero)))
```

This code uses MATCH to find the index position of the balance and the INDEX to get the same number down the labels to generate the text.

It is then a good idea to add the ErrorCheck to every sheet in the same place to provide a visual alert in case of error (see Figure 18.3). Alerts are usually marked in red and there is a style in the model called SFL_Alert for this purpose. If a schedule is printed out with an error, then it should be obvious to any user that there is something wrong with the inputs and calculations.

Figure 18.3   **Error check on every sheet**

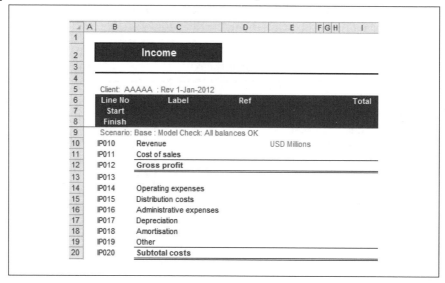

EXCEL AUDIT TOOLS

There are a number of audit tools built into Excel and, as stated earlier, you should assume that there are errors until it can be proved otherwise. It is assumed here that you have followed the systematic design method in this book such that inconsistent and hard-coded cells, etc., must be errors. You are always looking for exceptions to the simple coding rules. The tools are in Formulas on the Ribbon (see Figure 18.4).

Figure 18.4   **Ribbon auditing tools**

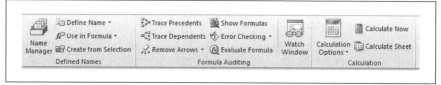

After checking a sheet for obvious errors, you should then click Show Formulas to switch to formula view (see Figure 18.5). This has the advantage of illustrating patterns in the data since you expect formulas and labels to be separated into distinct groups. This is suitable for small spreadsheets but if you have a model with thousands of cells you may need to use the methods covered later in the chapter to automate the process.

Show formulas

Figure 18.5

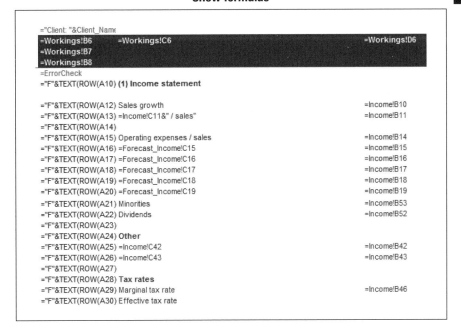

The Ribbon contains the same commands as found on the auditing toolbar in earlier versions of Excel. Trace Precedents and Dependents allow you to show the source and destination of the contents of the cell. Where the link shows a spreadsheet you can double-click the arrow to find the link off-sheet. This is also true for any links on-sheet. When an arrow is coloured red rather than blue, the link arrow will point to an error cell (see Figure 18.6). You can remove all the arrows or if you click to the right of the box you can choose to remove them one at a time.

This method provides the facility to check the cells used in individual formulas. You should work through the schedules to ensure that the cells work down the columns in a consistent manner. Non-parallel lines could mean that a wrong cell in a formula has been picked up.

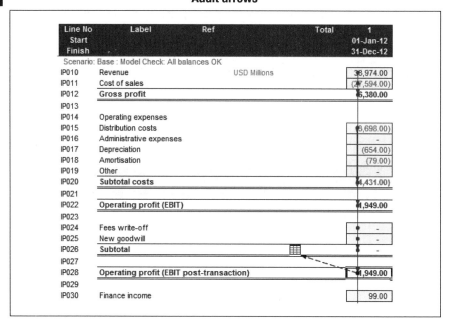

Figure 18.6 **Audit arrows**

You can also use `Evaluate Formula` to check complex formulas such as the one below from the Assets schedule. Each time you click Evaluate, Excel executes another stage of the calculation so that you can see how the answer emerges (see Figures 18.7).

```
Assets O19: =IF(AND(YEAR(Assets!O$7)>=YEAR($N19),
YEAR(Assets!O$7)<YEAR($N19)+$E$18),IF(Forecast!$H
$56=cstZero,SLN($L19,cstZero,$E$18),SYD($L19,cstZ
ero,$E$18,Assets!O$10-$M19)),cstZero)
```

Figure 18.7 **Evaluate formula**

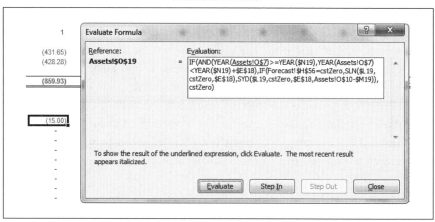

Background error checking in Excel can also highlight errors dynamically. You set the options in Excel, Options, Formulas as in Figure 18.8. If Excel encounters cells with any of these attributes, it will display a green triangle in the cell. Right-clicking on the cell activates options to gain help, ignore or resolve the issue.

Excel error checking

Figure 18.8

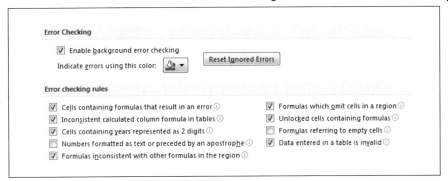

If you encounter complex formulas, these are often a source of errors, particularly when using functions such as IF. Some people say that a formula should possess no more than 75 characters or be limited to one line. In general, you should rewrite complex formulas such as the tax depreciation below. If not you should check the logic with Evaluate Formula.

```
Tax Deprn Cell O19: =IF(AND(YEAR(Tax_
Deprn!O$7)>=YEAR($N19),YEAR(Tax_Deprn!O$7)<YEA
R($N19)+$E$18),IF(Forecast!$H$62=0,$L19/$E$18,-
DDB(ABS($L19),cstZero,$E$18,O$10-$M19,Forecast!$E
$61*10)),cstZero)
```

You often come across labels which are incorrectly spelt. Labels should be checked with F7, which is the Windows shortcut key for spelling. Similarly, you should use F11 or Alt + F1 to draw quick charts to check patterns in data. F11 draws a new chart sheet whereas Alt + F1 places the chart on the same sheet. People are not exceptional at looking at pages of numbers, but they do understand patterns of data (see Figure 18.9). If you get an unusual chart pattern it could indicate errors somewhere in the model or incorrect inputs.

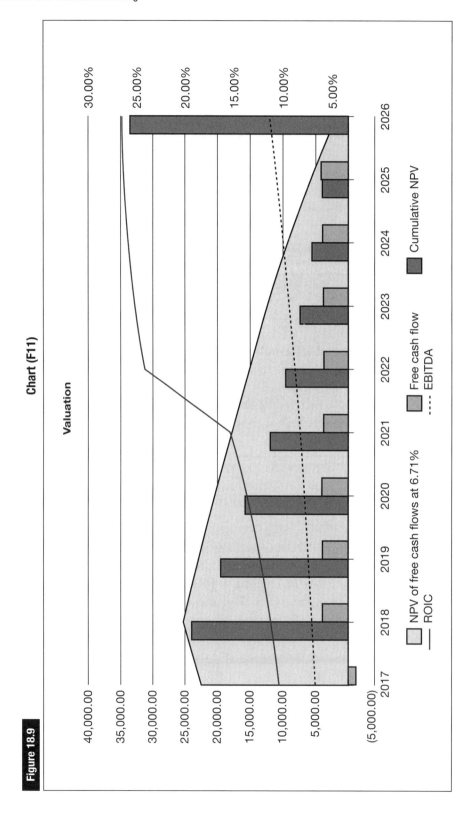

Figure 18.9

There are a range of number and cell formats in the model. Sometimes it is advantageous to see the numbers to their full extent without any wrapper. Usually you only see one or two decimal places, whereas Excel is working to 10 or 12 places. If you copy a sheet by right-clicking the tab, you can then format the sheet as numbers general format. The shortcut is Control + ~ (tilde).

The example in Figure 18.10 is taken from the Ratios sheet. The unformatted version (Figure 18.11) shows a constant sales growth which is correct against the Forecast sheet. The other numbers are correct to several decimal places. If any of them were simple numbers it could indicate an overwritten cell since individuals are usually unlikely to type nine decimal places.

Ratios sheet formatted

Figure 18.10

| Line No | Label | Ref | | 6 | 7 | 8 |
| Start | | | | 01-Jan-17 | 01-Jan-18 | 01-Jan-19 |
Finish				31-Dec-17	31-Dec-18	31-Dec-19
Scenario: Base : Model Check: All balances OK						
RT010	**Core ratios**					
RT011	Return on sales (NPAT/sales %)	FP050/FP010	%	4.2%	4.2%	4.3%
RT012	Asset turnover (sales / total assets)	FP010/FB033	X	1.4x	1.4x	1.5x
RT013	Asset leverage (total assets/equity)	FB033/FB068	X	6.4x	5.2x	4.3x
RT014	Return on equity (NPAT/equity %)	FP050/FB033	%	36.5%	31.5%	28.2%
RT016						
RT017	**Profitability**					
RT018	Sales growth	FP010	%	10.0%	10.0%	10.0%
RT019	Gross profit / sales (%)	FP012/FP010	%	20.5%	20.5%	20.5%
RT020	Operating profit / sales (%)	FP028/FP010	%	6.6%	6.5%	6.4%
RT021	Earnings before tax / sales (%)	FP044/FP010	%	5.1%	5.3%	5.5%
RT022	Return on capital employed (ROCE)	FP028/FB060+FB068		15.7%	17.3%	19.1%
RT023	Return on invested capital (ROIC)	FP028*(1-T)/FB060+FB068+FB036+FB0:		10.4%	11.2%	12.2%
RT024	Return on assets (ROA)	FP028/	%	9.0%	9.4%	9.8%

Ratio sheet unformatted

Figure 18.11

| Line No | Label | Ref | | 6 | 7 | 8 |
| Start | | | | 42736 | 43101 | 43466 |
Finish				43100	43465	43830
Scenario: Base : Model Check: All balances OK						
RT010	**Core ratios**					
RT011	Return on sales (NPAT/sales %)	FP050/FP010	%	0.04206075	0.04236151	0.04281395
RT012	Asset turnover (sales / total assets)	FP010/FB033	X	1.35796153	1.44038193	1.53149928
RT013	Asset leverage (total assets/equity)	FB033/FB068	X	6.39798941	5.16993937	4.29435259
RT014	Return on equity (NPAT/equity %)	FP050/FB033	%	0.36543322	0.31545292	0.28157872
RT016						
RT017	**Profitability**					
RT018	Sales growth	FP010	%	0.1	0.1	0.1
RT019	Gross profit / sales (%)	FP012/FP010	%	0.205	0.205	0.205
RT020	Operating profit / sales (%)	FP028/FP010	%	0.06631156	0.06499338	0.06406931
RT021	Earnings before tax / sales (%)	FP044/FP010	%	0.05114747	0.05320593	0.05517318
RT022	Return on capital employed (ROCE)	FP028/FB060+FB068		0.15676562	0.17312866	0.19069274
RT023	Return on invested capital (ROIC)	FP028*(1-T)/FB060+FB068+FB036+FB0:		0.10447034	0.11233701	0.12239037
RT024	Return on assets (ROA)	FP028/	%	0.09004855	0.09361529	0.09812211

Figure 18.12

Paste names

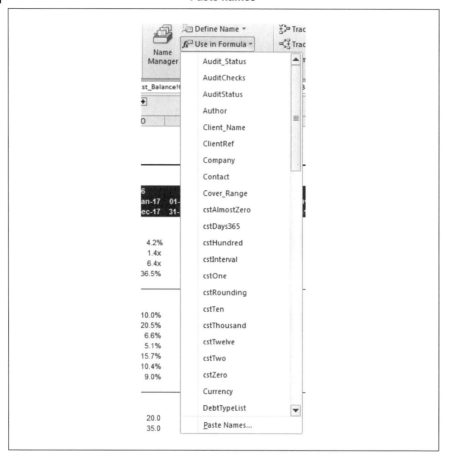

You should also check the range names in the model to make sure that they are all still current. If you copy a sheet with names, Excel will create sheet level or local names which can sometimes be confusing against the workbook level names.

Choose a blank range of cells. In Formulas, you can click Use in Formula and at the bottom there is a Paste Names option (see Figure 18.12). If you see a Ref! error then you know that a name has been deleted and is no longer valid. The list of names is shown in Figure 18.13.

When setting up the initial schedules, the model used validation to restrict entry to the input cells. You should make sure that the current values meet the rules entered for the cells. If any cells do not match, the tool sets a red ring around the cell (see Figure 18.14). When you amend the validation and run the tool again, the error rings should disappear.

Names list

Figure 18.13

Audit_Status	=Menu!$C$16
AuditChecks	=Workings!$K$32:$K$40
AuditStatus	=Menu!$C$17
Author	=Menu!$C$6
Client_Name	=Control!$E$5
ClientRef	=Control!$O$5
Company	=Menu!$C$7
Contact	=Menu!$B$20
Cover_Range	=Cover!$A$1:$P$30
cstAlmostZero	=Workings!$E$39
cstDays365	=Workings!$E$40
cstHundred	=Workings!$E$35
cstInterval	=Control!$E$8
cstOne	=Workings!$E$37
cstRounding	=Workings!$E$43
cstTen	=Workings!$E$42
cstThousand	=Workings!$E$36
cstTwelve	=Workings!$E$33
cstTwo	=Workings!$E$38
cstZero	=Workings!$E$34
Currency	=Control!$E$9

Validation

Figure 18.14

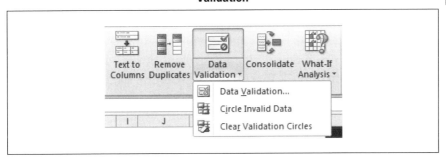

Data sometimes gets hidden and so it is a good idea to check for the last cell on each sheet. The shortcut is Control + End or you can go to Find & Select, Go To Special, Last Cell. As part of the design specification, Systematic always places a red or coloured border around a sheet to denote the last cell. There should be no data beyond this delineation line.

You should make further checks on circular references and links. Go to File, Options, Formulas and make sure that the iteration switch is unticked. In the example in Figure 18.15 it is ticked and this means that Excel will try to resolve any unplanned circular references without notification. This could mean that the model generates incorrect answers or becomes unstable. If you untick the box and there are no warnings, there are no circular references in open models. Whilst some banks are prepared to accept circular references it is preferable not to have any iteration in the models.

Figure 18.15

Circular references

Change options related to formula calculation, performance, and error handling.

Calculation options

Workbook Calculation ⓘ
- ⚪ Automatic
- ⚫ Automatic except for data tables
- ⚪ Manual
  - ☑ Recalculate workbook before saving

☑ Enable iterative calculation
Maximum Iterations: 5
Maximum Change: 0.001

Working with formulas

- ☐ R1C1 reference style ⓘ
- ☑ Formula AutoComplete ⓘ
- ☑ Use table names in formulas
- ☑ Use GetPivotData functions for PivotTable references

Links often cause problems since Excel does not provide sufficient warning – especially when you save files. It is too easy to create links when copying cells and forget to resolve them before saving the file. You should ensure that links are greyed out in Data, Connections (see Figure 18.16). If you sent a file to a colleague with an unresolved link, a file would generate a link request when opened. It is up to you to resolve the links as Excel will not warn you when you save the file.

Figure 18.16

Links

Finally in this section, each sheet should print correctly in portrait or landscape. Since you used template sheets they should still work. This is the benefit of standardisation since you copied the template sheet with the timeline a number of times. If you go to View, Workbook Views (Figure 18.17) you can size sheets on to pages and check the results. Each sheet should have standard headers and footers and if possible the date and time of the last save or print date.

Workbook views

Figure 18.17

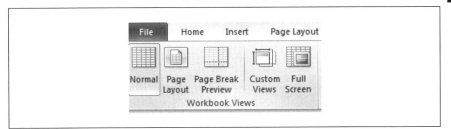

You can access page settings at File, Print, Settings (see Figure 18.18). This takes you to the same dialog box as in Excel 2003 where you can enter the standards for headers and footers (see Figure 18.19).

Page properties

Figure 18.18

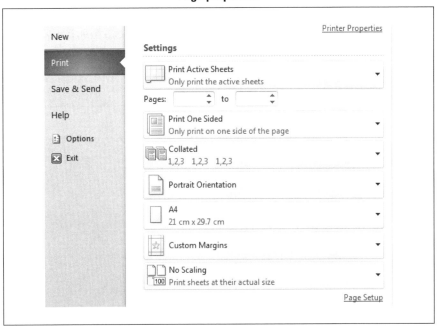

Figure 18.19   **Page setup**

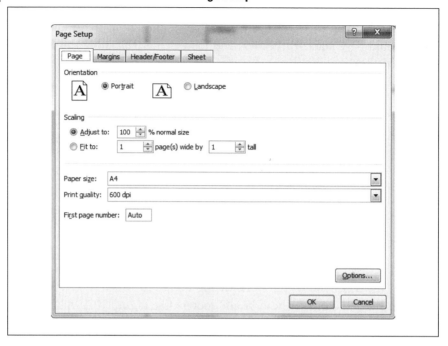

Alternatively you could write macros to automate the process (see Figure 18.20). This macro can be placed in the VBA `Workbook` section with the action set as `BeforePrint`. By placing the macro in this section it will

Figure 8.20   **Save Date macro**

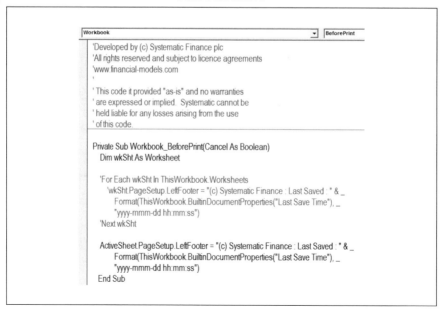

apply to all sheets and this is more efficient than using the general modules in the Visual Basic editor. The unused portion of the macro (which is remarked out with an apostrophe) would go through each sheet in the workbook every time you printed a sheet, whilst the active part of the macro would merely mark the current sheet.

CONSISTENCY CHECKS

Consistency checks are also useful for reviewing different blocks of code that involve using `Home, Find and Select, Go To Special` or press F5 and click `Special`. For each of these tests it is a good idea to follow these instructions:

- Make three copies of a sheet.
- Select all and strip out the colour (no fill).
- Remove any borders or other formatting.
- Make all the font colours black or automatic.
- Make all the number formats general (Control + ~).

The result is Figure 18.21.

Figure 18.21

Basic sheet

	A	B	C	D	E
1					
2			**Control_Copied**		
3					
4					
5		IN005	Client Name		AAAAA
6		IN006	Revision reference		Rev 1-Jan-2012
7		IN007	Start Date		40909
8		IN008	Interval		12
9		IN009	Currency		USD
10		IN010	Units:		Millions
11		IN011	Forecast Period		10
12		IN012			
13		IN013	**Uses of funds**		
14		IN014	Current stock price		1.5
15		IN015	Offer premium		0.1
16		IN016	Offer price per share	IN014*1+IN015	1.65
17		IN017			
18		IN018	Shares outstanding (MM)		7000
19		IN019	**Equity purchase price**		**11550**
20		IN020			
21		IN021	Equity purchase price	IN019	11550
22		IN022	Debt retired	FB057	16776
23		IN023	Initial advisory fee		0.005
24		IN024	Financing fee		0.01
25		IN025	Transaction costs		292.75
26		IN026	**Total uses**		**28618.765**

You can then pattern match a sheet (see Figure 18.22) by using F5, Special to select different types of cells and give them specific colours:

■ Constant numbers.

■ Constant text.

■ Formula numbers.

■ Formula text.

■ Formula logic (e.g. =C5<=EndDate).

■ Formula Errors.

Figure 8.22

Pattern match

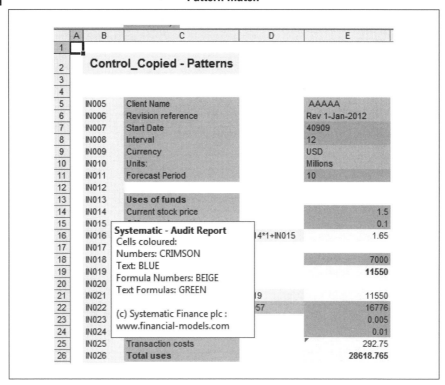

This method can be extended to select more specific types. When you want to check if a schedule adds up, a '1' test can help to automate the process. If you copy the working sheet as above, the process is:

■ F5, Special, Constant Numbers.

■ 1 + Control + Enter.

■ Control + ~.

■ Format the selected cells with a specific colour.

The result from the income statement in Figure 18.23 shows the same numbers across the range. If somebody had entered a formula in the input cells you would see the error immediately. The identical totals add some confidence to the sheet since you are looking at similar cells across the module.

One test

Figure 8.23

Line No	Label	Ref	Total	1	1	1	1	1
Start				1	1	1	1	1
Finish				1	1	1	1	1
Scenario: Base : Model Check: All balances OK								
IP010	Revenue	USD Millions		1	1	1	1	1
IP011	Cost of sales			1	1	1	1	1
IP012	Gross profit			2.00	2.00	2.00	2.00	2.00
IP013								
IP014	Operating expenses							
IP015	Distribution costs			1	1	1	1	1
IP016	Administrative expenses			1	1	1	1	1
IP017	Depreciation			1	1	1	1	1
IP018	Amortisation			1	1	1	1	1
IP019	Other			1	1	1	1	1
IP020	Subtotal costs			5.00	5.00	5.00	5.00	5.00
IP021								
IP022	Operating profit (EBIT)			7.00	7.00	7.00	7.00	7.00

If you have a block of cells such as the ratios, you may want to confirm that the same cell pattern exists across the sheet. If you select a group of cells and press F5, Special you can then select Row or Column differences (see Figure 18.24). If the routine highlights any cells you can format them in a different colour to mark them. If no cells are found, the model uses the same type of formula across or down the range.

Consistency check

Figure 8.24

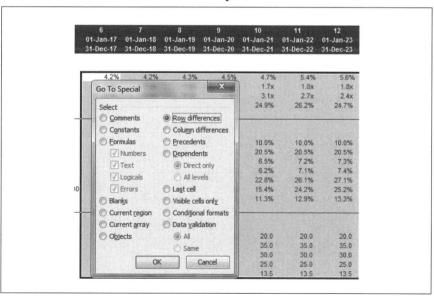

Finally, you could range and stress a model by entering unusual data to check what would happen. If you have validated cells then it should be impossible for you to enter the wrong kind of data. However, somebody may want to use larger numbers than the current example so the columns have to be wide enough. Similarly, a user may input a date in 'MMDDYY' rather than 'DDMMYY' order. The model should be able to cope with zeros, negatives and text in the wrong places without generating error values.

AUDIT SHEET

To assist others a note of the tests carried out may be helpful. This is a simple memo sheet recording how the model was reviewed, the individual in control, the date and any action taken. Notes in the model are always more useful than separate Word or Notepad files. The sheet forms part of the model documentation for future reference (see Figure 18.25).

Figure 18.25   **Audit sheet**

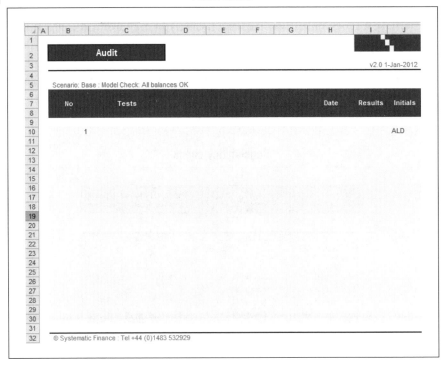

SUMMARY

The completed model should be reviewed through a number of Excel and other tests and you should develop a 'tick' sheet for checking models. With every test that the model 'passes', you become more confident that there are no serious errors although you can never be sure that there are no errors. You have to carry out and record each routine in turn before you can use and rely on a model.

Documentation

Documentation

Navigation

Protection

Version check

Final review

Summary

File: MCFM_Final.xls

DOCUMENTATION

Many models are not documented and the author has often heard that the original developer has left the department or company and the current users do not understand how the model works or how the different sections interact. Some modellers seem to want to make everything as complex as possible to prevent changes by others. However, it makes more sense that models should be clearly documented so that people are able to use and, where necessary, further develop them.

While you could write down lots of notes on the structure, a model map is often the best way of communicating the structure. There are plenty of shapes available on the Excel menus, which can be coloured to denote different functions and hyperlinked or linked via macros to different sections (see Figure 19.1).

Shapes

Figure 19.1

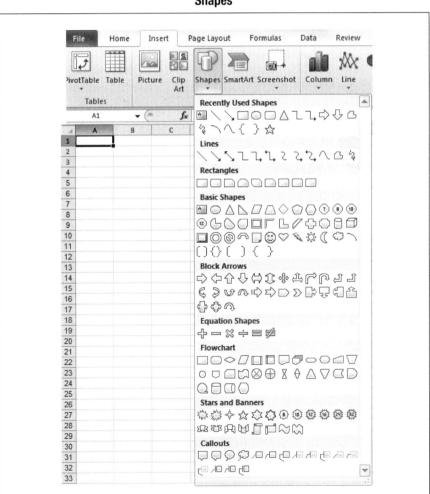

You can use the selection tools in Home, Editing, Find and Select to align the different objects or select multiple objects for formatting. If you copy the portrait template, you can put together a simple map of the model as one of the first sheets.

Figure 19.2 shows a completed sheet of the progression from the original inputs statements through the forecast to the outputs, sensitivity and reporting.

Figure 19.2

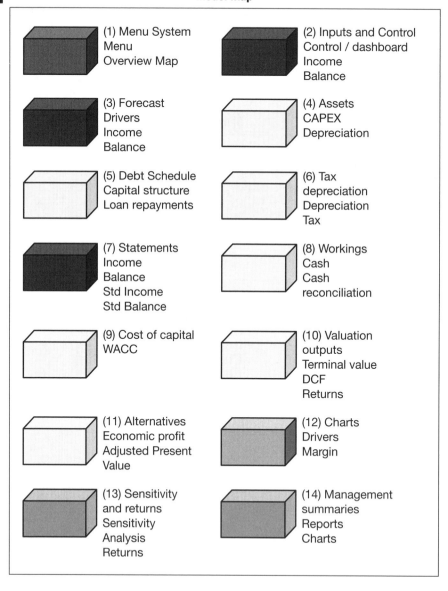

Model map

(1) Menu System
Menu
Overview Map

(2) Inputs and Control
Control / dashboard
Income
Balance

(3) Forecast
Drivers
Income
Balance

(4) Assets
CAPEX
Depreciation

(5) Debt Schedule
Capital structure
Loan repayments

(6) Tax
depreciation
Depreciation
Tax

(7) Statements
Income
Balance
Std Income
Std Balance

(8) Workings
Cash
Cash
reconciliation

(9) Cost of capital
WACC

(10) Valuation
outputs
Terminal value
DCF
Returns

(11) Alternatives
Economic profit
Adjusted Present
Value

(12) Charts
Drivers
Margin

(13) Sensitivity
and returns
Sensitivity
Analysis
Returns

(14) Management
summaries
Reports
Charts

You should go through the model inserting comments if you have not already done so. It is usually better to have notes and documentation in the model rather than held in separate Notepad or Word files. The shortcut to insert a comment is Shift + F2 or you can right-click a cell and select the Insert Comment option. Your name will always show in the comment since Excel gets your name from Excel, Options, General. Remove your name from the Excel options if you do not want it to appear.

Use Review to show and hide comments (see Figure 19.3) and you can also print sheets with comments showing. If you go to Home, Page Layout, Page Set Up and click the arrow, the box shown in Figure 19.4 appears. You then have two options in the drop-down box:

■ as displayed on the sheet;
■ as a list on a separate sheet.

Show comments

Figure 19.3

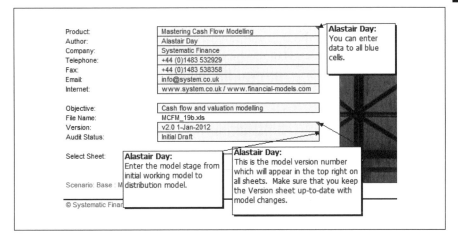

Print comments

Figure 19.4

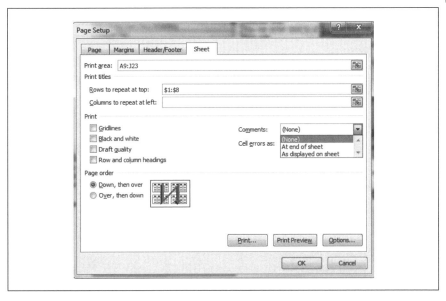

NAVIGATION

There are nearly 40 sheets and charts in the model and navigation can be difficult. You can right-click the arrows at the bottom left of an Excel screen and this gives you a crude menu, but it does not work well with large numbers of sheets. Alternatively, you can use the shortcuts Control + Page Up and Control + Page Down to shift along the sheets in either direction.

A previous chapter introduced a sheets macro to populate a range on the Workings sheet with the current array of sheets. This can be used to set up a simple navigation system to jump to any place in the workbook in two clicks:

- Click once to get back to a menu sheet.

- Click again to select a specified sheet.

You can insert a combo box on the Menu sheet and use the SheetsList range and SheetsLink ranges on the Workings sheet (see Figure 19.5). If you right-click the combo box you can assign the GetAllSheetNames to it. As you click and close the combo box it will update the index number in SheetsLink and then select the sheet by number rather than by name. This is an efficient way of selecting the sheet as it is independent of the hard-coded sheet name.

Figure 19.5

Combo box

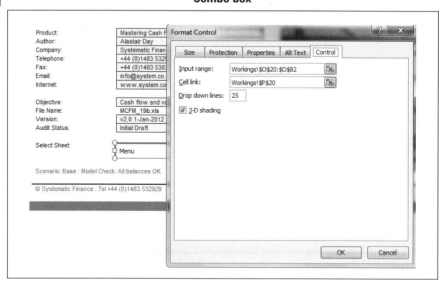

You then need a way to select the Menu sheet. Since the menu is the second sheet you simply need a macro:

```
Worksheets("Menu").Select
Range("A2").Select
Range("sheetslink") = 2
```

You could also add macros to select the last and next sheets:

```
Sub NextSheet()
On Error Resume Next
ActiveSheet.Next.Select
Range("A2").Select
End Sub

Sub LastSheet()
On Error Resume Next
ActiveSheet.Previous.Select
Range("A2").Select
End Sub

Sub UseModel()

Sheets(2).Select
Range("A2").Select
End Sub
```

You could use the standard button in the `Developer, Controls, Insert` menu, but it is often more interesting to use elements from the Shapes menu. The item in Figure 19.6 uses a base and then pastes arrows and a further button as a shape. You can right-click the shapes to assign macros. Once you are satisfied with the shape and have checked that it works, you can use `Home, Editing, Find and Select, Select Objects` to select all the objects before copying them. You can then paste these objects in the same place on all the sheets since you always want to return to the second sheet (see Figure 19.7).

Menu sheet with navigation

Figure 19.6

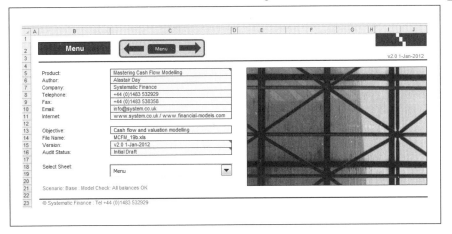

Figure 19.7

Navigation on every sheet

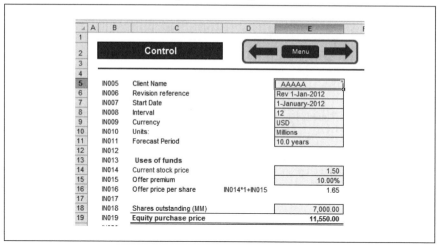

You could also place a button on the Cover sheet to jump to the menu on acceptance of the disclaimer (see Figure 19.8). The idea is to make it easy and intuitive to move around the model. Using these methods any user should be able to find their way around and quickly ascertain the general structure of the model.

Figure 19.8

Cover sheet

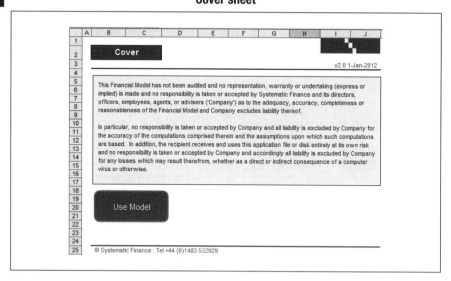

PROTECTION

If you are going to be sending the file to others or you do not want others to change the code, you could protect the file for data entry. You can protect:

- cells against formula changes;
- the workbook against structural changes, such as inserting and deleting sheets;
- Visual Basic for Applications (VBA);
- open and modify.

Protecting the cells is a two-stage process. Since you have followed a basic design method, input cells are clearly marked and physically separate from formula cells. Similarly, most sheets are dedicated purely to calculations and can be fully protected. The process is:

- Select the whole sheet by clicking in the top corner or using the shortcut Control + A.
- Use the arrow to the right of Home, Font to open the box in Figure 19.9.
- Tick both boxes (locked and hidden) to set the cells up for protection.
- Select Review, Changes, Protect Sheet, then enter and repeat a password.

Protect cells

Figure 19.9

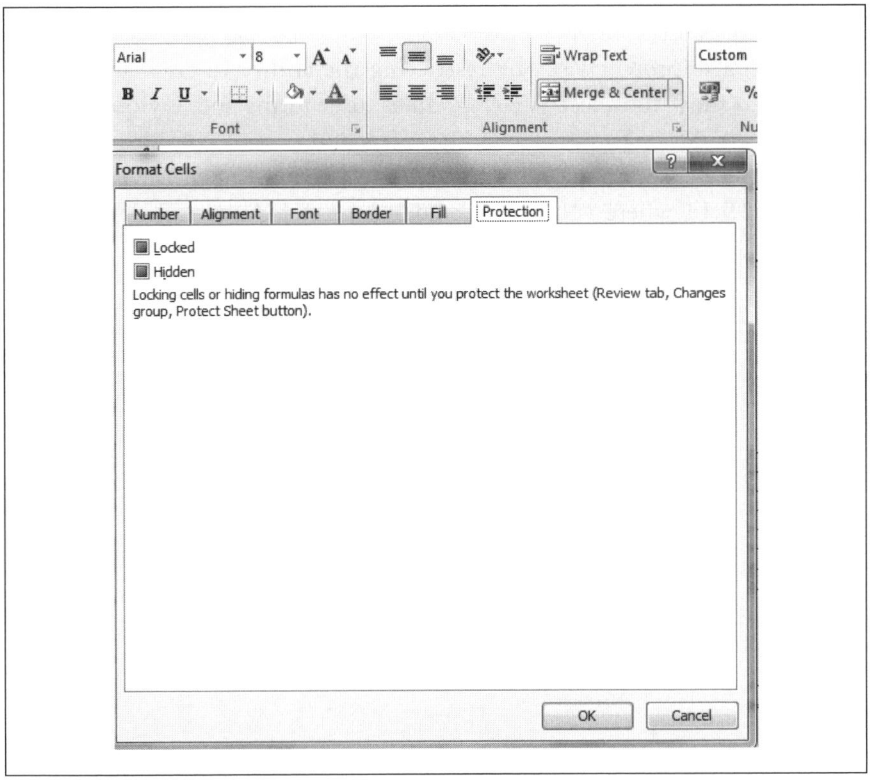

You will notice that certain items are greyed out on the menus since they are no longer available (see Figure 19.10). If there are inputs on the sheet use F5, Special to select the constant numbers and use Home, Font to deselect these cells before protecting the sheet. If somebody clicks on a protected cell, Excel will generate a protection error. The objective is to restrict access to the input cells, which should of course be validated for non-allowable input values.

Figure 19.10

Protect sheet and workbook

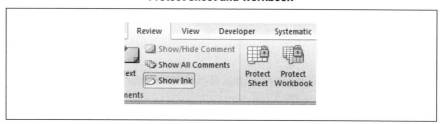

You can also protect the workbook against sheet and structural changes as above. This will stop users moving and deleting sheets or unhiding (revealing) hidden sheets. Again you click Protect, then enter and repeat a password to secure a model.

You can also protect VBA by restricting the ability to click and expand a project to show the sheet, VBA modules, user forms and any other object classes. Press Alt + F11 to access the VBA and press VBA Tools, VBA Project Properties, Protection. This will open the box shown in Figure 19.11 where you can tick Lock project for viewing. If you enter

Figure 19.11

VBA protection

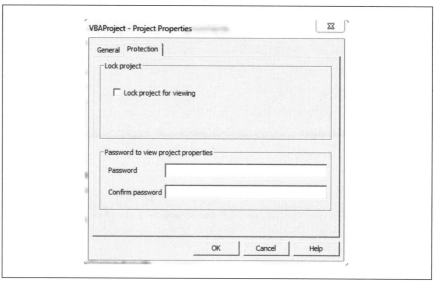

a password and repeat the password and save the file, this will secure the code. When you next open the file, you will be prompted for a password to expand the project and view the code.

If the file is placed on a server you may want further protection to prevent casual amendments. As with Word, you can specify sheet open and modify passwords. When you select `File, Save As, Tools`, you can access `General Options` as in Figure 19.12.

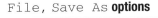 `File, Save As` **options**

Figure 19.12

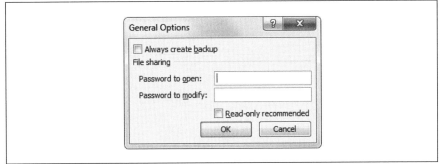

Using these methods, you can secure the file against casual access, although you should be aware that Excel is not supposed to be secure and can always be cracked with inexpensive security software.

VERSION CHECK

Models change over time as you enhance the features, find mistakes or require a different mix of outputs. Since the model is structured in modular form on separate sheets, it should be straightforward to add more schedules. For example, you could add a multi-stage dividend discount calculation without disrupting any of the current calculations. All the required data is available on input and accounting schedules.

It is easy to forget what and why you change code and therefore a memo sheet for version changes is useful as in Figure 19.13. Each time you make a change, you can write notes here and then change the version number on the Menu sheet. It is important that you have consistency such that version 1.1 XX-Jan-XXX continues to derive the same answers. Any change could indicate that somebody has changed the code without authority.

Figure 19.13

Version log

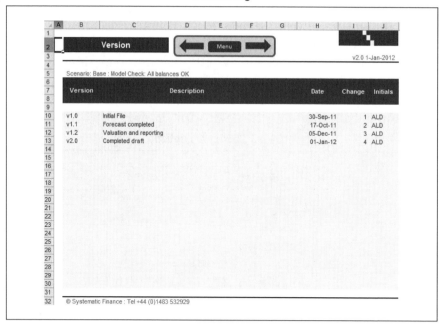

FINAL REVIEW

Upon completion you need to give the file a final review and perhaps ask others to review the outputs and the workings of the file. They may have some useful suggestions on usability or features. You could also consider using some commercial software to provide further confidence on the code. There is a list of packages at **www.financial-models.com**. You should also enter other cases in the model in order to check the output further and make sure you are confident of the answers produced by your code.

SUMMARY

This chapter reviews ways of making the file more usable by exploring elements that are often overlooked due to time constraints or other reasons. While there are always time pressures in a commercial environment, you should consider producing some documentation and certainly add comments on key cells in the model. The file may be in use for several years and you may forget the reasons for coding in a specific manner. A navigation system is useful for this and future files so the code will remain reusable. In addition, it is preferable to protect distribution files against casual amendment by users to ensure some control and ownership of the model. With the file complete, you can enter different data and process more cases ready for distributing the finished model.

Appendix 1

Useful Maths and Analysis ToolPak functions listed by category

Software installation

Licence

File list

Systematic Finance plc

File: MCFM_Office_2011_Menus

USEFUL MATHS AND ANALYSIS TOOLPAK FUNCTIONS LISTED BY CATEGORY

Function name	Category	Analysis ToolPak	Description
EDATE	Date/Time	Yes	Serial number of the date that is the indicated number of months before or after the start date
EOMONTH	Date/Time	Yes	Serial number of the last day of the month before or after a specified number of months
NETWORKDAYS	Date/Time	Yes	Number of whole workdays between two dates
WEEKNUM	Date/Time	Yes	Converts a serial number to a number representing where the week falls numerically with a year
WORKDAY	Date/Time	Yes	Serial number of the date before or after a specified number of workdays
YEARFRAC	Date/Time	Yes	Year fraction representing the number of whole days between start_date and end_date
ACCRINT	Financial	Yes	Accrued interest for a security that pays periodic interest
ACCRINTM	Financial	Yes	
AMORDEGRC	Financial	Yes	Depreciation for each accounting period by using a depreciation coefficient
AMORLINC	Financial	Yes	Depreciation for each accounting period
COUPDAYBS	Financial	Yes	Number of days from the beginning of the coupon period to the settlement date
COUPDAYS	Financial	Yes	Number of days in the coupon period that contains the settlement date
COUPDAYSNC	Financial	Yes	Number of days from the settlement date to the next coupon date
COUPNCD	Financial	Yes	Next coupon date after the settlement date
COUPNUM	Financial	Yes	Number of coupons payable between the settlement date and maturity date
COUPPCD	Financial	Yes	Previous coupon date before the settlement date
CUMIPMT	Financial	Yes	Cumulative interest paid between two periods
CUMPRINC	Financial	Yes	Cumulative principal paid on a loan between two periods

Function name	Category	Analysis ToolPak	Description
DB	Financial	–	Depreciation of an asset for a specified period using the fixed-declining balance method
DDB	Financial	–	Depreciation of an asset for a specified period using the double-declining balance method or some other specified method
DISC	Financial	Yes	Discount rate for a security
DOLLARDE	Financial	Yes	Converts a dollar price, expressed as a fraction, into a dollar price, expressed as a decimal number
DOLLARFR	Financial	Yes	Converts a dollar price, expressed as a decimal number, into a dollar price, expressed as a fraction
DURATION	Financial	Yes	Annual duration of a security with periodic interest payments
EFFECT	Financial	Yes	Effective annual interest rate
FV	Financial	–	Future value of an investment
FVSCHEDULE	Financial	Yes	Future value of an initial principal after applying a series of compound interest rates
INTRATE	Financial	Yes	Interest rate for a fully invested security
IPMT	Financial	–	Interest payment for an investment for a given period
IRR	Financial	–	Internal rate of return for a series of cash flows
ISPMT	Financial	–	Calculates the interest paid during a specific period of an investment
MDURATION	Financial	Yes	Macauley modified duration for a security with an assumed par value of $100
MIRR	Financial	–	Internal rate of return where positive and negative cash flows are financed at different rates
NOMINAL	Financial	Yes	Annual nominal interest rate
NPER	Financial	–	Number of periods for an investment
NPV	Financial	–	Net present value of an investment based on a series of periodic cash flows and a discount rate
ODDFPRICE	Financial	Yes	Price per $100 face value of a security with an odd first period
ODDFYIELD	Financial	Yes	Yield of a security with an odd first period

Function name	Category	Analysis ToolPak	Description
ODDLPRICE	Financial	Yes	Price per $100 face value of a security with an odd last period
ODDLYIELD	Financial	Yes	Yield of a security with an odd last period
PMT	Financial	–	Periodic payment for an annuity
PPMT	Financial	–	Payment on the principal for an investment for a given period
PRICE	Financial	Yes	Price per $100 face value of a security that pays periodic interest
PRICEDISC	Financial	Yes	Price per $100 face value of a discounted security
PRICEMAT	Financial	Yes	Price per $100 face value of a security that pays interest at maturity
PV	Financial	–	Present value of an investment
RATE	Financial	–	Interest rate per period of an annuity
RECEIVED	Financial	–	Amount received at maturity for a fully invested security
SLN	Financial	–	Straight-line depreciation of an asset for one period
SYD	Financial	–	Sum-of-years' digits depreciation of an asset for a specified period
TBILLEQ	Financial	Yes	Bond-equivalent yield for a Treasury bill
TBILLPRICE	Financial	Yes	Price per $100 face value for a Treasury bill
TBILLYIELD	Financial	Yes	Yield for a Treasury bill
VDB	Financial	–	Depreciation of an asset for a specified or partial period using a declining balance method
XIRR	Financial	Yes	Internal rate of return for a schedule of cash flows that is not necessarily periodic
XNPV	Financial	Yes	Net present value for a schedule of cash flows that is not necessarily periodic
YIELD	Financial	Yes	Yield on a security that pays periodic interest
YIELDDISC	Financial	Yes	Annual yield for a discounted security; for example, a Treasury bill
YIELDMAT	Financial	Yes	Annual yield of a security that pays interest at maturity
ABS	Maths	–	Absolute value of a number
ACOS	Maths	–	Arccosine of a number

Function name	Category	Analysis ToolPak	Description
ACOSH	Maths	–	Inverse hyperbolic cosine of a number
ASIN	Maths	–	Arcsine of a number
ASINH	Maths	–	Inverse hyperbolic sine of a number
ATAN	Maths	–	Arctangent of a number
ATAN2	Maths	–	Arctangent from x- and y-coordinates
ATANH	Maths	–	Inverse hyperbolic tangent of a number
CEILING	Maths	–	Rounds a number to the nearest integer or to the nearest multiple of significance
COMBIN	Maths	–	Number of combinations for a given number of objects
COS	Maths	–	Cosine of a number
COSH	Maths	–	Hyperbolic cosine of a number
COUNTIF	Maths	–	Counts the number of nonblank cells within a range that meet the given criteria
DEGREES	Maths	–	Converts radians to degrees
EVEN	Maths	–	Rounds a number up to the nearest even integer
EXP	Maths	–	Returns e raised to the power of a given number
FACT	Maths	–	Factorial of a number
FACTDOUBLE	Maths	Yes	Double factorial of a number
FLOOR	Maths	–	Rounds a number down, toward zero
GCD	Maths	Yes	Greatest common divisor
INT	Maths	–	Rounds a number down to the nearest integer
LCM	Maths	Yes	Least common multiple
LN	Maths	–	Natural logarithm of a number
LOG	Maths	–	Logarithm of a number to a specified base
LOG10	Maths	–	Base-10 logarithm of a number
MDETERM	Maths	–	Matrix determinant of an array
MINVERSE	Maths	–	Matrix inverse of an array
MMULT	Maths	–	Matrix product of two arrays
MOD	Maths	–	Remainder from division
MROUND	Maths	Yes	Returns a number rounded to the desired multiple
MULTINOMIAL	Maths	Yes	Multinomial of a set of numbers

Function name	Category	Analysis ToolPak	Description
ODD	Maths	–	Rounds a number up to the nearest odd integer
PI	Maths	–	Value of pi
POWER	Maths	–	Result of a number raised to a power
PRODUCT	Maths	–	Multiplies its arguments
QUOTIENT	Maths	Yes	Integer portion of a division
RADIANS	Maths	–	Converts degrees to radians
RAND	Maths	–	Returns a random number between 0 and 1
RANDBETWEEN	Maths	Yes	Returns a random number between the numbers you specify
ROMAN	Maths	–	Converts an arabic numeral to roman, as text
ROUND	Maths	–	Rounds a number to a specified number of digits
ROUNDDOWN	Maths	–	Rounds a number down, toward zero
ROUNDUP	Maths	–	Rounds a number up, away from zero
SERIESSUM	Maths	–	Sum of a power series based on the formula
SIGN	Maths	–	Sign of a number
SIN	Maths	–	Sine of the given angle
SINH	Maths	–	Hyperbolic sine of a number
SQRT	Maths	–	Returns a positive square root
SQRTPI	Maths	Yes	Square root of (number * pi)
SUBTOTAL	Maths	–	Returns a subtotal in a list or database
SUM	Maths	–	Adds its arguments
SUMIF	Maths	–	Adds the cells specified by a given criteria
SUMPRODUCT	Maths	–	Sum of the products of corresponding array components
SUMSQ	Maths	–	Sum of the squares of the arguments
SUMX2MY2	Maths	–	Sum of the difference of squares of corresponding values in two arrays
SUMX2PY2	Maths	–	Sum of the sum of squares of corresponding values in two arrays
SUMXMY2	Maths	–	Sum of squares of differences of corresponding values in two arrays
TAN	Maths	–	Tangent of a number
TANH	Maths	–	Hyperbolic tangent of a number
TRUNC	Maths	–	Truncates a number to an integer

Function name	Category	Analysis ToolPak	Description
AVEDEV	Statistical	–	Average of the absolute deviations of data points from their mean
AVERAGE	Statistical	–	Average of its arguments
AVERAGEA	Statistical	–	Average of its arguments, including numbers, text and logical values
BETADIST	Statistical	–	Cumulative beta probability density function
BETAINV	Statistical	–	Inverse of the cumulative beta probability density function
BINOMDIST	Statistical	–	Individual term binomial distribution probability
CHIDIST	Statistical	–	One-tailed probability of the chi-squared distribution
CHIINV	Statistical	–	Inverse of the one-tailed probability of the chi-squared distribution
CHITEST	Statistical	–	Test for independence
CONFIDENCE	Statistical	–	Confidence interval for a population mean
CORREL	Statistical	–	Correlation coefficient between two data sets
COUNT	Statistical	–	Counts how many numbers are in the list of arguments
COUNTA	Statistical	–	Counts how many values are in the list of arguments
COVAR	Statistical	–	Returns covariance, the average of the products of paired deviations
CRITBINOM	Statistical	–	Smallest value for which the cumulative binomial distribution is less than or equal to a criterion value
DEVSQ	Statistical	–	Sum of squares of deviations
EXPONDIST	Statistical	–	Exponential distribution
FDIST	Statistical	–	F probability distribution
FINV	Statistical	–	Inverse of the F probability distribution
FISHER	Statistical	–	Fisher transformation
FISHERINV	Statistical	–	Inverse of the Fisher transformation
FORECAST	Statistical	–	Returns a value along a linear trend
FREQUENCY	Statistical	–	Returns a frequency distribution as a vertical array
FTEST	Statistical	–	Result of an F-test
GAMMADIST	Statistical	–	Gamma distribution
GAMMAINV	Statistical	–	Inverse of the gamma cumulative distribution

Function name	Category	Analysis ToolPak	Description
GAMMALN	Statistical	–	Natural logarithm of the gamma function, (x)
GEOMEAN	Statistical	–	Geometric mean
GROWTH	Statistical	–	Returns values along an exponential trend
HARMEAN	Statistical	–	Harmonic mean
HYPGEOMDIST	Statistical	–	Hypergeometric distribution
INTERCEPT	Statistical	–	Intercept of the linear regression line
KURT	Statistical	–	Kurtosis of a data set
LARGE	Statistical	–	K-th largest value in a data set
LINEST	Statistical	–	Parameters of a linear trend
LOGEST	Statistical	–	Parameters of an exponential trend
LOGINV	Statistical	–	Inverse of the lognormal distribution
LOGNORMDIST	Statistical	–	Cumulative lognormal distribution
MAX	Statistical	–	Maximum value in a list of arguments
MAXA	Statistical	–	Maximum value in a list of arguments, including numbers, text and logical values
MEDIAN	Statistical	–	Median of the given numbers
MIN	Statistical	–	Minimum value in a list of arguments
MINA	Statistical	–	Smallest value in a list of arguments, including numbers, text and logical values
MODE	Statistical	–	Most common value in a data set
NEGBINOMDIST	Statistical	–	Negative binomial distribution
NORMDIST	Statistical	–	Normal cumulative distribution
NORMINV	Statistical	–	Inverse of the normal cumulative distribution
NORMSDIST	Statistical	–	Standard normal cumulative distribution
NORMSINV	Statistical	–	Inverse of the standard normal cumulative distribution
PEARSON	Statistical	–	Pearson product moment correlation coefficient
PERCENTILE	Statistical	–	K-th percentile of values in a range
PERCENTRANK	Statistical	–	Percentage rank of a value in a data set
PERMUT	Statistical	–	Number of permutations for a given number of objects
POISSON	Statistical	–	Poisson distribution

Function name	Category	Analysis ToolPak	Description
PROB	Statistical	–	Probability that values in a range are between two limits
QUARTILE	Statistical	–	Quartile of a data set
RANK	Statistical	–	Rank of a number in a list of numbers
RSQ	Statistical	–	Square of the Pearson product moment correlation coefficient
SKEW	Statistical	–	Skewness of a distribution
SLOPE	Statistical	–	Slope of the linear regression line
SMALL	Statistical	–	K-th smallest value in a data set
STANDARDIZE	Statistical	–	Returns a normalised value
STDEV	Statistical	–	Estimates standard deviation based on a sample
STDEVA	Statistical	–	Estimates standard deviation based on a sample, including numbers, text and logical values
STDEVP	Statistical	–	Calculates standard deviation based on the entire population
STDEVPA	Statistical	–	Calculates standard deviation based on the entire population, including numbers, text and logical values
STEYX	Statistical	–	Standard error of the predicted y-value for each x in the regression
TDIST	Statistical	–	Student's t-distribution
TINV	Statistical	–	Inverse of the Student's t-distribution
TREND	Statistical	–	Returns values along a linear trend
TRIMMEAN	Statistical	–	Mean of the interior of a data set
TTEST	Statistical	–	Probability associated with a Student's t-test
VAR	Statistical	–	Estimates variance based on a sample
VARA	Statistical	–	Estimates variance based on a sample, including numbers, text and logical values
VARP	Statistical	–	Calculates variance based on the entire population
VARPA	Statistical	–	Calculates variance based on the entire population, including numbers, text and logical values
WEIBULL	Statistical	–	Weibull distribution
ZTEST	Statistical	–	Two-tailed P-value of a z-test

SOFTWARE INSTALLATION

A CD containing the Excel files and templates accompanies the book. The file names relate to their chapter numbers and you should refer to the file list for the sequence of files (see page 295). The file notation is MCFM and then the chapter number. For your reference, the files for a particular chapter are quoted at the beginning of each chapter. Each of the files are skeletons for you to complete the model in stages.

Follow the instructions below to install the files and create a programme group using the simple SETUP command.

System requirements

This section summarises the requirements for using the application.

- Personal computer with a CD drive.
- Hard disk with 20 Mb of free space.
- Microsoft® Mouse or other compatible pointing device.
- VGA or compatible display.
- *Microsoft® Windows* and *Excel* 2003 or later.

The files should work under Mac OS, but you may have to copy the files yourself. For this purpose, the files are supplied as an executable and in a separate directory of uncompressed files.

Installation

- Insert the CD into your CD-ROM drive.
- Select the Start button in the bottom left of your screen.
- Select Run.
- Write in the space provided: D:\SetUp.exe – then click on OK.
- D is your CD-ROM drive: if this is not correct for your machine then change the letter accordingly.
- The application will now install itself. Follow the instructions on screen to select a destination directory.
- If you are prompted, then restart Windows.

Important

When the installation has finished, open Excel and select `File, Excel Options, Add-Ins` (see Figure A1.1). You need to make sure that Analysis ToolPak and Solver are selected. When you tick the boxes you may be prompted for your original Office install disk.

The files in this book make use of some of the advanced functions from the Analysis ToolPak such as `EDATE` and `XNPV` or Solver routines. Analysis ToolPak is not installed using a typical Excel installation and you may see 'NAME' errors if Excel cannot understand or parse the function names. If this is the case use your original Office disks to install the option.

Figure A1.1	Tool add-ins

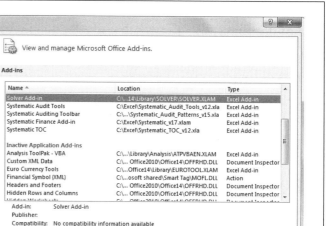

Analysis ToolPak contains extra statistical and financial functions needed by the applications (see Figure A1.2). Click it to select it and press OK. If you do not select it, you will encounter errors on opening certain files.

Analysis ToolPak

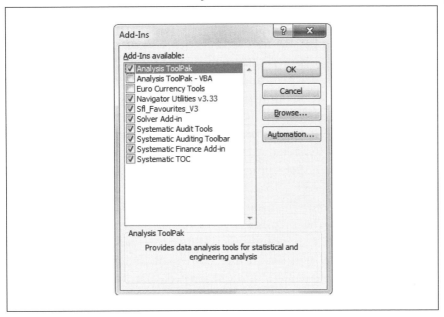

Accessing the application files

- You will see that a programme group has been created for you. The application will also now appear under Programs on the Start menu.

- When installed, the program group should include all the files on the accompanying file list.

- To access any of the files, simply double-click the icons in the program group.

- You can also open a ReadMe file of installation instructions and a file list.

- Press OK to continue and the selected file will open.

- There is a master file list in the form of an Excel model and a list within the book.

LICENCE

This notice is intended to be a 'no nonsense' agreement between you ('the licensee') and Systematic Finance Ltd ('Systematic'). The software and associated documentation ('software') are subject to copyright law. They are protected by the laws of England. If you use this software, you are deemed to have accepted the terms and conditions under which this software was supplied.

Files accompanying *Mastering Cash Flow and Valuation Modelling* are copyright © Systematic Finance Ltd ('Systematic').

The software has not been audited, and no representation, warranty or undertaking (express or implied) is made and no responsibility is taken or accepted by Systematic and its directors, officers, employees, agents or advisers as to the adequacy, accuracy, completeness or reasonableness of the financial models and Systematic excludes liability thereof.

In particular, no responsibility is taken or accepted by Systematic and all liability is excluded by Systematic for the accuracy of the computations comprised therein and the assumptions upon which such computations are based. In addition, the recipient receives and uses the software entirely at its own risk and no responsibility is taken or accepted by Systematic and accordingly all liability is excluded by Systematic for any losses which may result therefrom, whether as a direct or indirect consequence of a computer virus or otherwise.

No part of the accompanying documentation may be reproduced, transmitted, transcribed, stored in a retrieval system or translated without the prior permission of the copyright holder. You have a limited licence to use the software for the period stated on the software copyright notice and to make copies of the software for backup purposes. This is a single copy software licence granted by Systematic. You must treat this software just like a book except that you may copy it onto a computer to be used and you may make an archival backup copy of the software for the purposes of protecting the software from accidental loss.

The phrase 'just like a book' is used to give the licence maximum flexibility in the use of the licence. This means, for example, that the software can be used by any number of people, or freely moved between computers, provided it is not being used on more than one computer or by more than one person at the same time as it is in use elsewhere. Just like a book, which can only be read by one person at a time, the software can only be used by one person on one computer at one time. If more than one person is using the software on different machines, then Systematic's rights have been violated and the licensee should seek to purchase further single copy licences by purchasing more copies of the book. (In the case of multiple licences or network licences, then the number of users may only equal the number of licences.)

You may not decompile, disassemble or reverse-engineer the licensed software. You may not rent or lease the software to others or claim ownership. If you wish to pass the software to another person, you may. However, you must provide all original disks, documentation and remove the software from your own computer(s) to remain within the single copy licence agreement. To do otherwise will violate the rights of Systematic.

Systematic does not warrant that the functions contained in the software will meet your requirements or that the operation of the software will be uninterrupted or error free. This warranty does not extend to changes made to the software by third parties, nor does it extend to liability for data loss, damages or lost profits due to the use of the software.

Systematic does not have any responsibility for software failure due to changes in the operating environment of the computer hardware or operating system made after delivery of the software.

FILE LIST

Filter	Topic	Items
1	Basic template	MCFM_Template
2	Skeleton	MCFM_Skeleton
3	Final file	MCFM_Final
4	Appendices	MCFM_Office_2011_Menus

The above files comprise skeleton Excel templates for you to work on as you develop the model.

Important: Make sure that you follow the installation instructions and ensure that the Analysis ToolPak and Solver are loaded in your version of Excel.

SYSTEMATIC FINANCE PLC

Systematic Finance plc is an independent company specialising in:

■ Financial modelling and consulting – design, build, audit, review.

■ Financial training – financial modelling techniques, credit analysis, leasing and corporate finance on an in-house and public basis in Europe, Africa, Middle East, Asia and America.

■ Leasing as a corporate lessor and arranger.

For further information and support, please go to **www.financial-models. com**, where there is a contact and information form, or contact:

Alastair L Day
Systematic Finance
Orchard House
Green Lane
Guildford
Surrey GU1 2LZ

Tel: +44 (0)1483 532929
Fax: +44 (0)1483 538358

Email: aday@system.co.uk
Web: **www.financial-models.com**

Appendix 2

An introduction to Microsoft® Office 2010 (Office 14)

File: MCFM_Office_2011_Menus

AN INTRODUCTION TO MICROSOFT® OFFICE 2010 (OFFICE 14)

This appendix provides an introduction to Microsoft® Office 2010 (Office 14) to show the differences in the menus and commands to earlier versions. Office 2007 and 2010 mark a substantial departure from earlier versions of Office from Excel version 3 to version 11 (2003) and attempts to make the menus, toolbars and options more accessible in combined form. This appendix provides an overview and some screenshots of the menu ribbon at the top of the screen. There is also a function reference on the disk (MCFM_Office_2011_Menus).

Microsoft® Office User Interface Overview

The whole Office interface has been redesigned to contain more features and new file formats. Microsoft explains that most Office users accessed only 8 to 10 per cent of the functions on the many toolbars and menus in previous versions of the applications, because most of the programs' features were buried in layers of menus and sub-menus. This figure of 10 per cent has been quoted in other studies. In response, Microsoft has placed the functions on a single, changeable Ribbon to make them more visible, and thus more likely to be used. The result is a user interface that should make it easier for people to get more out of Microsoft® Office applications so they can deliver better results faster. Microsoft® Office Word 2010, Office Excel 2010, Office PowerPoint 2010 and Office Access 2010 feature a similar workspace to offer the same style across the Office family. Whilst you cannot amend the Ribbon without resorting to HTML in Excel 2007, the Ribbon in Excel 2010 can be customised by the user.

Key features

In previous releases of Microsoft® Office applications, people used a system of menus, toolbars, task panes and dialog boxes to get their work done. This system worked well when the applications had a limited number of commands. Now that the programs do so much more, the menus and toolbars system does not work as well. Too many program features are said to be too hard for many users to find. For this reason, the overriding objective for the Ribbon user interface is to make it easier for people to find and use the full range of features these applications provide. The result should be more efficient use of the applications in Word, PowerPoint, Access and Excel.

The Ribbon

The previous menus and toolbars have been replaced by the Ribbon, which presents commands organised into a set of tabs. The tabs on the Ribbon display the commands that are most relevant for each of the task areas in Office Word 2010, Office PowerPoint 2010, Office Excel 2010 or Office Access 2010.

Home Screen

Contextual tabs

Certain sets of commands are only relevant when objects of a particular type are being edited. For example, the commands for editing a chart are not relevant until a chart appears in a spreadsheet and the user is focusing on modifying it. These are in effect sub-menus. In earlier versions of Office, these commands can be difficult to find. In Office Excel 2010, clicking on a chart causes a contextual tab to appear with the commands used for chart editing. Contextual tabs only appear when they are needed and make it much easier to find and use the commands needed for the operation at hand.

Galleries

Galleries provide users with a set of clear results to choose from when working on their document, spreadsheet, presentation or Access database. By presenting a simple set of potential results, rather than a complex dialog box with numerous options, Galleries simplify the process of producing professional-looking work. The traditional dialog boxes are still available for those wishing a greater degree of control over the result of the operation.

Live Preview

Live Preview is a new addition that shows the results of applying an editing or formatting change as the user moves the pointer over the results presented in a Gallery. This new capability simplifies the process of laying out, editing and formatting so users can create excellent results with less time and effort. As you move your mouse the page updates dynamically with the formatting and other changes.

Migration

Office 2010 uses different file formats to Office 2003 primarily due to the switch to XML file formats as the defaults in Word, Excel and PowerPoint. Office 2010 applications can open and work on files created in previous releases back to Office 97, and you will be able to create files in all existing Office formats. However, to take full advantage of the smaller file sizes and other benefits of Office 2010, you are forced to use the new XML formats: .docx in Word, .xlsx in Excel and .pptx in PowerPoint. For example, later versions of Excel use a more secure protection system but this is not backward compatible to earlier versions.

1. Office Menus – Home

The screen below shows the difference in the menu commands starting with Home. To open, modify or print a document you click the File icon in the top left. Home provides all cell formatting currently on the Formatting toolbar and under Edit. The elements on the right such as conditional formatting, tables and styles are currently found under Format. Clicking the arrow at the bottom of the ribbon will generally open an Excel 2003-like dialog box.

Home screen

Figure A2.2

2. Insert

This screen combines further toolbars and options: Shapes are currently on the Drawing toolbar, pivot tables are under Data and Charts can be found on the Insert menu. These commands all insert objects on the spreadsheet so the new Office Ribbon brings them together here. Where you see a triangle on the Ribbon item, further menus open out with options. When you click these buttons, they open to reveal further options. For example, inserting a column chart opens up all the variants of column charts or you can open a dialog box with all charts similar to the 2003 menus.

Figure A2.3

Insert

Figure A2.4

Submenu

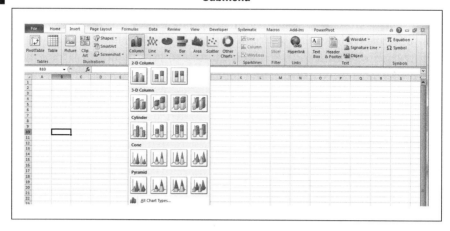

3. Page Layout

This menu brings together all the layout commands from the different Excel 2003 menus. All the commands relate to the layout of individual sheets. Print comments are currently on the File menu while Custom Views are on View. Commands such as `Bring to Front` are on the drawing menu.

Figure A2.5

Page Layout

4. Formulas

Inserting formulas in Excel 2003 can be complex when you need to find one of the 300 different functions. This menu helps with finding individual functions since they are arranged in categories with elements of the auditing toolbar. Commands such as `Evaluate Formula` and `Watch Window` allow you to trace commands and understand the process of calculation and result. The audit commands are hard to find in Excel 2003 and this layout tries to make them more accessible.

Formulas

5. Data

The Data menu contains some of the 2003 commands menu such as Connections and Data Validation. Sorting and Filtering is also on Data. What-if analyses such as Data Tables, Scenarios and Goal Seek are Tools options in Excel 2003. These are key commands for risk and variance analysis in Excel. The commands for linking data and workbooks are also here since Excel works well with Access databases and other external sources.

Data

6. Review

Reviewing includes Tools options such as spelling and protection together with Comments from the Insert menu. The idea is to utilise this set of commands when the initial workbook has been written. Good practice includes annotating and commenting cells, together with protecting formula cells against unauthorised changes. This option provides a checklist of some of the ways of generating reports.

Review

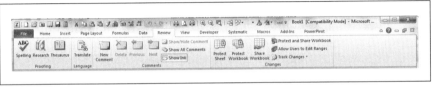

7. View

There are a number of tools for changing the appearance of Excel, such as Gridlines, Formula Bar, etc., which can be found in Tools Options or View on earlier versions. Again, these are all the commands that stipulate the viewing of Excel, many of which are currently found under Window. The protection commands are arranged logically in a block rather than being scattered in different places.

Figure A2.9

View

8. Developer

The Developer options are not available unless you click the box using the Options tab below. This allows you to record macros and make use of extended possibilities in Visual Basic. Macros are currently on the Tools menu or the Visual Basic toolbar and this option brings all the commands together. The commands for combo boxes and other controls from the 2003 Forms and Controls toolbars are also located here.

Figure A2.10

Developer

Figure A2.11

Excel options

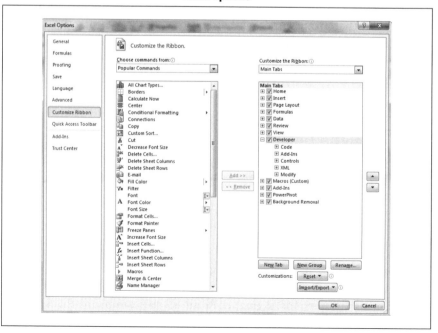

You need to go to `Excel Options, Customize Ribbon` and then tick `Show Developer tab` on the right and the extra option appears on the Ribbon. In 2007 this is in Excel options under Popular.

Show Developer toolbar

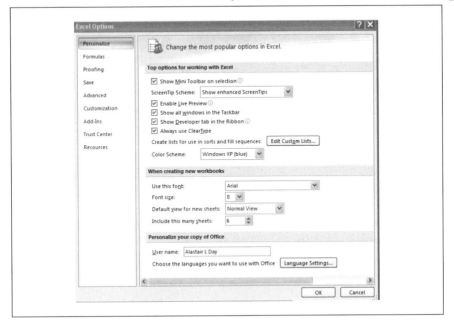

9. Add-Ins

In Excel 2003, you select add-ins with Tools and Add-Ins. In Office 2010 this is a separate option and you choose the add-ins with the options below. Tool bars open out when you select the add-ins such as Solver.

Add-Ins

10. Options – General

Click `File, Options, General` to personalise the Excel environment. This section is the equivalent to Setup in Excel 2003, for example to change the default number of sheets in an Excel workbook. The user name is used as the default for comments, macros and other places where a name is needed. To make your workbooks anonymous, enter a default name such as 'Excel User' here.

Figure A2.14

General

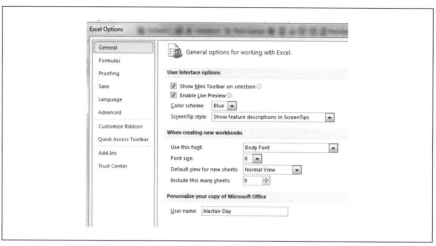

11. Options – Formulas

These options determine the automation of calculation and the error check-ing options currently in `Tools, Options, Calculation and Error Checking`. You can go down the list and select or deselect specific options such as the instances that Excel will flag as potential errors.

Figure A2.15

Formulas

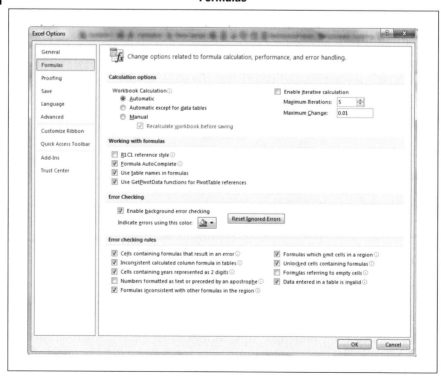

12. Options – Proofing

This option is common with other parts of Office 14 and chooses how proofing is carried out and how Excel seeks to correct potential errors. The Auto Correct and dictionary options are also here. You can download and install further dictionaries from the Microsoft website.

Proofing

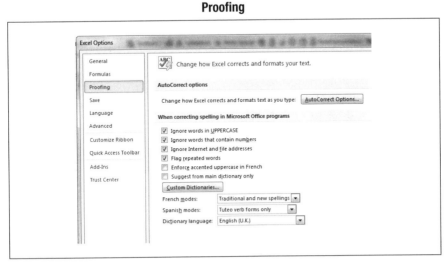

13. Options – Save

Here you set up file locations, the auto-save interval and the visual appearance. It is a good idea to use Auto Save or save your files often to avoid losing work. Also here you can choose to save files by default in an earlier file format.

Save

14. Options – Advanced

This section deals with advanced options for editing and other actions currently found in Tools, Options. This includes the controls for editing options such as Auto Complete together with editing and display options.

Advanced

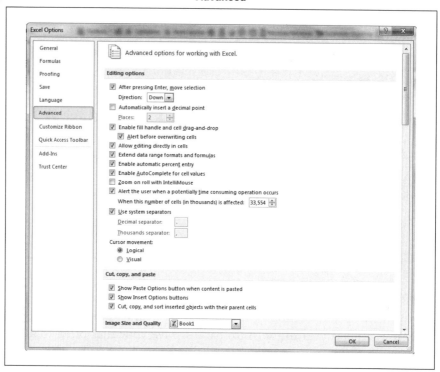

15. Options – Customisation

You can customise toolbars with quick commands and this menu option allows you to select commands for the Quick Access Toolbar. The Quick Access Toolbar is visible at the top left of the Ribbon. Excel 2007 did not allow you to customise the ribbon but this option has been reinstated in Excel 2010.

Customization

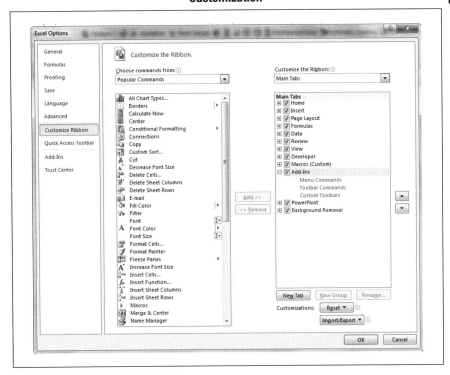

Quick Access Toolbar

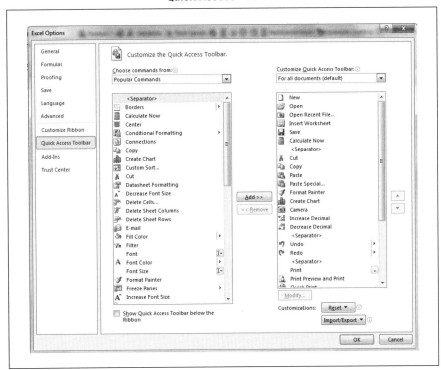

16. Options – Trust Center

This section on security provides tools for securing documents and privacy. In Excel 2003 these tools are scattered in the different option boxes.

Figure A2.21

Trust Center

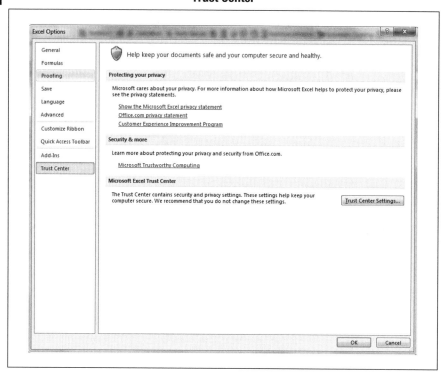

17. Options – Resources

This section organises all the assistance available in Office 14 for fixing problems, getting updates and downloading updates as they become available. The Office suite contains more advanced tools for finding and fixing installation problems. This is more streamlined than Excel 2003, which uses a Trust Center setting for the commands.

Resources

Figure A2.22

Index